Screening by International Aid Organizations Operating in the Global South

"This welcomed book sheds light on an opaque organizational practice intersecting humanitarian,international aid, risk governance, and counter-terrorism regimes. By analyzing screening as aprocedure where aid organizations check the background of individuals to comply with national andinternational sanctions laws, Beata Paragi succeeds in contributing to humanitarian and surveillancestudies, as well as to International Relations more broadly."

—Bruno Oliveira Martins, *Senior researcher, Peace Research Institute Oslo (PRIO)*

Beata Paragi

Screening by International Aid Organizations Operating in the Global South

Mitigating Risks of Generosity

Beata Paragi
Institute of Global Studies
Corvinus University of Budapest
Budapest, Hungary

ISBN 978-3-031-54164-3   ISBN 978-3-031-54165-0   (eBook)
https://doi.org/10.1007/978-3-031-54165-0

Cover illustration: © John Rawsterne/patternhead.com

This Palgrave Macmillan imprint is published by the registered company Springer Nature Switzerland AG
The registered company address is: Gewerbestrasse 11, 6330 Cham, Switzerland

Paper in this product is recyclable.

And for the want of a word
I renew my life
For I was born to know you
To name you
Liberty.

(*Liberté* by Paul Eluard, 1942, translated from French by Carla Yasmine
Atwi https://allpoetry.com/Libert-)
https://www.poetica.fr/poeme-279/liberte-paul-eluard/

where there is tyranny,
everyone is a link in the chain;
its stench emanates and spreads from you,
you too are tyranny;

(*One sentence about tyranny* by Gyula Illyes, 1950, translated from
Hungarian by Andris Heks)
https://www.cambridge.org/core/books/abs/legalized-identities/epi
graph/9375D5743E159222B860147120EFA0CA

ACKNOWLEDGEMENTS

This book has grown out of 'slow' research project behind which there was no major research funding. The minor financial contributions and non-material support I enjoyed, however, proved priceless because they kept the idea alive over the years. The initial phase of the research behind this book, the purpose of which was to explore data protection dilemmas in the aid sector, was funded by the Tempus Public Foundation (Hungary) and hosted by the *Senter for Rettsinformatikk* (Norwegian Research Centre for Computers and Law) at the University of Oslo (UiO). A study programme (MA in ICT Law) I participated in from 2020 to 2022 enabled me to explore legal-regulatory technologies and considerations characterizing screening. The counterterrorism and surveillance dimension could be incorporated into the analysis due to some symbolic funding from the Legal Innovation Lab Oslo (University of Oslo) and Lovdata Norway during the same years. A workshop discussing the data protection dimension of screening with practitioners was hosted by the Peace Research Institute in Oslo (PRIO) with seed funding provided by the Norwegian Centre for Humanitarian Studies (NCHS). I would also like to say thanks to VOICE (Voluntary Organisations in Cooperation in Emergencies), the largest humanitarian NGO network in Europe and NCHS for sharing the link to questionnaire to the second survey with their membership.

The responsibility for the conclusions drawn is mine, but I am more than grateful to Dag Wiese Schartum (UiO), Kristin B. Sandvik (UiO and PRIO), Maria Gabrielsen Jumbert (PRIO) and their colleagues affiliated with PRIO—Bruno Oliveira Martins, Kristoffer Lidén, Ben Hayes and Ayşe Bala Akal—for their professional support and kind encouragement and also to Johannes P. Lorentzen, a fellow student, who shared his valuable insights, gathered in the financial sector, upon reading parts of this manuscript. I am indebted to participants of the workshop and the interviews and to those having filled out the online questionnaires—directors, consultants, legal advisors, compliance and data protection officers—for sharing their experiences and the dilemmas aid organizations face. I know that we raise different questions and do not necessarily think alike in all regards. I would also like to express my gratitude to the directors of two European advocacy organizations who did their best to make me understand why this matter is delicate and why it is so hard to raise questions around transparency in certain contexts and by certain inquirers as well as to the anonymous reviewer for confirming the validity of political lessons expressed in literary works too: not only civil society organizations and aid projects, but also universities and research institutes, scholars and researchers—books like this—may play certain inescapable role in ambivalent power games. Last, but not least many thanks to my editors at Routledge for having seen the potential in this subject and for editing the text according to professional standards.

Reviewers and editors of these papers have also contributed to the development of the idea, thank you.

RELATED PUBLICATIONS, THE CONTENT
OF WHICH OVERLAP WITH PARTS OF THIS BOOK:

Paragi, B. (2022a). *Challenges in Using Online Surveys for Research Involving Sensitive Topics: Data Protection Practices of European NGOs Operating in the Global South.* SAGE Research Methods Cases—Doing Research Online. Retrieved July 18, 2023, from https://methods.sagepub.com/case/online-surveys-delicate-sensitive-topics-data-protection-european-ngos

Paragi, B. (2022b). *The Ambiguous Politics of Screening.* Blog post, Oslo: Norwegian Centre for Humanitarian Studies. Retrieved August 18, 2023, from https://www.humanitarianstudies.no/the-ambiguous-politics-of-screening/

Paragi, B. (2023). *Opacity or Transparency? Screening by NGOs in the Context of Aid Work* (NCHS-Paper). Norwegian Centre for Humanitarian Studies. Retrieved July 18, 2023, from https://www.humanitarianstudies.no/resource/opacity-or-transparency-screening-by-ngos-in-the-context-of-aid-work/

Paragi, B. (2024). The Art of Screening: Reasonable Efforts and Measures at the Nexus of Aid Work and Counterterrorism. *Surveillance & Society, 22*(2), 138–159.

CONTENTS

ABBREVIATIONS

AML	Anti-Money Laundering
AWSD	Aid Workers Security Database
CDD	Customer Due Diligence
CFT	Counter-Terrorist Financing
CJEU	Court of Justice of the EU
CSO	Civil society Organization
CVA	Cash and Voucher Assistance
DG ECHO	Directorate-General for European Civil Protection and Humanitarian Aid Operations, EC, EU
DG INTPA	Directorate-General for International Partnerships, EC, EU
DPO	Data Protection Officer
EC	European Commission, EU
ECtHR	European Court of Human Rights
EDPB	European Data Protection Board
EEA	European Economic Area
EU	European Union
FATF	Financial Action Task Force
FSPs	Financial Service Providers
GDPR	EU General Data Protection Regulation (2016/679)
HO	Humanitarian Organization
ICRC	The International Red Cross and Red Crescent Movement
ICT4D	Information-Communication Technologies for Development
IFRC	The International Federation of Red Cross and Red Crescent Societies
IO	International Organization
IR	International Relations

KYC	Know Your Customer
MSF	Médecins Sans Frontières
NGDO	Non-Governmental Development Organization
NGO	Non-Governmental Organization
NRC	Norwegian Refugee Council
OECD DAC	OECD Development Assistance Committee
OECD	Organisation for Economic Co-operation and Development
P/CVE	Preventing and Countering Violent Extremism
PN	Privacy Notice
UN SR HR/CT	United Nations Special Rapporteur of CT
UNHCR	The United Nations High Commissioner for Refugees
UNRWA	United Nations Relief and Works Agency
UNSC	United Nations Security Council
USAID	U.S. Agency for International Development
VOICE	Voluntary Organisations in Cooperation in Emergencies
WHO	World Health Organization

LIST OF TABLES

CHAPTER 1

Introduction

Abstract Due to a diverse set of reasons, aid work has become increasingly securitized by various means and by various actors for more than two decades. Donors and aid organizations themselves play a role in this process by implementing reasonable measures to mitigate risks. The purpose of this first chapter is to introduce the core theme of this book—screening as a risk-mitigating measure by aid organizations registered in the European Union and operating in the Global South—by recalling the four research questions that guided the research, summarizing the methods applied and drawing the structure of the remaining part of the book. It also offers an introduction to key terms, such as aid organizations and risks and draws the frameworks than can be used to interpret screening from various disciplinary perspectives.

Keywords Aid organizations · Screening · Risks and risk-mitigation · Compliance · Securitization

Aid projects implemented in the Global South by international governmental and non-governmental organizations are widely seen as symbols of generosity, solidarity, altruism and humanitarianism in case of conflict and disaster situations. Activities of aid organizations are subject to public scrutiny, certain political and legal oversight due to their spending their

B. Paragi, *Screening by International Aid Organizations Operating in the Global South*, https://doi.org/10.1007/978-3-031-54165-0_1

donors'—in many cases taxpayers'—money, but accountability has its limits in the civil sector (Jordan & Van Tujil, 2006). While isolated anthropological studies may offer insights to the 'lifewords' of specific civil society organizations and their relationships with given communities in particular geographical locations outside the Global North (Kalfeis & Knodel, 2021) as well as into the relationship between aid organizations and their international staff (Fechter, 2014), industry-specific internal operations and organizational practices are rarely investigated in the scholarship. While the risks embedded in and benefits promised by ICT4D and humanitarian technologies have been scrutinized for about a decade (Harris, 2016; Jacobsen, 2015; Qureshi, 2019; Sandvik, 2023; Sandvik et al., 2014, 2017; Walsham, 2017), little information is available on the details of how various technologies are designed, deployed and used by aid organizations.

This book explores dilemmas of transparency around an opaque organizational practice known as screening. While transparency is a controversial and ambiguous matter in every context (Adams, 2020), screening is one among the many tools offered by the compliance industry that ensures contemporary governability "in name of the undisputable good, in the name of the elimination of all the things we all can agree are evil" (Kuldova, 2022, vi). It refers to background checks by means of which organizations (corporations, immigration or customs authorities, financial institutions and even civil society organizations, CSOs) systematically, but in a rather mysterious manner, collect certain information on individuals. The general purpose of various background check procedures, such as screening, is to distinguish individuals and organizations that may pose a risk from reliable and trustworthy ones. While the concerned individuals can be (would-be) clients, employees, other transaction partners, the information being subject to interest concerns their real or perceived 'adverse behaviour': criminal activities, adverse (social) media appearances, direct or indirect affiliation with terrorist organizations or other sanctioned entities.

Background checks in criminal contexts and for-profit settings can be analyzed within the frameworks of the 'surveillance-industrial' complex (Hayes 2012b) and 'compliance-industrial complex' which latter translates "noble ideas into practices of control and pre-emption of future risks, into new forms of hybrid policing [and] shapes the ways in which we are governed, profiled, sorted, surveilled, nudged, risk-assessed, punished, sanctioned—as workers, clients, customers, suppliers, and humans" (Kuldova, 2022, vi). Screening, however, is also conducted by a narrow set of aid organizations implementing projects in Global South countries.

This practice deserves attention because large aid organizations—or their alliances—are increasingly perceived to have the 'same ontological status as states' and, as a result, they can be seen as key institutions 'in the provision of security and a threat to it' (Watson & Burles, 2018, 437) especially in the contemporary context of global governance. The power of aid organizations is also reflected in concepts such as the 'empire of humanity' (Barnett, 2002) or 'humanitarian governance' (Barnett, 2013). As indicated by these terms, the relationship between aid organizations and their subjects is characterized by power imbalances, resembling relations between the empire and its subject (the 'governed') in an era when "politics is dead" (Kuldova, 2022, v). Building mostly on Michel Foucault's work, governmentality scholars conceptualize governments and governance as attempts "to shape with some degree of deliberation aspects of our behaviour according to particular sets of norms and for a variety of ends" (Dean, 2010, 18). Instead of politics, behaviour, and as a result, power relations are ordered by "regulations, directives, standards, guidelines, and codes of conduct and ethics" and experts "translating policies that aim to fight corruption, money laundering, financial crimes, human rights abuses, and more, into technobureaucratic compliance systems, integrity training and algorithmic monitoring and surveillance systems" (Kuldova, 2022, v–vi). Experts knowing technologies and procedures and offering expert solutions have become more important than humans that are capable only to understand things. An expert, recalling Zygmunt Bauman (1991, 199), "spans the otherwise distant words of the objective and the subjective". However, "by separating knowing from doing and knowers from doers, the mediating expertise and the attendant technology [made] the life-world of all members of society (...) into a territory of permanent and acute ambivalence and uncertainty" (Bauman, 1991, 212). Indeed, considering the role played by large international (non-governmental and/or aid) organizations in various (humanitarian, migration, etc.) domains of international or global governmentality (Dean, 2010, 228–249), screening can be seen as a tool serving the ambivalent purpose of privatized risk governance in the post-9/11 world.

The term 'screening' has been widely used by scholars exploring how various screens (CCTV, mobiles and other smart devices, films/TV) representing 'vigilant or watchful visuality' have been appropriated, mobilized or instrumentalized to serve the 'watchful politics of the war on terror' (Amoore, 2007; Amoore & Goede, 2008) from public places to airports (Lyon, 2007b). Yet, for the purpose of this study it is also necessary to recall the understanding of 'screening' in medical contexts for an interrelated set of reasons. First, terrorism, violent extremism[1] and crime are frequently conceptualized as a 'disease' in public discourse threatening the 'healthy' social body. Such 'medicalization of social life' covers 'conditions previously not considered to be of any medical interests' (Bauman, 1991, 213). As a result, medico-political metaphors are also instrumentalized in the counterterrorism discourse (Beyribey, 2020; Spencer, 2012). The consequences of such metaphors, however, are both ambivalent and ambiguous. Recalling criticism from medical ethics, the extent to which illnesses and diseases are not of political nature, recovery may be easily hindered by harmful and humiliating analogies (Mongoven, 2006). Such metaphors are also harmful from societal and community perspectives because they normalize certain preventive measures and political responses (strict immigration policies, counterterrorism laws, military interventions) as appropriate, while excluding others, such as negotiations (Spencer, 2012). Yet, as the practice of screening fits the general logic of risk prevention and mitigation, medical metaphors merit scrutiny.

In the context of medical and life sciences the general purpose of screening is the detection of illness or disease for sake of public health. Considering the fine balance between individual (human, health-related) rights and public health concerns, screening in medical contexts is regulated in line with the guidelines issued in 1968 by the World Health Organization (WHO). Following a US CCI Conference on Preventive Aspects of Chronic Disease (1951) the *Principles and Practice of Screening for Disease* (WHO, 1968, 11) defined screening as

> the presumptive identification of unrecognized disease or defect by the application of tests, examinations, or other procedures (...). Screening tests

---

[1] The book uses the only the term (counter)terrorism, noting that "the globalisation of Countering Violent Extremism (CVE) policies is the most significant development in counterterrorism policy in the last decade ... CVE policies have significantly widened the range of methods used by governments for countering terrorism and shifted their target from terrorist organisation to religious ideology and identity" as a result of which "the war on terror has given itself a new vocabulary and a wider set of partnering agencies, from educators to artists" (Kundnani & Hayes, 2018, 3).

sort out apparently well persons who probably have a disease from those who probably do not.

It is important to note that medical screening tests, by definition and on purpose, can only be applied to populations, not individuals (Rayner, 2017; Steele, 2018), even though it is the individual whose body is screened by various technologies. Screening is not intended to be diagnostic and "persons with positive or suspicious findings must be referred to their physicians for diagnosis and necessary treatment" (WHO, 1968, 11). Although the distinction between screening and surveillance is a grey area even in medical science, the main difference concerns their overall aim or function. Screening usually involves feedback of results to the individuals concerned and includes intention to treat; surveillance, in contrast, only "aims to quantify prevalence and does not generally include feedback to individuals, nor is it linked to treatment" (Rayner et al., 2017). In any case, medical ethics of screening prompt that clear information must be provided to participating individuals "so that they can weigh up the balance of benefit and harm before deciding on whether or not to engage in the process" (Steele, 2018).

Considering screening as a sort of background check in business settings by for-profit and non-profit organizations, the 'fault' may be transferring donor money for illicit purposes, hiring a convicted criminal or sexual offender, offering a glass of water to someone deemed terrorist by a donor country or renting an office space from a sanctioned individual. While it has been scrutinized how aid organizations attempt to reduce or avert various risks for ensuring organizational operability and survival (Duffield, 2001, 2010; Fejerskov et al., 2023, 1–5), little attention has been paid to the expert practices of NGOs, the purpose of which is to mitigate real or perceived risks emerging not so much in insecure political contexts but stemming from their interactions with individuals. Indeed, as noted by Bauman long ago, the life-world of individuals is "saturated by expertise", whereby the "expert-produced and managed technique […] constitutes the true environment of individual life" (Bauman, 1991, 214). It is those who "possesses the skills and administer the technology" that increasingly determine and command life-activities (Bauman, 1991, 214) in humanitarian and development settings too.

Acknowledging that aid organizations may also be subject to screening and surveillance by governments and financial actors (Anwar et al., 2022;

Hayes, 2017, 28; També, 2021) and understanding that screening may carry different connotations in the aid industry,[2] *screening for the sake of this book* refers to a procedure whereby certain aid organizations check the background of individuals to comply with international and domestic (sanctions) law, with conditional clauses enshrined in funding agreements or to pursue other organizational interests. Common is the objective to comply with 'global' norms and 'universal' standards: to prevent the use of donor money for illicit purposes, for example, money-laundering, terrorism finance and corruption or avert reputational hazards. The general purpose of screening is to enable aid organizations to distinguish persons (and legal entities) with 'normal' background from those having 'risky' profiles. In other words, screening is about verifying the identity, more precisely, the 'clearness' of a particular individual (or an entity) before an NGO signs contract with them as an individual donor, supplier, consultant or employee or includes them as beneficiary into an aid project and further monitoring the risks until the contractual or non-contractual relation lasts.

Screening in general and the use of tech solutions for screening in particular raise questions not only with regard to the law and politics of listing (De Goede & Sullivan, 2016; Sullivan, 2020), privatised legal-regulatory compliance (Kuldova, 2022) and related financial surveillance in the context of security and counterterrorism studies (De Goede, 2012; Hayes, 2012b; Rébé, 2020) or international humanitarian law (Eckert, 2022; Gillard, 2021a, 2021b), but also regarding the broader human rights issues, personal data protection included. The principle of transparency and the right to information deserves particular attention not simply because screening can be conceptualized as a data processing operation mostly unknown to the wider public, but also because aid organizations themselves are vocal advocates of transparency when it comes to governmental conduct targeting them, their operations and their beneficiaries both in donor and aid recipient countries.

---

[2] For example, while "screening" beneficiaries or refugees might also refer to verifying if beneficiaries are part of a community receiving aid or individuals are real asylum-seekers (e.g. camp residents, *see* Jubany, 2011), "wealth screening" is conducted by aid INGOs for fundraising purposes. As their practices, modalities and technologies are different, none of them is discussed in this book.

Transparency is seen both as a norm guiding aid policies, practices and effectiveness[3] and a legal principle carrying relevance in the context of data protection. As for the former, transparency—as one of the core principles guiding aid work—aims to ensure the effectiveness of development assistance by mitigating corruption risks, among others, by providing access to information on reliable data (on aid finances) in a manner that is transparent to all stakeholders. As for the latter, privacy and data protection studies interpret transparency as a legal principle which is enacted, applied, implemented by lawmakers and courts. Its primary function is to protect individual human rights vis-à-vis the state that may abuse their power by preventing access to information (Klareen, 2013), but states are also obliged to protect human rights when interactions take place between private actors.

NGOs registered in the European Union (EU) and in European Economic Area (EEA) processing the personal data of individuals are bound by the EU General Data Protection Regulation 2016/679 (EU GDPR, 2016; hereinafter GDPR). This fact is relevant from legal perspectives not only because the EU's data protection framework ambitions to reinforce the data controllers' liability and the data subjects' rights at the same time by promoting norms in global terms (Bennett, 2018), but also because states tend to criminalize foreigners for being foreigners in migration contexts (Franko, 2020) and view them being less entitled to privacy rights than their own citizens (Milanovic, 2013). Considering the importance it attributes to the protection of fundamental rights, the GDPR, however, not only applies to its single market, but is also extended to the EU's external trade—and aid—relationships for its territorial scope (Schmidt, 2022, 246). Therefore, EU/EEA-registered NGOs are bound by the GDPR even when they implement projects in the Global South

---

[3] The principle of transparency was enshrined in the *Paris Declaration on Aid Effectiveness* (2005), the *Accra Agenda for Action* and the *4th High Level Forum on Aid Effectiveness* held in Busan (2011) which projected the following actions: aid recipient countries "will facilitate parliamentary oversight by implementing greater transparency in public financial management, including public disclosure of revenues, budgets, expenditures, procurement and audits. Donors will publicly disclose regular, detailed and timely information on volume, allocation and, when available, results of development expenditure to enable more accurate budget, accounting and audit by developing countries" (OECD, 2008, 20). For the EU's commitment to aid transparency, *see* https://ec.europa.eu/neighbourhood-enlargement/about-us/aid-transparency_en.

(Frantz et al., 2020; Gazi, 2020; Paragi, 2021) as long as their data processing operations fall under the scope defined in the GDPR.

Transparency, as a legal principle "takes the form of a duty to inform data subjects"—among others—which is enshrined in various articles of the GDPR (Article 12–14; Recitals 11, 58, 59, 60, 63, 166). This obligation coupled with the right to information "require that the data subject be informed of the existence of the processing operation and its purpose … taking into account the specific circumstances and context in which the personal data are processed" (EU GDPR, Recital 60) in line with the overarching principle of transparent, lawful and fair processing (Article 5(1)). It may apply to screening too, but transparency around this practice is not a straightforward matter as the right to data protection is not an absolute human right.

Contextualization: Aid Organizations, Risks and Disciplinary Frameworks

Aid organizations. Thousands of aid organizations operate in the Global South with the aim of providing development assistance, humanitarian aid or doing advocacy work for the benefit of less privileged populations. To understand the differences in terms of their rights and obligations, intergovernmental organizations, such as The United Nations High Commissioner of Refugees (UNHCR), the World Food Program (WFP) and international organizations enjoying specific privileges and immunities under international and domestic law, such as the ICRC (The International Red Cross and Red Crescent Movement) and IFRC (The International Federation of Red Cross and Red Crescent Societies) are to be distinguished from charities, non-governmental and civil society organizations (NGOs, CSOs) even though they are usually and commonly labelled as 'humanitarian organizations' (HOs) or 'aid organizations'.

Both academic scholarship (development and humanitarian studies) and law (in certain jurisdictions) make a conceptual distinction between NGOs operating in the field of international development (NGDOs) from those organizations (charities, relief organizations) that are mostly active in the humanitarian field (humanitarian NGOs charities, relief organizations). While various donors motives are integral part of development assistance from policies through the implementation of projects and programmes to evaluation, humanitarian assistance is usually not characterized by overtly formulated donor interests. Charities and humanitarian organizations are not only legally required to refrain from political advocacy, activism and actions even in liberal donor countries (Murray et al., 2023), but it is also their best interest to frame their activities as purely humanitarian especially in politically sensitive fields. Counterarguments and criticism put aside, the ideal humanitarian project is implemented in line with humanitarian principles (neutrality, impartiality, humanity and independence) and with the normative purpose of saving lives and mitigating suffering without causing further harm (Anderson, 1999; Donini & Gordon, 2015). The distinction, however, is not always so clear in practice, because aid organizations can implement both types of projects.

Conceptual clarity also requires us to distinguish national aid organizations (registered in a single donor country, for example, the Danish Church Aid in Denmark) from international non-governmental organizations (INGOs and their alliances) having local branches and offices in multiple donor and recipient countries (such as PLAN, Caritas, Care, Oxfam). Seen from aid recipient countries, they can be equally labelled 'international' or 'foreign' as opposed to local CSOs or grassroots initiatives. Permissions to operate are needed in almost all jurisdictions in line with the legal principle of territorial sovereignty. As domestic registration of foreign/international aid organizations is usually required in aid recipient Global South countries too, the border between local and foreign is not as clear-cut in analytical terms as in public or political discourse. The matter is further complicated by the fact that NGOs may be sometimes, if not simultaneously, referred to as beneficiaries (of private and official funds) and donors funding aid projects in the Global South in partnership with other international or local organizations.

Blurred borders also apply to the profile and activities of aid organization whereby the label 'political' or 'advocacy' can hardly be separated from the 'non-political'. It is particularly true in the context of global governance where the transnational, international or global civil society, composed of the loose network of individual (non-profit or intergovernmental) organizations with shared norms and common values, plays an increasingly powerful role. While their function is "to mitigate the more damaging forces of the global economy" (Amoore & Langley, 2004, 101 cited by Dean, 2010, 243), their participation in the international government of poverty is not free from organizational interests. Development NGOs' advocacy and engagement are influenced not only by moral vision and reputational considerations, but also by funding concerns (Szent-Iványi, 2023). Aid organizations are also increasingly (self-)securitized because the notion of (in)security is detectable in a "host of apparently heterogenous domains: of food, water, the environment, population, and even the human" (Dean, 2010, 246). As a result, NGOs, even humanitarian organizations become inherently political (Fassin, 2007), "even when engaging activity commonly understood as cultural, social and/ or humanitarian" (Watson & Burles, 2018, 444, fn 2). The fact that they are represented both in public discourse and in practice as non-political, apolitical or depoliticized emerges from their legal categorization (imposed by states), analytical categories (developed in IR and securitization scholarship) (Watson & Burles, 2018) and also from organizational branding strategies. Such labels—local/domestic, foreign/international, civil society/state, non-political/political, humanitarian/development—may equally pose risks to the given NGOs if used by others and may be strategically used (self-imposed) by them to prevent being dragged into politics.

This book uses the general term 'aid organizations' for four main reasons. First, non only non-governmental organizations (NGOs) and international aid organizations, but also organizations with special legal status conduct screening. Second, donors have also started including sanctions- and counterterrorism-related restrictions in their agreements with NGDOs being less familiar with the challenges associated with screening than humanitarian organizations (Gillard, 2021b, 519–520, 531–536). Third, mainstream data protection standards and principles are identical—at least in OECD countries—regardless of legal jurisdictions and categorizations. It should, however, be emphasized that the differences may carry relevance when it comes to rights and obligations prescribed in legislation regulating participation in national security and counterterrorism (CT/PVE) activities. Last, but not least, considering the international dimension, legal compliance equally includes the consideration of laws applicable in their country of origin (where the given organization is established or registered) and in the given location they operate (depending on the legal status of the NGO in the aid recipient country).

Risks and power. Although risks and uncertainties were long ago acknowledged as part of social life (Beck, 1992) and that of preconditions enabling governmentality, "there is no such thing as risk in reality"

(Dean, 2010, 206). Risks do not necessarily arise from the presence of a tangible, particular danger, as emphasized by Beck (1992) and Dean (1999/2010), but are the effect of a "combination of abstract factors, which render more or less probable the occurrence of undesirable modes of behaviour" (Rose, 1989, ix).

Recalling the medical context for analytical comparisons, clinical risk management not only "mobilises psychological expertise to create risk profiles and contain the risk of various categories of people deemed to have mental and/or emotional problems" (Aradau, 2004, 268), but also various technologies too. One example is screening which is widely used in health care with positive connotations, as "[s]creening tests sort out apparently well persons who probably have a disease from those who probably do not" (WHO, 1968, 11). Expertise combined with technology is further used for constructing risk profiles which makes risks identifiable and calculable. Risk management and care provision depend on the construction of medical and biographical profiles as long as various risk categories are applied to various (bodies of) persons who are then placed under surveillance or treatment (Aradau, 2004, 268). Indeed, screening and surveillance are related, but not identical concepts in medical contexts either whereby a major difference concerns the notification of individuals.

Furthermore, prevention of occurrences is about anticipating or predicting the emergence of undesirable outcome both in medical and non-medical contexts. In this regard, "what is important about risk is not risk itself", rather "the forms of knowledge that makes it thinkable, such as statistics, ... management...; the techniques that discover it; the technologies that seek to govern it" among others (Dean, 2010, 206). This feature and function of risk explains why it enjoyed little attention in original conceptual framework offered by international relations (IR) and securitization theories (Buzan et al., 1998). This body of scholarship could not accommodate the concept of 'risk' because risks themselves generally do not threaten survival (Aradau, 2004, 264–274). As its growing popularity may be explained by the calculability or the quantification of predictability it promises, the many kinds of risk rationality have become "central to the forms of calculative rationality that seek to secure governmental mechanisms" in international domains too (Dean, 2010, 227).

Risk as a significant theme emerged in the fields of IR, security and counterterrorism studies only after 9/11 (Aradau, 2004). Yet, states within their own jurisdictions have long been interested in making 'legible' populations for the purpose of controlling populations and territories (Scott, 1998). As a result, risk management has come to be seen by powerful actors as useful for governing societies and managing various cross-border problems from migration management through human trafficking (Aradau, 2004), from countering terrorism (Jackson, 2015b; Jarvis, 2019) to aid work (Fejerskov et al., 2023, 1–5) to mention only few international contexts. As terrorism has been constructed as unknowable and unpredictable, the "potential terrible consequences of imagined risks are to be prevented with whatever measures available" regardless of the actual statistical probably of risks materializing (Jackson, 2015b, 44–46). Considering that the world in general—and individual life-worlds in particular—became increasingly perceived through the lens of risk and security (Beck, 1992), 'whatever measures available' implies that "intelligence work spill[ed] rapidly from the imaginary bounds of nation-state security and foreign relations to every nook and corner of society" (Kuldova, 2022, 11 and 23–28).

Due to the abundance of risk thinking, the operation of aid organizations have also increasingly become securitized by powerful actors since 11 September (Duffield, 2001, 2007; Howell, 2014; Jackson, 2015a; Howell & Lind, 2009). As aid work is now free neither of real, nor of perceived security and other risks, larger organizations spend considerable amount of time and other resources on identifying, managing or reducing them, sometimes at the expense of creating or contributing to new ones. Scholarship on risks and uncertainties in the aid sector is mostly concerned with the practices of humanitarian organizations (for they operate in so-called high-risk environments where vulnerable populations are affected by disasters or man-made conflicts), but NGDOs may also be affected.

Therefore, aid organizations not only have invested heavily in governing (reducing, averting, mitigating) various risks and uncertainties by fortifying physical infrastructure (Duffield, 2010), developing due diligence policies and employing compliance officers (Muhomed et al., 2021), implementing various remote management practices (Akal, 2022; Duroch & Neuman, 2021) and using various technologies and data (Harris, 2016; Qureshi, 2019; Walsham, 2017), but they have also been criticized for doing it in a manner that, in effect, may entail further risks or harms especially in humanitarian contexts. Such criticism apply not only to the unintended consequences of how various technologies are designed, developed, tested or used in experimental Global South settings

(Duffield, 2016; Jacobsen, 2015; Sandvik et al., 2014, 2017), but also to the growing humanitarian non-knowledge or ignorance. All this makes digital humanitarianism, and as an integral part of that, contemporary risk-management, itself, risky (Fejerskov et al., 2023).

Disciplinary frameworks. Both screening of non-governmental organizations (NGOs) by financial service providers and screening of individuals by aid organizations—the latter being the main focus of this book—can be found at the nexus of a wide range of academic (sub)disciplines. While insights from the overlapping fields of international relations (IR), security, (counter)terrorism, development and humanitarian studies, as well as, privacy (data protection) studies and surveillance studies—as well as their critical domains—are helpful to understand this practice, it is worthwhile to recall Tereza Kuldova's observation on the challenges characterizing research on risks and compliance: "when the reality on the ground is one of progressive hybridization and blurring, it also becomes impossible to remain constrained by disciplinary boundaries" (Kuldova, 2022, v).

Scholarship on the use of technology and data for aid-supported purposes is concerned with how digitalization can be used to promote development, mitigate poverty (Harris, 2016; Qureshi, 2019; Walsham, 2017) or deliver humanitarian aid in a manner that does not contribute to prolonging conflicts (Sandvik et al., 2014, 2017). Such approaches may prompt the benefits of reasonable measures, such as screening, the extent to which it may prevent the misuse of donor money as claimed by the compliance industry (Hayes, 2017, 28). However, practitioners have been long concerned with donor conditionality considering screening as an example of how (mostly Western, resourceful) donors, that is influential OECD DAC (Organisation for Economic Co-operation and Development, Development Assistance Committee) and larger EU member states try to advance their interests by including technical conditions on 'reasonable measures' into funding agreements. While political, peace-related, economic or technical conditions embedded in (development) aid relations can be distinguished for analytical purposes (Stokke, 1995), demanding the implementation of 'reasonable efforts' is not simply a technical condition, but at the same time also a political one in its consequences both in development and humanitarian contexts.

Recalling insights from the critical domains of humanitarian studies (Duffield, 2016; Fast & Jacobsen, 2019; Pallister-Wilkins, 2021; Vaughn, 2009), IR, development and security studies (Duffield, 2001, 2007;

Howell, 2014; Howell & Lind, 2009), screening also serves a securitization agenda by means of which aid organizations operating in the Global South are not only dragged or co-opted into the counterterrorism game as (in)voluntary or reluctant players (Hayes, 2012a, 2017, 39), but also become 'policing' agents in the compliance-industrial complex (Kuldova, 2022). Therefore, screening against various lists (of sanctioned individuals, entities or terrorists, convicted criminals) can be explored and interpreted by lenses offered by the law and politics of listing (De Goede & Sullivan, 2016; Federer, 2022; Minella, 2019; Sullivan, 2020) for two main reasons. On the hand, while aid organizations as bank clients are subject to ordinary financial surveillance (Amicelle & Favarel-Garrigues, 2012; Rébé, 2020), organizations themselves, their staff, as well as human rights activists may also be listed by governments that consider their activities hostile (Amnesty International, 2020, 16; UN SR HR/CT, 2019, 2023). On the other hand, civil society and non-governmental organizations are seen as potential policing partners in CFT/PVE activities the same way as financial service providers and corporations (Kuldova, 2022), welfare services (Heath-Kelly & Gruber, 2023) and lawyers (Helgesson & Mörth, 2019).

The broader nexus of human rights, humanitarian law and counterterrorism is not irrelevant either. While screening of *final* beneficiaries has been widely discussed and rejected in the context of international humanitarian law by practitioners (Eckert, 2022; Gillard, 2021a, 2021b; O'Leary, 2021), screening *in general* also raises questions with regard to privacy and data protection rights of employees and transaction partners and related surveillance issues.

Recalling the synergies between surveillance (law) and privacy studies (Goold & Neyland, 2009; Skinner-Thompson, 2022), these domains are linked by their common interest in individuals and personal data. On the one hand, screening can be conceptualized as a series of data processing operations, at the core of which are personal data (IFRC, 2021, 23–24; Paragi, 2023; VOICE, 2021, *see also* Chapter 3 in this book). On the other hand, surveillance studies may also be relevant when it comes to understanding screening for it focuses on visibility and ways of seeing people and watching their corresponding digital(ized) bodies. Both official donors and aid organizations are known to cooperate with private tech companies in delivering various kinds of surveillance technologies in aid-recipient countries for purposes of population management control

(Hosein & Nyst, 2013) or the expected benefits of 'aidwashing' (Martin, 2023). While screening by NGOs may fit this set of literature too, it should be mentioned that 'surveillance' in the context of aid work is used originally with a connotation portraying control and care, surveillance and recognition inseparable (Fast & Jacobsen, 2019; Weitzberg et al., 2021).

The Motives and Essence of Screening

Being simultaneously recipients of official donor money and potential donors to local beneficiaries, guardians of public awareness and employers of thousands working in the Global South, development and humanitarian organizations have been demanded to participate in security-related activities for more than two decades. National legislative bodies, banks and financial service providers and official donors equally demand that INGOs prevent terrorism financing and money laundering through different structures and mechanisms engrained in law, related regulations and guidelines (Hayes, 2012a; UN SR HR/CT, 2019, 2023). Aid organizations not receiving official funding are subject to financial surveillance only by their banks before they open a bank account or when they initiate an international money transfer (Hayes, 2012a, 2017; També, 2021). In addition to such financial surveillance, organizations working with official donors (the US government, the EU or national aid agencies of member states) usually also sign funding agreements with conditional clauses (NRC, 2018a, 2018b). While these conditional clauses aim to prevent money transfers that might be used for financing terrorism or other illicit purposes in the Global South, reasonable measures of risk mitigation have been increasingly digitalized by larger, international aid organizations.

What legal compliance and prevention by reasonable measures means in practice is not necessarily specified by law or in funding agreements, rather it is left to the market (Hayes, 2012b; Kuldova, 2022). As a result, to minimize transactions with designated organizations, sanctioned persons or anyone affiliated with listed entities, or just to avoid being accused of financing terrorism, larger aid organizations conduct screening.[4] While manual screening requires a lot of work, neither

---

[4] The conceptual difference between vetting and screening also deserves to be mentioned. Screening is carried out by aid actors (INGOs) themselves, vetting requires

business organizations, nor aid organizations have access to population registries, law enforcement and other databases available to the police and security agencies. Therefore, as regulatory requirements flowing from international and domestic sanctions have become increasingly complex, commercial actors have started to consolidate the different lists of convicted criminals, designated or sanctioned individuals and legal entities into searchable services and products by offering digitalized solutions to their customers, such as banks, governmental agencies or non-profits (De Goede & Sullivan, 2016; Hayes, 2017, 28). To organize this practice in a time-efficient manner and to demonstrate compliance with law, international standards and internal due diligence procedures (Kuldova, 2022), large international aid organizations also resort to such technologies, especially if the scope of their activities involves multiple countries and sectors in the Global South; various donors (EU, US, national); numerous projects, contracts, and financial transactions; and thousands of employees.

To sum up, for the sake of this book, screening refers to a procedure whereby aid organizations implementing (mostly humanitarian) aid projects in the Global South regularly or on an ad hoc basis check the background of individuals against various watchlists consolidated in commercially available databases to comply with international and domestic (sanctions) law, with conditional clauses enshrined in funding agreements or to pursue other organizational interests. While the technical functionality of screening tools implies that the personal data of *any* individual getting in direct touch with NGOs can be screened—processed in automated ways—when they are deemed to pose financial, legal or reputational risk, internal organizational procedures may ensure (self)-restraint. While screening has been problematized by practitioners as screening of final beneficiaries is at odds with humanitarian principles (Gillard, 2021a, 2021b), its data protection dimension is not only less exposed, but it also means a huge challenge to aid organizations (VOICE, 2021, 3).

---

them to provide the identity information (personal data or) of individuals and entities to the official donor mostly in case of the United States (USAID, 2021), which carries out the checks itself (Gillard, 2021a, 48). For the data protection dimension of wealth screening see Franz et al. (2020).

Research Objectives and Questions

This book communicates the results of a longer, design-wise somewhat fragmented research process which equally included a small, externally funded research project (2021) and a study programme with course assignments and thesis writing (University of Oslo, 2022).

Considering that very little was known with regard to how the General Data Protection Regulation (GDPR) affected European donor policies and aid organizations operating in the Global South after it had entered into force in 2016 (2018) (Franz et al., 2020; Gazi, 2020; Kuner & Marelli, 2020; Paragi, 2021), the initial purpose was only to explore EU-based NGOs' experiences with the GDPR in the context of aid projects implemented in the Global South.[5]

As the theme of screening emerged as one the most important data protection concerns during the first interviews, further efforts were invested to explore the technology used for screening initially for the sake of a course assignment.[6] Later on, during the thesis writing process, more attention was paid to the impact of screening conducted by aid organizations on the privacy and personal data rights of individuals in general, focusing on the principle of transparency and right to information on the one hand and to the relationship between screening and surveillance on the other hand.[7]

To reconstruct the fragmented objectives of different research phases, the purpose of this book is to contextualize screening, to introduce and conceptualize it as a data processing activity, to interpret screening in light of surveillance studies and to discuss the politics of (missing) transparency by including the context into the analysis in which many NGOs operating in the Global South navigate. Therefore, the book looks to answer the following questions (RQ 1–4):

---

[5] See also the Annexes.

[6] University of Oslo, JUS5671: Legal Technology: Artificial Intelligence and Law; Spring Semester, 2020/2021.

[7] *The opacity of screening. An analysis of the principle of transparency and right to information in case of screening conducted by NGOs in the context of aid work in the Global South.* MA-thesis in ICT Law, University of Oslo, 2022, https://www.duo.uio.no/handle/10852/101138.

1. How aid organizations and their operations are securitized and what does the term 'reasonable efforts' mean in the context of counterterrorism?
2. How (under what conditions: purpose and legal basis) can screening be conceptualized as a data processing operation? What does the principle of transparency and the right to information mean in the GDPR? How do NGOs registered in the European Union communicate screening to data subjects?
3. Considering the opacity around screening, can it be conceptualized as a form of surveillance?
4. What dilemmas aid organizations face with regard to disclosing information on screening in privacy notices or in other formats when they operate in Global South settings?

While the core subject of the book is screening, it is the matter of transparency which serves as an overarching theme linking development and humanitarian studies, privacy studies and surveillance studies across the chapters. Therefore, the implied purpose of this work is to raise the question if aid organizations, let them be purely humanitarian or development (aid) organizations, contribute to the existing inequalities and injustices by screening or by screening in secret. It should be acknowledged that the question can be raised as a sort of conclusion towards the end of the book, but further research will be needed to find a reply if there is any.

METHODS, MATERIALS AND ETHICAL CONSIDERATIONS

The research design combined social science methods and some legal methods. The former included a literature review on the context of screening (RQ 1), the collection and analysis of data with regard to the empirics of screening: an online survey exploring general data protection concerns of a non-representative sample of EU/EEA-registered NGOs (RQ 2, RQ 4); qualitative interviews with stakeholders on data protection challenges in the context of aid work in the Global South (RQ 2) and a workshop on screening with stakeholders (RQ 1, RQ 2, RQ 4); an analysis of publicly available privacy notices (RQ 2). Legal methods were used to analyse certain NGO practices (communication of screening via publicly available privacy notices) limiting the discussion to relevant rules enshrined in the GDPR and related legal guidelines (RQ 2) in Chapter 3.

Regardless of the types of technologies used in the aid sector, while various aid organizations struggle to implement data protection measures (Franz et al., 2020; Gazi, 2020; Kuner & Marelli, 2020), official aid policies rarely consider this domain in aid work as a priority (Paragi, 2021). To explore NGOs' dilemmas with regard to GDPR semi-structured qualitative interviews ($n = 12$) were conducted in Spring and Autumn 2021 with representatives of European NGOs (Norway: $n = 4$; France: $n = 1$; Switzerland: $n = 1$; Austria: $n = 1$; Denmark: $n = 1$, Belgium $n = 1$; NL: $n = 1$; UK: $n = 1$). The discussions usually lasted for an hour and were not recorded; only notes were taken. Screening appeared as a common concern for most interviewees, either for ethical reasons or for legal compliance. Therefore, the few quotes cited in this article are not results of a content analysis of written transcripts but are only used to illustrate dilemmas shared across organizations.

Simultaneously, an online survey was conducted from January 2021 to April 2021 (Paragi, 2022). Respondents' data is summarized in Table 1.1 (see also Annex).

Screening also illustrates how a given technology can be used by aid organizations beyond their stated (development and/or humanitarian) objectives (Walsham, 2017, 28). Acknowledging that there are various products available on the market for non-profit clients too, documentation on 'CP-WatchList-Tech' obtained by email was selected to demonstrate the technical side of screening. 'CompliancePartner' (CP)

Table 1.1   Profiles of INGOs participating in the online survey

Location within Europe (n = 35)	Main area (n = 35)	Geographic areas of operations (multiple)	Number of local employees (n = 35)
Scandinavia (12)	Development (9)	Middle East (21)	Fewer than 10 (10)
Central-Eastern Europe (5)	Humanitarian (4)	North Africa (14)	11–20 (3)
Western Europe (11)	Both (18)	Sub-Saharan Africa (29)	21–50 (4)
Southern Europe (3)	None, other (4)	Asia (21)	More than 51 (18)
United Kingdom (4)		Latin America, Caribbean (20)	
		EU Eastern neighbourhood (14)	
		Other (2)	

offers access to a cloud-based consolidated database containing multiple and integrated watchlists[8] (CP-WatchList-Tech). This information was complemented with the description of a similar screening software, World-Check[9] (De Goede & Sullivan, 2016, 76–81), information available on the corporate websites of LexisNexis Risk Solutions[10] and CSI WatchDOG Elite[11] and a qualitative interview with a European representative of LexisNexis (as of Autumn 2021). While the latter contributed to a better understanding of the technical side, the information obtained was verified by triangulation, namely, correspondence with an advisor working at a European aid organization using the tool.

While the matter of screening is known both in academic and practitioner circles, it is usually discussed in the context of aid organizations' involuntary involvement or reluctant participation in counterterrorism. As very few aid organizations acknowledge publicly—let us say, on its website—that it screens individuals at large scale, collecting scientifically reliable data on the number and profile of aid organizations that conduct screening posed a huge challenge. Noting that the online survey contained two questions regarding screening,[12] and screening also emerged as a data protection concern during the interviews, publicly available privacy notices (PNs) posted on organizations' websites were assessed for mapping how organizations communicated screening, if at all, vis-à-vis the data subjects (RQ 2). Having considered the disadvantages—privacy notices are not mentioned in the GDPR as a modality of communications,

---

[8] Researchers cannot escape the matter of secrecy either when "they encounter confidential material" (De Goede et al. 2019). Therefore, both the company name (CompliancePartner) and the product name (CP-WatchList-Tech) are fictional because the person providing information has left the company since our email correspondence. While the original company and product names have been anonymized, the year of publication (version) and page numbers are encrypted wherever the internal documents are cited.

[9] World-Check used to be a Thomson-Reuters product, but has been operated by Refinitiv/LSEG for years, https://www.lseg.com/en/risk-intelligence/screening-solutions/world-check-kyc-screening.

[10] https://risk.lexisnexis.com/products/worldcompliance-data. Lexis Nexis offers other risk management solutions to its clients, see: https://risk.lexisnexis.com/products.

[11] https://www.csiweb.com/how-we-help/regulatory-compliance/sanctions-screening/.

[12] Q10 asked about the typical purposes for data collection; Q15c (a follow-up question) inquired about the specific purposes of collecting personal data for meeting donor requirements.

they are heavily criticized for being incomprehensible regardless of jurisdictions (Becher & Benoliel, 2021; Zarsky, 2022, 1461–1464) and NGOs themselves share information about their data processing operations in privacy notices in different ways—privacy notices posted on websites were selected simply for their accessibility.

Yet, it should also be acknowledged that privacy notices were used as proxies (an alternative to ethnographic data, *see later*) assuming that if screening can be conceptualized as a data processing operation, data subjects (individuals screened) have right to know about it. The availability and accessibility of these documents also ensured comparison across organizations. While PNs were scrutinized for any reference to screening in Autumn 2022, terms such as (ethical) screening, vetting, background check, due diligence, fraud prevention, and AML/CFT were deemed 'direct' evidence. Indirect formulation was also considered for the extent to which screening may have been inferred from other wording. Considering that there are thousands of NGOs registered in the EU/EEA, NGOs were selected based on their VOICE membership[13] ($n = 88$) as well as on a random basis ($n = 5$) so that larger actors present in multiple areas with a diverse profile and employee pool were part of the sample. All in all, the content of 92 publicly available privacy notices was assessed for evidence on screening (usually under the subthemes derived from GDPR: purposes of processing, legitimate interest, data transfer to third parties as data processors) in November 2022.[14]

A hybrid workshop was also arranged at Peace Research Institute Oslo (PRIO) in September 2022, with the primary purpose to provide an opportunity for practitioners to discuss the practices and data protection dilemmas of screening (RQ-2; RQ-5). Invitation was sent out to humanitarian organizations by email and by an open call posted on the website of

---

[13] VOICE stands for Voluntary Organisations in Cooperation in Emergencies. It is the largest European humanitarian NGO network promoting efficient and effective humanitarian aid worldwide since 1992, *see* https://voiceeu.org/.

[14] Only one privacy notice per aid NGO was publicly available with the exception of two organizations (NRC, PLAN UK). Larger NGOs may have multiple privacy notices (PNs) (for internal use only) addressed to various groups of people (data subjects: candidates, employees, etc.), which may be subject to change. For example, PLAN UK has revised its privacy notices since the data collection was closed (in November 2022); it used to have six PNs, but in early 2023 there were four. Three NGOs did not have a privacy notice as of November 2022. Please, note that the content of and access to privacy notices on websites may dynamically change.

the Norwegian Centre for Humanitarian Studies.[15] Both forms contained a notification about the dual purpose of the event (facilitating discussion on the topic, data collection for the purpose of research). Altogether 16 different organizations indicated intention to participate by responding to the invitation, about one-third of which showed up. Actual participants included and legal advisors, compliance or data protection officers (DPOs) ($n = 11$) of European humanitarian organizations ($n = 6$), researchers working with themes such as humanitarianism, security and technology as scholars, consultants or both ($n = 7$).

With regard to research ethics and following the EU guidelines (EU, 2021), information on the details of the research was shared with the participants by email based on which they could consider informed participation. Key informants also were provided with the opportunity to read the original manuscripts, incorporated also into this book, before submission.[16]

Concerning the limitations, the book can offer neither a full picture on screening, nor a comprehensive assessment of NGO conduct with regard to any data protection law. As for the latter while restrictions might apply in certain jurisdictions, relevant provisions of the EU GDPR[17] (2016) will be used to illustrate the transparency obligations that are applicable in the case of INGOs that are registered in the EU/European Economic Area (EEA). As for the former, mapping internal organizational practices and procedures would have required field ('ethnographic') research at multiple venues (organizations' headquarters) to see how due diligence and compliance procedures are implemented in practice and how screening-related decisions are made. As it was neither ambitioned, not a realistic option, pure legal analysis could not be aspired either as it would have required access to internal sources documenting facts, that is, NGO policies (on due diligence, data protection, screening) and procedures of their notification practices. Such legal analysis—yet to be conducted by someone—is necessary to answer the open-ended question placed at the end of the previous section and prompted by Chapter 5.

---

[15] *Screening as a data processing operation in aid work.* Closed workshop (with Chatham House rules). Oslo, Peace Research Institute, September 23, 2022, Oslo, https://www.humanitarianstudies.no/events/screening-as-a-data-processing-operation-in-aid-work/.

[16] Earlier versions of Chapter 3 (Paragi, 2023) and Chapter 4 (Paragi, forthcoming).

[17] The GDPR is relevant the extent to which screening can be conceptualized as a data processing operation alongside the provisions of the GDPR.

To compensate for the lack of ethnographic data during the research process and the low response rate concerning a vein attempt of a second online survey,[18] desk research was used to complement the information provided by the practitioners throughout the interviews and workshops. Reports and guidelines communicating NGOs' experiences with counter-terrorism, financial surveillance and data protection were re-reviewed for gathering open-source information on screening. The most relevant sources to be mentioned: the *International Review of the Red Cross* and featured articles on the ICRC's website[19]; a toolkit developed by the Norwegian Research Council (*Toolkit for principled humanitarian action: Managing counterterrorism risks*)[20]; publications and resources available on the website of US-based Charity & Security Network[21] and that of the European Center for Not-for Profit Law Stichting (ECLN).[22]

Last, but not least, it should also be briefly acknowledged that the author of this book may not have been the best-positioned researcher to explore this subject. Being affiliated with a Hungarian university[23]

---

[18] The second survey (questionnaire on reasonable measures and related notification procedures) contained seven open-ended questions, without collecting any personal data or demographic info from the respondents. The invitation to fill out the second survey was sent out in a targeted manner to those that had indicated their interest in the workshop in September 2022; was posted on the NCHS-website (June 29, 2023, https://www.humanitarianstudies.no/news/survey-screening-data-protec tion-and-transparency-in-aid-work/) and was also circulated in a VOICE newsletter in June 2023 (ca. 600 email-recipients). Two reminders were sent to participants of the earlier qualitative interviews and those that indicated their interest in the workshop. Altogether only five organizations shared their experiences by filling out the form, insights from which will be cited to illustrate specific features of the screening process. Considering that the research started in Spring 2021 and the manuscript of this book was delivered in Autumn 2023, multiple reasons can be cited for low response rate. In addition to the researcher's positionality one can mention general survey fatigue, permanent or temporary (sick, maternity) leave, organizational changes affecting the staff and potentially also the delicacy of the research topic itself.

[19] https://casebook.icrc.org/highlight/terrorism-counterterrorism-and-ihl   and http://international-review.icrc.org/reviews/irrc-no-916-917-counterterrorism-sancti ons-and-war.

[20] https://www.nrc.no/toolkit/principled-humanitarian-action-managing-counterterro rism-risks/.

[21] https://charityandsecurity.org/.

[22] https://ecnl.org/focus-areas/security-and-counter-terrorism.

[23] The commission (EC) froze grants from Horizon Europe and Erasmus+ student exchange for 21 universities (entities that are organised in the form of or maintained by

and doing research on some opaque practices of international (Western European) NGOs while the Hungarian government labelled certain civil society organizations operating in Hungary either as 'foreign agents', or as risks to national security (Romaniuk, 2022) may not have been an ideal combination. As the managing director of a European advocacy organization kindly summarized it while we discussed my perceptions on NGOs' distrust towards my research on transparency-related matters: "when transparency around screening is scrutinized, one can easily deliver arguments to those governments that persecute aid and human rights organizations by demanding full transparency only to restrict their operational environment. Your citizenship and affiliation most unfortunately do not help in this regard".[24] Yet, one cannot disregard the argument put forth by Fejerskov et al. (2023, 2) either:

> Datafication inherent in humanitarian in digital humanitarianism does the opposite of what humanitarian organizations expect: [it] opens new expanses of ignorance and unknowns in humanitarian affairs.

These words are to be read in line with the 'politics of anti-knowledge' and the counterterrorist's criticized 'passion for ignorance' unpacked in critical counterterrorism studies (Jackson, 2015b). Such expressions reflect the understanding that neither the moral status of 'terrorists' deserve attention for "them being evil and irrational by default", nor "context, culture or language matters when judging certain individuals or acts in name of protecting and preventing others" (Zulaika, 2012, 54 cited by Jackson, 2015b, 45). Considering that the pool of individuals screened by aid organizations is not limited to (potential) terrorists and

---

public interest) as a measure "for the protection of the Union budget against breaches of the principles of the rule of law in Hungary". *Joint statement by Commissioners Hahn and Gabriel on the application of Council Implementing Decision of 15 December 2022 in relation to Hungarian public interest trusts.* January 26, 2023, https://erasmus-plus.ec.europa.eu/news/joint-statement-by-commissioners-hahn-and-gabriel-on-the-application-of-council-implementing-decision-of-15-december-2022-in-relation-to-hungarian-public-interest-trusts.

[24] I had two independent discussions during the research process with similar conclusions, a Zoom-call in March 2021 (with the director of a human rights advocacy organization, *see also* Paragi, 2022) and a Whatsapp-call with the director of a legal advocacy organization (September 2023).

criminals—the entire point of screening is to sort out persons listed in various databases—the question how much information is provided to 'data subjects' is not simply a legal issue emerging in the context of data protection, but closely related to control and power, certain mechanisms of which are appropriated by aid organizations—(in)voluntary members of security chains (De Goede 2018)—in name of providing care and recognition.

STRUCTURE

The book unfolds as follows. This Introduction is followed by a brief contextualization of reasonable efforts required from aid organizations, screening included, in light of the scholarship discussing securitization in and of the aid sector (Chapter 2). Chapter 3 introduces and conceptualizes screening as a data processing operation and focuses on the principle of transparency to explore how the right to information is fulfilled by aid organizations. As findings indicate considerable opacity prevails around screening, which facilitates analysing screening in light of surveillance studies in Chapter 4. As its core empirical part, this chapter introduces a tool used for screening following the analytical logic offered by Lyon (2007a, 26–27). Screening—as a digital tool and space of surveillance— is explored by focusing on rationalization, urgency, sorting, technology, knowledgeability, and the power relations between the watchers and the watched. Knowledgeability and data subjects' reasonable expectations deserve attention because they are inherently linked with data protection principles and the right to information in the context of privacy studies (Bygrave, 2014; Klareen, 2013; Vrabec, 2021), with human rights and counterterrorism (Tzanou, 2017) and also because they illustrate power imbalances between the watchers and the watched as discussed. Chapter 5, as a sort of discussion, focuses on the politics of transparency by highlighting the delicate political environment contextualizing constraining aid organizations' moral dilemmas.

REFERENCES

Adams, R. (2020). *Transparency. New Trajectories in Law*. Routledge.

Akal, A. B. (2022). *Tacit Engagement as a Form of Remote Management: Risk Aversity in the Face of Sanctions Regimes* (NCHS Paper). Retrieved November 8, 2022, from https://www.humanitarianstudies.no/resource/tacit-engagement-as-a-form-of-remote-management-risk-aversity-in-the-face-of-sanctions-regimes/

Amicelle, A., & Favarel-Garrigues, G. (2012). Financial Surveillance: Who Cares. *Journal of Cultural Economy, 5*(1), 105–124. https://doi.org/10.1080/175 30350.2012.640560

Amnesty International. (2020). *AI Report 2020/2021: The State of the World's Human Rights*. Retrieved May 20, 2022, from https://reliefweb.int/sites/ reliefweb.int/files/resources/POL1032022021ENGLISH.PDF

Amoore, L. (2007). Vigilant Visualities: The Watchful Politics of the War on Terror. *Security Dialogue, 38*(2), 215–232. https://doi.org/10.1177/096 7010607078526

Amoore, L., & De Goede, M. (Eds.). (2008). *Risk and the War on Terror*. Routledge.

Amoore, L., & Langley, P. (2004). Ambiguities of Global Civil Society. *Review of International Studies, 30*(1), 89–110.

Anderson, M. B. (1999). *Do No Harm: How Aid Can Support Peace - or War.* Boulder, CO: Lynne Rienner.

Anwar, T., Wesseling, M., & Soares, R. R. (2022). *New Tech, Perpetual Challenges. How Emerging Technologies for Financial Compliance are Impacting the Nonprofit Sector* (European Center for Not-for-Profit Law). Retrieved October 15, 2023, from https://ecnl.org/sites/default/files/2022-09/ ECNL%20FINTECH%20Report.pdf

Aradau, C. (2004). The Perverse Politics of Four-Letter Words: Risk and Pity in the Securitisation of Human Trafficking. *Millennium, 33*(2), 251–278. https://doi.org/10.1177/03058298040330020101

Barnett, M. N. (2002). *Empire of Humanity. A History of Humanitarianism*. Cornell University Press.

Barnett, M. N. (2013). Humanitarian Governance. *Annual Review of Political Science, 16*(1), 379–398.

Bauman, Z. (1991). *Modernity and Ambivalence*. Polity Press.

Becher, S. I., & Benoliel, U. (2021). Law in Books and Law in Action: The Readability of Privacy Policies and the GDPR. In K. Mathis & A. Tor (Eds.), *Consumer Law and Economics. Economic Analysis of Law in European Legal Scholarship* (Vol. 9, pp. 179–204). Springer. https://doi.org/10.1007/978-3-030-49028-7_9

Beck, U. (1992). *The Risk Society. Towards a New Modernity*. SAGE.

Bennett, C. J. (2018). The European General Data Protection Regulation: An Instrument for the Globalization of Privacy Standards? *Information Polity, 23*(2), 239–246. https://doi.org/10.3233/IP-180002

Beyribey, T. (2020). Medico-Political Metaphors of Counter-Terrorism: The Case of Turkey. *Critical Studies on Terrorism, 13*(3), 418–440. https://doi.org/ 10.1080/17539153.2020.1791388

Buzan, B., Wæver, O., & de Wilde, J. (1998). *Security: A New Framework for Analysis*. Lynne Rienner.

Bygrave, L. A. (2014). Core Principles of Data Privacy Law. In *Data Privacy Law: An International Perspective* (Online ed., pp. 145–168). Oxford Academic. Retrieved October 13, 2022, from https://doi.org/10.1093/acprof:oso/9780199675555.003.0005

Dean, M. (1999/2010). *Governmentality: Power and Rule in Modern Society.* (2nd ed.). Sage.

De Goede, M. (2012). *Speculative Security: The Politics of Pursuing Terrorist Monies.* University of Minnesota Press.

De Goede, M. (2018). The Chain of Security. *Review of International Studies, 44*(1), 24–42. https://doi.org/10.1017/S026021051700035

De Goede, M., & Sullivan, G. (2016). The Politics of Security Lists. *Environment and Planning D: Society and Space, 34*(1), 67–88. https://doi.org/10.1177/0263775815599309

De Goede, M., Bosma, E., (eds) Pallister-Wilkins, P. (2019) Secrecy and Methods in Security Research: A Guide to Qualitative Fieldwork. London: Routledge

Donini, A., & Gordon, S. (2015). Romancing Principles and Human Rights: Are Humanitarian Principles Salvageable? *International Review of the Red Cross, 97*(897–8), 77–109.

Duffield, M. (2001). *Global Governance and the New Wars: The Merging of Development and Security.* Zed Books.

Duffield, M. (2007). *Development, Governing the World of Peoples.* Polity Press.

Duffield, M. (2010). Risk-Management and the Fortified Aid Compound: Everyday Life in Post-Interventionary Society. *Journal of Intervention and State Building, 4*(4), 453–474. https://doi.org/10.1080/17502971003700993

Duffield, M. (2016). The Resilience of the Ruins: Towards a Critique of Digital Humanitarianism. *Resilience, 4*(3), 147–165. https://doi.org/10.1080/21693293.2016.1153772

Duroch, F., & Neuman, M. (2021). *Should We Discriminate in Order to Act? Profiling: A Necessary but Debated Practice* (HPN Paper). Retrieved April 8, 2022, from https://odihpn.org/publication/should-we-discriminate-in-order-to-act-profiling-a-necessary-but-debated-practice/

Eckert, S. (2022). Counterterrorism, Sanctions and Financial Access Challenges: Course Corrections to Safeguard Humanitarian Action. *International Review of the Red Cross, 103*(916–917), 415–458. https://international-review.icrc.org/articles/counterterrorism-sanctions-and-financial-access-challenges-916#footnote81_27rk033

EU (European Union). (2021). *Ethics in Social Science and Humanities.* European Commission. https://ec.europa.eu/info/funding-tenders/opportunities/docs/2021-2027/horizon/guidance/ethics-in-social-science-and-humanities_he_en.pdf

EU GDPR (European Union General Data Protection Regulation). (2016). *Regulation 2016/679 of the European Parliament and of the Council of 27 April 2016 on the Protection of Natural Persons with Regard to the Processing of Personal Data and on the Free Movement of Such Data.* Retrieved April 8, 2022, from https://eur-lex.europa.eu/eli/reg/2016/679/oj

Fassin, D. (2007). Humanitarianism as a Politics of Life. *Public Culture, 19*(3), 499–520. https://doi.org/10.1215/08992363-2007-007

Fast, L., & Jacobsen, K. L. (2019). Rethinking Access: How Humanitarian Technology Blurs Control and Care. *Disasters, 43*(S2), S151–S168. https://doi.org/10.1111/disa.12333

Fechter, A.-M. (Ed.). (2014). *The Personal and the Professional in Aid Work.* Routledge.

Federer, J. P. (2022). The Politics of Proscription and Peacemaking: Implications of Labelling Armed Groups as Terrorists and Extremists. *Journal of Intervention and Statebuilding, 17*(2), 207–213. https://doi.org/10.1080/175 02977.2022.2107361

Fejerskov, A. M., Clausen, M. -L., & Seddig, S. (2023). Humanitarian Ignorance: Towards a New Paradigm of Non-Knowledge in Digital Humanitarianism. *Disasters.* Advance online publication. https://doi.org/10.1111/disa.12609

Franko, K. (2020). *The Crimmigrant Other—Migration and Penal Power.* Routledge.

Franz, V., Hannah, L., & Hayes, B. (2020). *Civil Society Organizations and General Data Protection Regulation Compliance Challenges, Opportunities, and Best Practice.* Open Society Foundation. Retrieved April 18, 2022, from https://www.opensocietyfoundations.org/publications/civil-society-org anizations-and-general-data-protection-regulation-compliance

Gazi, T. (2020). Data to the Rescue: How Humanitarian Aid Organizations Should Collect Information Based on the GDPR. *International Journal Humanitarian Action, 5*(9), 1–7. https://doi.org/10.1186/s41018-020-00078-0

Gillard, E. (2021a). *IHL and the Humanitarian Impact of Counterterrorism Measures and Santions. Unintended Ill Effects of Well-Intended Measures* (Chatham House Report). Retrieved April 28, 2022, from https://www.chathamhouse.org/2021/09/ihl-and-humanitar ian-impact-counterterrorism-measures-and-sanctions/04-funding-agreements

Gillard, E. (2021b). Screening of Final Beneficiaries—A Red Line in Humanitarian Operations. An Emerging Concern in Development Work. *International Review of the Red Cross, 103*(916–917), 517–537. https://int ernational-review.icrc.org/articles/screening-of-final-beneficiaries-a-red-line-in-humanitarian-operations-916

Goold, B. J., & Neyland, D. (2009). *New Directions in Surveillance and Privacy.* Routledge.

Harris, R. W. (2016). How ICT4D Research Fails the Poor. *Information Technology for Development, 22*(1), 177–192. https://doi.org/10.1080/026 81102.2015.1018115

Hayes, B. (2012a). Counter-Terrorism, "Policy Laundering," and the FATF: Legalizing Surveillance, Regulating Civil Society. *The International Journal of Not-for-Profit Law, 12*(1–2), 1–40. https://www.icnl.org/resources/res earch/ijnl/1-introduction-2

Hayes, B. (2012b). The Surveillance-Industrial Complex. In K. Ball, K. D. Haggerty, & D. Lyon (Eds.), *Routledge Handbook of Surveillance Studies* (pp. 167–175). Routledge. https://doi.org/10.4324/9780203814949.ch2_2_c

Hayes, B. (2017). *The Impact of International Counter-Terrorism on Civil Society Organisations: Understanding the Role of the Financial Action Task Force.* Bread for the World. Retrieved May 8, 2022, from http://efc.issuelab.org/resources/27481/27481.pdf

Heath-Kelly, C., & Gruber, B. (2023). *Vulnerability. Governing the social through security politics.* Manchester University Press.

Helgesson, K. S., & Mörth, U. (2019). Instruments of Securitization and Resisting Subjects: For-Profit Professionals in the Finance-Security Nexus. *Security Dialogue, 50*(3), 257–274. https://doi.org/10.1177/096701061 9835655

Hosein, G., & Nyst, C. (2013). *Aiding Surveillance: an Exploration of How Development and Humanitarian Aid Initiatives are Enabling Surveillance in Developing Countries.* Privacy International. https://privacyinternational.org/sites/default/files/2017-12/Aiding%20Surveillance.pdf

Howell, J. (2014). The Securitisation of INGOs Post-9/11. *Conflict, Security and Development, 14*(2), 151–179. https://doi.org/10.1080/14678802.2014.903692

Howell, J., & Lind, J. (2009). *Counter-Terrorism, Aid and Civil Society: Before and After the War on Terror.* Palgrave.

IFRC (International Federation of Red Cross) (2021). *Practical Guidance for Data Protection in Cash and Voucher Assistance.* https://www.ifrc.org/doc ument/practical-guidance-data-protection-cash-and-voucher-assistance

Jackson, P. (Ed.). (2015a). *Handbook of International Security and Development.* Routledge.

Jackson, R. (2015b). The Epistemological Crisis of Counterterrorism. *Critical Studies on Terrorism, 8*(3), 33–54. https://doi.org/10.1080/17539153.2015.1009762s

Jacobsen, K. L. (2015). *The Politics of Humanitarian Technology: Good Intentions, Unintended Consequences and Insecurity.* Routledge.

Jarvis, L. (2019). Terrorism, Counter-Terrorism, and Critique: Opportunities, Examples, and Implications. *Critical Studies on Terrorism, 12*(2), 339–358. https://doi.org/10.1080/17539153.2019.1575607

Jordan, L., & Van Tujil, P. (2006). *NGO Accountability. Politics, Principles and Innovations.* Earthscan.

Jubany, O. (2011). Constructing Truths in a Culture of Disbelief: Understanding Asylum Screening from Within. *International Sociology, 26*(1), 74–94. https://doi.org/10.1177/0268580910380978

Kalfeis, M., & Knodel, K. (2021). *NGOs and Lifewords in Africa. Transdisciplinary Perspectives*. Berghahn Books.

Klareen, J. (2013). The Human Right to Information and Transparency. In A. Bianchi & A. Peters (Eds.), *Transparency in International Law* (pp. 223–238). Cambridge University Press.

Kuldova, T. Ø. (2022). *Compliance-Industrial Complex the Operating System of a Pre-Crime Society*. Palgrave Macmillan.

Kundnani, A., & Hayes, B. (2018). *The Globalisation of Countering Violent Extremism Policies: Undermining Human Rights, Instrumentalising Civil Society* (TNI Report). Transnational Institute (TNI) in Association with SOURCE Network on Societal Security. Retrieved October 1, 2023, from https://www.tni.org/files/publication-downloads/the_globalisation_of_countering_violent_extremism_policies.pdf

Kuner, C., & Marelli, M. (Eds.). (2020). *Handbook on Data Protection in Humanitarian Action* (2nd ed.). ICRC—Brussels Privacy Hub. Retrieved March 3, 2022, from https://www.icrc.org/en/data-protection-humanitarian-action-handbook

Lyon, D. (2007a). *Surveillance Studies: An Overview*. Polity Press.

Lyon, D. (2007b). Airport Screening, Surveillance, and Social Sorting: Canadian Responses to 9/11 in Context. *Canadian Journal of Criminology and Criminal Justice, 48*(3), 397–411. https://doi.org/10.3138/cjccj.48.3.397

Martin, A. (2023). Aidwashing Surveillance: Critiquing the Corporate Exploitation of Humanitarian Crises. *Surveillance & Society, 21*(1), 96–102. https://doi.org/10.24908/ss.v21i1.16266

Milanovic, M. (2013). Foreign Surveillance and Human Rights: Do Foreigners Deserve Privacy? Part 1–5. *EJIL: Talk! Blog of the European Journal of International Law*. Retrieved October 14, 2022, from https://www.ejiltalk.org/foreign-surveillance-and-human-rights-introduction/

Minella, C. M. (2019). Counter-Terrorism Resolutions and Listing of Terrorists and Their Organizations by the United Nations. In E. Shor & S. Hoadley (Eds.), *International Human Rights and Counter-Terrorism* (pp. 31–53). Springer.

Mongoven, A. (2006). The War on Disease and the War on Terror: A Dangerous Metaphorical Nexus? *Cambridge Quarterly of Healthcare Ethics, 15*(4), 403–416. https://doi.org/10.1017/S0963180106060518

Muhomed, S., Puri, J., Stickler, H., & Sugand, D. (2021). *NGOs' Due Diligence and Risk Mititagion: A Holistic Approach*. London School of Economics and Political Science and The Charity and Security Network. Retrieved September

13, 2023, from https://charityandsecurity.org/wp-content/uploads/2021/04/NGOs-Due-Diligence-and-Risk-Mitigation.pdf

Murray, I., Umbers, L., & Wesson, M. (2023). Regulating Political Advocacy by Charities Liberally. *Nonprofit and Voluntary Sector Quarterly, 53*(1), 236–256. Advance online publication. https://doi.org/10.1177/08997640221145116

NRC (Norwegian Refugee Council). (2018a). *Principles Under Pressure: The Impact of Counterterrorism Measures and Preventing/Countering Violent Extremism on Principled Humanitarian Action.* Retrieved March 13, 2021, from https://reliefweb.int/sites/reliefweb.int/files/resources/nrc-principles_under_pressure-report-screen.pdf

NRC (Norwegian Refugee Council). (2018b). *Understanding Conditional Clauses.* Retrieved March 13, 2021, from https://www.nrc.no/shorthand/stories/understanding-counterterrorism-clauses/index.html and https://www.nrc.no/globalassets/pdf/reports/toolkit/nrc_toolkit_03_reviewing-counterterrorism-clauses.pdf

O'Leary, E. (2021). Politics and principles: The impact of counterterrorism measures and sanctions on principled humanitarian action. *International Review of the Red Cross, 103*(916–917), 459–477. https://doi.org/10.1017/S1816383121000357

OECD (Organisation for Economic Co-operation and Development). (2008). *The Paris Declaration on Aid Effectiveness and the Accra Agenda for Action.* https://www.oecd.org/dac/effectiveness/34428351.pdf

Paragi, B. (2021). Digital4development? European Data Protection in the Global South. *Third World Quarterly, 42*(2), 254–273. https://doi.org/10.1080/01436597.2020.1811961

Paragi, B. (2022) Challenges in Using Online Surveys for Research Involving Sensitive Topics: Data Protection Practices of European NGOs Operating in the Global South. *SAGE Research Methods Cases – Doing Research Online.* https://methods.sagepub.com/case/online-surveys-delicate-sensitive-topics-data-protection-european-ngos

Paragi, B. (2023). *Opacity or transparency? Screening by NGOs in the context of aid work.* NCHS-paper. Oslo: Norwegian Centre for Humanitarian Studies. https://www.humanitarianstudies.no/resource/opacity-or-transparency-screening-by-ngos-in-the-context-of-aid-work/

Pallister-Wilkins, P. (2021). Saving the Souls of White Folk: Humanitarianism as White Supremacy. *Security Dialogue, 52*(1_suppl), 98–106. https://doi.org/10.1177/0967010621102441

Qureshi, S. (2019). Perspectives on Development: Why Does Studying Information and Communication Technology for Development (ICT4D) Matter? *Information Technology for Development, 25*(3), 381–389. https://doi.org/10.1080/02681102.2019.1658478

Rayner, M., et al. (Eds.). (2017). Screening and Surveillance. In M. Rayner, K. Wickramasinghe, J. Williams, K. McColl, & S. Mendis (Eds.), *An Introduction to Population-Level Prevention of Non-Communicable Diseases* (Online ed., pp. P.7.1–P7.86). Oxford Academic. https://doi.org/10.1093/med/9780198791188.003.0007

Rébé, N. (2020). *Counter-Terrorism Financing: International Best Practices and the Law*. Brill.

Romaniuk, S. (2022). *Under Siege: Counterterrorism and Civil Society in Hungary*. Lexington Books.

Rose, N. (1989). *Governing the Soul: The Shaping of the Private Self*. New York: Routledge.

Sandvik, K. B. (2023). *Humanitarian Extractivism. The Digital Transformation of Aid*. Manchester University Press.

Sandvik, K. B., Jacobsen, K. L., & McDonald, S. M. (2017). Do Not Harm: A Taxonomy of the Challenges of Humanitarian Experimentation. *International Review of the Red Cross, 99*(1), 319–344. https://doi.org/10.1017/S181638311700042X

Sandvik, K., Gabrielsen Jumbert, M., Karlsrud, J., & Kaufmann, M. (2014). Humanitarian Technology: A Critical Research Agenda. *International Review of the Red Cross, 96*(893), 219–242. https://doi.org/10.1017/S1816383114000344

Schmidt, J. (2022). The European Union and the Promotion of Values in Its External Relations—The Case of Data Protection. In J. Lee & A. Darbellay (Eds.), *Data Governance in AI, FinTech and Legal Tech* (pp. 238–262). Edward Elgar Tech.

Scott, J. C. (1998). *Seeing Like a State. How Certain Schemes to Improve the Human Condition Have Failed*. Yale University Press.

Skinner-Thompson, S. (2022). Introduction: Privacy Studies, Surveillance Law. *Surveillance & Society, 20*(3), 294–296. https://doi.org/10.24908/ss.v20i3.15774

Spencer, A. (2012). The Social Construction of Terrorism: Media, Metaphors and Policy Implications. *Journal of International Relations and Development, 15*, 393–419. https://doi.org/10.1057/jird.2012.4

Steele, R. J. (2018). Screening and Surveillance-Principles and Practice. *The British Journal of Radiology, 91*(1090). https://doi.org/10.1259/bjr.20180200

Stokke, O. (1995). *Aid and Political Conditionality*. Routledge.

Sullivan, G. (2020). *The Law of the List. UN Counterterrorism Sanctions and the Politics of Global Security Law*. Cambridge University Press.

Szent-Iványi, B. (2023). *European Civil Society and International Development Aid*. Routledge.

També, N. (2021). *Unintended Consequences of AML/CFT Regulation: The Challenges of Banking Non-Profit Organisations.* European Center for Not-for-Profit Law. Retrieved September 1, 2023, from https://ecnl.org/public ations/unintended-consequences-amlcft-regulation-challenges-banking-non-profit-organisations

Tzanou, M. (2017). *The Fundamental Right to Data Protection: Normative Value in the Context of Counter-Terrorism Surveillance.* Hart Publishing.

UN SR HR/CT. (2019). *Impact of Measures to Address Terrorism and Violent Extremism on Civic Space and the Rights of Civil Society Actors and Human Rights Defenders: Report of the Special Rapporteur on the Promotion and Protection of Human Rights and Fundamental Freedoms While Countering Terrorism* (A/HRC/40/52). UN Human Rights Council. Retrieved June 8, 2022, from https://documents-dds-ny.un.org/doc/UNDOC/GEN/G19/057/59/PDF/G1905759.pdf?OpenElement

UN SR HR/CT. (2023). *Global Study on the Impact of Counter-Terrorism on Civil Society and Civic Space.* UN Human Rights Council. Retrieved August 8, 2023, from https://defendcivicspace.com/wp-content/uploads/2023/06/SRCT_GlobalStudy.pdf

USAID (U.S. Agency for International Development). (2021). *ADS Chapter 319 Partner Vetting.* New Edition Date: 01/15/2021 Responsible Office: M/MPBP File Name: 319_011521. USAID. Retrieved October 24, 2023, from https://www.usaid.gov/sites/default/files/2023-07/319.pdf

Vaughn, J. (2009). The Unlikely Securitizer: Humanitarian Organizations and the Securitization of Indistinctiveness. *Security Dialogue, 40*(3), 263–285. https://doi.org/10.1177/0967010609336194

VOICE (Voluntary Organisations in Cooperation in Emergencies). (2021). *Adding to the Evidence the Impacts of Sanctions and Restrictive Measures on Humanitarian Action* (VOICE Survey Report). Retrieved January 20, 2022, from https://voiceeu.org/search?q=adding+to+the+evidence

Vrabec, H. U. (2021). The Right to Information. In *Data Subject Rights Under the GDPR* (Oxford Academic, Online ed., pp. 64–101). Oxford University Press. https://doi.org/10.1093/oso/9780198868422.003.0004

Walsham, G. (2017). ICT4D Research: Reflections on History and Future Agenda. *Information Technology for Development, 23*(1), 18–41. https://doi.org/10.1080/02681102.2016.1246406

Watson, S., & Burles, R. (2018). Regulating NGO Funding: Securitizing the Political. *International Relations, 32*(4), 430–448. https://doi.org/10.1177/0047117818782604

Weitzberg, K., Cheesman, M., Martin, A., & Schoemaker, E. (2021). Between Surveillance and Recognition: Rethinking Digital Identity in Aid. *Big Data & Society, 8*(1), 1–8. https://doi.org/10.1177/20539517211006744

WHO (World Health Organization), Wilson, J. M., & Glover, J. G. (1968). *Principles and practice of screening for disease.* World Health Organization. https://iris.who.int/handle/10665/37650

Zarsky, T. (2022). Serious Notice: A Celebration, Discussion, and Recognition of Joel Reidenberg's Work on Privacy Notices and Disclosures. *Fordham Law Review, 90*(4), 1457–1487. Available at SSRN: https://ssrn.com/abstract= 4050682

Zulaika, J. (2012). Drones, Witches and Other Flying Objects: The Force of Fantasy in US Counterterrorism. *Critical Studies on Terrorism, 5*(1), 51–68. https://doi.org/10.1080/17539153.2012.659909

CHAPTER 2

Securitization and Compliance in Aid Work

Abstract This chapter provides a contextualization of screening by briefly summarizing the historical background of securitization characterizing the contemporary aid sector and recalling the main legal instruments and mechanisms used for this purpose. The mechanisms by means of which aid organizations are (in)advertently dragged into the counterterrorism game cover international and domestic laws regulating sanctions and terrorist listing, 'reasonable efforts' expected, conditional clauses in grant agreements and internal compliance procedures. Yet, it must be remembered that the donor side of the aid market is strongly concentrated: most of the contracts facilitating the implementation of aid projects with (conditional) funding in the Global South are signed with only five to ten OECD DAC donor countries. Furthermore, aid organizations also finance their activities from private funds that reveal other organizational interests in the domain of risk management.

Keywords Securitization · Counterterrorism regulations · Reasonable measures · Conditional funding · Risk management and compliance · Expert assistance

© The Author(s), under exclusive license to Springer Nature   35
Switzerland AG 2024
B. Paragi, *Screening by International Aid Organizations Operating in the Global South*, https://doi.org/10.1007/978-3-031-54165-0_2

Care, Assistance and Expertise Securitized

In Autumn 2021, six Palestinian human rights organizations were designated as terrorist organizations by Israel, the government of which officially asked donors to stop funding them. European Union (EU) member states hesitated to provide a straightforward answer to this 'call' in the absence of convincing evidence (Ziv & Abraham, 2022). They also had to be cautious because any official response would have entailed consequences, such as terminating funding to aid projects, in line with the so-called reasonable efforts expected in the context of anti-money laundering and combating the financing of terrorism (AML/CFT) (Rébé, 2020; Sullivan, 2020). This case, which will be sporadically referred to later in this book, illustrates the inescapabilty of the securitized chain of aid work. Key links in this chain include laws and regulations, among others, transactions, contracts, internal procedures that regulate or govern the relations of aid organizations operating in the Global South with international partners, foreign donors and financial service providers.

While practices and mechanisms of 'commercialized suspicion' merited academic attention (Hayes, 2012; Kuldova, 2022; Lyon, 2007), less is known about how non-state actors, more precisely, international aid organizations, implement 'reasonable measures' to mitigate risks in the era of surveillance societies. Therefore, this chapter addresses the question how aid organizations and their operations are securitized by compliance demands and what does the term 'reasonable efforts' mean in the context of aid work. The contemporary obsession with (preventing) risks, threats, extremism, radicalism or terrorism coupled with domestic and international legislation on counterterrorism, sanctions, national security implies that operations and transactions of actors that would nothing to do with national or public security have been increasingly securitized. It applies to diverse domains from the financial sector through the telecommunication industry to airlines (De Goede, 2018), from social welfare and health care sectors in and outside Europe (Heath-Kelly & Gruber, 2023) through border controls (Amelung et al., 2021) to international aid organizations operating in the Global South (Bloodgood & Tremblay-Boire, 2011; Howell, 2014; Howell & Lind, 2009; Jackson, 2015a; Watson & Burles, 2018).

Recalling that humanitarian action is considered a politics of life[1] (Fassin, 2007), securitization refers to a process whereby an issue is framed as an existential threat to survival, thereby justifying the use of immediate or emergency countermeasures by particular actors (Buzan et al., 1998, 23–24). The actors can be governments, political parties, authorities, international or non-governmental organizations—anyone that aspires to influence and capitalize on public opinion. This process is successful, if the audience—the public, the electorate, the voter or any other community—targeted with a message "tolerate[s] violations of rules that would otherwise have to be obeyed" (Buzan et al., 1998, 25). Both the nexus of security and development studies and that of humanitarian and security studies illustrate how aid allocation, projects and organizations are instrumentalized for security purposes and how aid work itself has become increasingly securitized due to its potential to mitigate risks (Duffield, 2001, 2007; Jackson, 2015a). If bioborders emerged "as a result of heterogeneous attempts to organize data border-crossing" to provide a sense of security to a diverse audience (Amelung et al., 2021), northern democracies—simultaneously also OECD DAC donors—not only regulate and control immigration in name of human rights and humanitarianism (Perkowiski, 2021) but have also been providing meaningful support to governments in the Global South with the aim of surveilling populations and preventing their movement towards the North (Bossong & Carrapico, 2016). As Hosein and Nyst (2013) demonstrated both development and humanitarian aid initiatives contributed to increasing surveillance in Global South countries, a practice which only became more prevalent since their study.

The general securitization agenda of the post-9/11 era could be escaped neither by aid organizations operating in the Global South, nor by Northern civil society organizations and citizens offering help to individuals arriving from the Global South. Hence, aid organizations are simultaneously seen as facilitators of security (by providing aid for increasing human and social security) and threats to security (by potentially raising funds for terrorist or criminal organizations) (Howell, 2014;

---

[1] Fassin (2007, 511) described politics in moral terms consisting of a war of 'an axis of good' against 'an axis of evil'. If "humanitarian aid is offered as a priority to those whose need to live is threatened by the indifference or the overt hostility of others", the politics of life (humanitarian agents) stands in contrast to the politics of death (criminal states or non-state actors).

Howell & Lind, 2009). As demonstrated both by academic scholarship and common sense too, their securitization involves both positive (inclusionary) and negative (repressive, exclusionary) measures depending on the context, jurisdictions, territory of operations, their size and reach and profile, to list only a few factors.

Aid organizations, as a result, are not only passively securitized entities, but also entities facilitating certain securitization. If securitizing discourses "identify a referent object that is threatened and endorse emergency measures to alleviate the threat", humanitarianism can also be conceptualized as a securitization process inasmuch as "certain actors are privileged in the identification of both human insecurity and the appropriate measures for 'restoring' affected humans to a condition of security" not just in conflict situations, but also in case of disasters (Watson, 2009, 15). For example, a main security goal of humanitarian organizations is to strengthen and demonstrate their distinctiveness by convincing others, especially, non-humanitarian actors that blurring the boundary between humanitarian and political means an existential threat to their organizational identity and physical-operational security too (Vaughn, 2009).

The impact of various risk-mitigating measures, counterterrorism included, on human rights in general (Minella, 2019) and on the civil space and aid organizations in particular, has been rather ambiguous. Civil society organizations have increasingly been co-opted as—voluntary or instrumentalized—actors for serving the purpose of prevention in the fight against terrorism and violent extremism for two main reasons. On the one hand, they are considered more reliable partners than official agencies in many contexts. On the other hand, aid organizations consider themselves experts—positioned better than traditional security actors— 'to cure' certain political 'illnesses'. Citing the UN Special Rapporteur on the promotion and protection of human rights and fundamental freedoms while countering terrorism (UN SR HR/CT, 2019, 5):

> where civil society actors are present in areas where the State is unable or unwilling to govern, they often play an intermediary role, owing to their credibility and access to remote communities … civil society restores confidence in national and international counter-terrorism efforts and the essential yet fragile trust between individuals, communities and the authorities in countering terrorism.

This observation resonates well with Bauman's argument on expertise which "creates and enhances the need of itself" due to the "principally unlimited multiplication of new problems which render expertise indispensable" (Bauman, 1991, 232). However, not only the definitions of and market-mediated solutions to such problems (risks) have been privatized by creating a compliance-industrial complex (Kuldova, 2022) and securitizing the aid sector, but ambivalence too. Recalling Bauman (1991, 197 and 220) ambivalence also "moved from the public to the private space" as

> [m]ost new developments in expertise and expertly produced 'targeted' technology are aimed at the repairing of damage perpetrated by older technology and expertise. Damage done by expertise may be cured only by more expertise. More expertise means, in its turn, yet more damage and more demand for expert cure.

The cycle seems vicious as aid organizations, admittedly or not, aspire either to compensate for the historical legacies of colonialism or to repair the wrongs stemming from global inequalities. Such inequalities, however, produce rather ambivalent risks (terrorism, organized crime on the one hand and responses, such as counterterrorism and PVE on the other hand) that may threaten aid organizations and workers too. Therefore, many NGOs relate to risk management in general, counterterrorism activities in particular in a rather ambivalent manner for the "complex and compounding misuse of counter-terrorism and P/CVE (preventing and countering violent extremism) measures and practices" in form of "judicial harassment, administrative measures, counterterrorism financing restrictions, listing and sanctions, and the weaponization of new technologies such as spyware and drones" against aid organizations, their staff and beneficiaries both in Global North and international (Global South) settings (UN SR HR/CT, 2023, 11). Humanitarian organizations working in conflict areas are particularly affected by the growing risk aversion among donors in relation to CT measures and sanction lists. As the technocratic and procedural conceptualization of risk (aversion) easily overwrites humanitarian principles, such measures can easily constrain humanitarian engagement with non-state armed groups—rebel or designated terrorist organizations—which may be in control of areas where people in need of aid are located (Federer, 2022; O'Leary 2021, 461).

Regardless of the academic critique of contemporary counterterrorism paradigm (Jackson, 2015b; Jarvis, 2019) and that of the compliance industry (Kuldova, 2022), to their organizational profile (development, humanitarian, human rights, advocacy) and legal status (non-governmental organization, governmental or intergovernmental agency or an entity enjoying special legal status), aid organizations are regulated by various legal instruments and market-mediated commercial solutions promising risk mitigation. Both official donors (spending taxpayers' money) and financial institutions facilitating money transfers between their clients implemented various measures with the intention to scrutinize aid organizations' local partners, private and official donors, monitoring their financial transactions and so on. International and domestic legislation, funding agreements offered by donors (Mackintosh & Duplat, 2013) and financial transactions of NGOs enjoy particular interest (Watson & Burles, 2018). The diverse set of instruments and mechanisms created engaged organizations that (in)voluntarily participate in risk management and securitization agendas (Bloodgood & Tremblay-Boire, 2011; Howell, 2014; Howell & Lind, 2009; Lazell and Petrikova, 2020). Hence, the purpose of the next sections is to summarize briefly how legal and other 'reasonable measures' are used to regulate aid organizations' operations and projects implemented in Global South countries in name of preventing terrorism and mitigating other kinds of risks.

INTERNATIONAL AND DOMESTIC LAWS REGULATING LISTING

The United Nations (UN), the European Union and other international organizations equally require their member states to combat terrorism by various interrelated measures, such as treaties and Security Council resolutions (Rébé, 2020, 18–20), intergovernmental organizations, such as UN Office of Counter-Terrorism, Council of Europe Committee on Counter-Terrorism, EU Counter-terrorism Coordinator, advisory tools (Rébé, 2020, 20–23), sanctions lists and domestic laws (De Goede & Sullivan, 2016; Rébé, 2020, 107–238; Sullivan, 2020).

Although sanctions and terrorist lists are not identical and used for different, but potential overlapping purposes, the politics of listing refers to official decisions about placing legal entities and natural persons on international or national sanctions lists or designating them as terrorists (Federer, 2022; Sullivan, 2020). Recalling Sullivan (2020, 56) listing as an 'operational form of writing' and a 'simple ordering technique' has become a key component of the global anti-terrorism campaign. However, while not every listed person is a terrorist, terms such as 'terrorism' or 'terrorist' do not have a universal definition. As a result, the list "helps bypass the problem of defining terrorism; it renders disparate localised threats commensurable; it enrols diverse actors into new preemptive security networks and quantifies potential future threats into something governable in the present" (Sullivan, 2020, 58).

In other words, lists and listing can be equally used, abused, or misused by those in power (Sullivan, 2020). For example, while contemporary Russia doubts the legality and legitimacy of sanctions against Russian citizens, Western governments consider it problematic that even imprisoned human rights defenders and journalists can be labelled as terrorists for "spreading misinformation, leaking state secrets and insulting authorities" in many parts of the world (Amnesty International, 2020, 16).

With the adoption of the UNSC Resolution 1373 (2001), the UN delegated extensive authoritative power to the Security Council. For more than two decades, the obligations listed in this legally binding resolution have required all member states to enact domestic laws that criminalize both terrorism and any support of terrorism by sanctions, freezing of assets, etc. Later on, UNSC Resolution 2396 (2017) was adopted under Chapter VII of the UN Charter which has since required states to develop systems for collecting biometric data "to properly identify terrorists, including foreign terrorist fighters", and to develop watchlists and databases "of known and suspected terrorists" and to share this data broadly, both domestically and internationally, to "screen travellers and conduct risk assessments" (UNSC, 2017, para 13 and 15). Although the resolution has been widely criticized for its grave human rights implications by legal scholars, UN experts and NGOs (Sullivan, 2020, 117), its main role and function has remained more or less intact since September 2001.

Recalling only the most relevant elements of the EU legislation—which is to be read in line with donor policies and funding agreements as well as the GDPR when it comes to certain data protection operations, such as screening—the European equivalent of UNSC 1373 was adopted a year later, in 2002 (Council Framework Decision 2002/475/JHA). Its main purpose has been to harmonize member states' legislative approaches to counterterrorism by requiring the introduction of criminal provisions on terrorism and lists of terrorist offences (Kaunert &

Léonard, 2019, 270). It was followed by the adoption of further protocols and directives and their subsequent revisions, such as the *Directive on money laundering* (2001/97/EC), the *Directive on AML/CFT* (2005/60/EC), the *Additional Protocol to Council of Europe Convention on the Prevention of Terrorism* (2015), the *Directive 2015/849 on preventing the use of financial system for money laundering or terrorist financing* (4th Anti-Money Laundering Directive) and the *Directive 2017/541 on Combating Terrorism and replacing Council Framework Decision 2002/475JHA and amending Council Decision 2005/671/JHA* (EU, 2017). These and related legal instruments regulate offences both of terrorism and terrorism financing. The comprehensive Directive on combating terrorism (EU, 2017/541) not only requires member states to establish criminal offences to target terrorist organizations and terrorist individuals as well as those who assist them, but it also allows considerable room for manoeuvring for law enforcement authorities by mentioning that even intention, that is, a terrorist offence yet to be committed is a crime itself. Article 11 (EU, 2017, Article 11, 88/15) carries particular relevance the extent to which it stipulates that

> [M]ember States shall take the necessary measures to ensure that providing or collecting funds, by any means, directly or indirectly, with the intention that they be used, or in the knowledge that they are to be used, in full or in part, to commit, or to contribute to the commission of, any of the offences referred to in Articles 3 to 10 is punishable as a criminal offence when committed intentionally;

> Where the terrorist financing referred to in paragraph 1 of this Article concerns any of the offences laid down in Articles 3, 4 and 9, it shall not be necessary that the funds be in fact used, in full or in part, to commit, or to contribute to the commission of, any of those offences, nor shall it be required that the offender knows for which specific offence or offences the funds are to be used.

Concerning the practical implications, since the adoption of the above-mentioned instruments, international financial institutions, accountants, lawyers and a wide range of other private actors have been obligated to follow a risk-based approach in their dealings with clients (EU, 2005) to prevent terrorism funding (Rébé, 2020). As explored, among others, by Helgesson and Mörth (2019, 258), these directives "include obligations to identify and monitor clients properly" as well as "to report suspicions of illicit financial transactions to the national financial police without informing the client concerned". International aid organizations are not exceptions as they are equally affected, sometimes even targeted, by counterterrorism legislations and regulations (Eckert, 2022; Hayes, 2012, 2017; O'Leary, 2021) and subject to financial surveillance (Amicelle, 2011; Amicelle & Favarel-Garrigues, 2012).

As this book is about larger international aid organizations, the majority of which benefits from official funding from the EU and/or its member states, the next section will focus on how various risks (primarily counterterrorism and related AML, but also organized crime or human trafficking) appear in funding agreements. Before moving forward, however, the nature of the 'aid market' should be approximated for it is strikingly concentrated. Although the OECD DAC has about 32 member states as of 2023 (labelled as Western or established donors), almost 70% of the official development assistance (ODA, a statistical category including also humanitarian and emergency assistance) comes from a small number of donor countries, namely, the USA, UK, Germany, France and Japan (Overton & Murray, 2021, 68).

Recalling data provided by the OECD DAC (2023) 80% of the total ODA (204 billion USD) was provided by ten countries in 2022: the big five donors—the United States (55.3 billion USD), the United Kingdom (15.7 billion USD), Germany (35 billion USD), France (15.8 billion USD)—and five medium donors—Canada (7.8 billion USD), Italy (6.4 billion USD), the Netherlands (6.4 billion), Sweden (5.4 billion USD) and Norway (5.1 billion USD). More than 10% (27.6 billion USD) of the total ODA was channelled via the European Union (EC) and 46% of it (93 billion USD) was provided by EU-member DAC donors. As implied, the listed donors exert far more and stronger influence via the funding agreements and contracts (with or without conditional clauses) than the remaining 20–25 OECD DAC members or non-DAC donors.

Countering Risks by Donors: Conditionality in Funding Agreements

In addition to legal frameworks summarized above briefly, conditional clauses in funding agreements also push aid organizations to implement reasonable measures—such as screening—to remain eligible for future tenders. Conditional clauses have become vital elements of funding agreements especially in the case of humanitarian organizations operating in conflict situations (Mackintosh & Duplat, 2013) as demonstrated by examples gathered by the Norwegian Research Council (NRC, 2018b).

Humanitarian organizations consistently reject the idea of screening their beneficiaries—vulnerable individuals that receive humanitarian aid— referring to their obligations enshrined in international humanitarian law (IHL) and principles (Gillard, 2021b).[2] However, while beneficiary screening in humanitarian contexts is usually rejected, the border between humanitarian and development realms is not so clear-cut for the growing interest of 'development donors' (aid budgets) in conflict settings. As a result, not only development NGOs may be increasingly required to sign funding agreements with conditional clauses (Gillard, 2021b), but humanitarian NGOs being interested in cooperating with donors (with development budgets and funding agreements) may also face difficulties when the contract to be signed is not of humanitarian in its nature (O'Leary, 2021, 465). Furthermore, aid organizations also employ tens, if not hundreds of thousands, in Global South countries, that may be subject to screening. If employment relations are characterized by power imbalances regardless of geographic location, the (labour) relations between international or Global North organizations (as employers) and local, Global South citizens (as employees, consultants, volunteers, activists) are even more unequal (see Chapter 5).

Focusing on funding agreements and taking the European Union as an example, contracts can be signed either with the Directorate-General for Neighbourhood and Enlargement Negotiations (DG NEAR), with the Directorate General for International Partnerships (DG INTPA) or with the DG in charge of humanitarian affairs (DG ECHO) in the context of aid projects financed by the European Commission (EC). Partner organizations implementing EU-financed projects may sign two main types of contracts—grant agreements or service contracts—depending on the activity to be financed from EU budget. Both types of contracts contain references to reasonable or preventive measures, a matter that has direct implications in the context of personal data protection too for the personal data involved, collected and processed by NGOs.

---

[2] Interview with an advisor working at a Norwegian NGO [8], Teams, 14 June 2021.

Considering development NGOs, DG INTPA and DG NEAR introduced the counterterrorism clause in its contracts with NGDOs from Summer 2019 with the purpose of ensuring that no funding is made available to designated terrorist organizations. As a result, the relevant annex to the current grant agreement[3] to be signed by NGOs in cases of projects managed by DG INTPA and DG NEAR reads as follows:

> 12.2. … in the following circumstances the contracting authority may … terminate this contract or the participation of any beneficiary(ies) in this contract without any indemnity on its part when (d) it has been established by a final judgment or a final administrative decision or by proof in possession of the contracting authority that the beneficiary(ies) has been guilty of fraud, corruption, involvement in a criminal organisation, money laundering or terrorist financing, terrorist related offences, child labour or other forms of trafficking in human beings or circumventing fiscal, social or any other applicable legal obligations, including through the creation of an entity for this purpose.

The list is rather long and includes not only activities related to money laundering or terrorism, but other kinds of risks too: criminal offences, fraud, corruption, child labour or human trafficking. Special efforts are expected from aid organizations in the context of counterterrorism in exchange for the EU financial support:

> 1.5.bis [g]rant beneficiaries and contractors must ensure that there is no detection of subcontractors, natural persons, including participants to workshops and/or trainings and recipients of financial support to third parties, in the lists of EU restrictive measures.

Acknowledging that delimitation is not always clear-cut, it is needed to emphasize the distinction between development NGOs and humanitarian NGOs again—the latter operating in line with the humanitarian principles—because conditional clauses such as the above affect them somewhat differently depending on the funding source.

---

[3] Annex II under *General conditions applicable to European Union-financed grant contracts for external actions*—Annex e3h2, version 2021.1 (e3h2_gencond_en.pdf), see: https://wikis.ec.europa.eu/pages/viewpage.action?pageId=95551590 and https://wikis.ec.europa.eu/display/ExactExternalWiki/Annexes.

Regarding the humanitarian sector and complementing earlier humanitarian exemptions in geographically defined sanctions regimes, such as Somalia or Syria (Eckert, 2022, 426–430; O'Leary, 2021, 468–472), a recently adopted UN Resolution (UNSC 2664/2022) permits exceptions to humanitarian organizations by not considering "the payment of funds, other financial assets, or economic resources, or the provision of goods and services necessary to ensure the timely delivery of humanitarian assistance" a "violation of the asset freezes imposed by this Council or its Sanctions Committees" (UNSC, 2022, para 1 on p. 2). The interpretation of exemptions, however, may vary from donor to donor and may be dynamically changing depending on how people are categorized.

Being one of the largest official humanitarian donors, the DG ECHO included the above cited clause in its grant agreements relating to Iran, Iraq, Syria and Sudan before 2021 (Gillard, 2021b, 530). It was revised in 2021 and a minor adjustment was made in its grant agreement excluding the vetting of final beneficiaries[4]:

> the need to ensure the respect for EU restrictive measures must not however impede the effective delivery of humanitarian assistance to persons in need in accordance with the humanitarian principles and international humanitarian law. Persons in need must therefore not be vetted.

To clarify the rules, the European Commission also published a guideline titled *Commission guidance note on the provision of humanitarian aid in compliance with EU restrictive measures* on June 30, 2022 according to which (EU EC, 2022, 11):

> Funds and economic resources cannot be provided to designated persons either directly or indirectly, unless those persons qualify as persons in need of humanitarian aid.

Regardless of such exemptions (applying to transactions), international and EU funding policies, however, also imply that all other individuals and entities—staff, partners, suppliers, individual donors—will continue to be required to be screened in line with the logic of the 'reasonable

---

[4] Annex 5 of the Humanitarian Aid grant agreement. See also *Working with DG ECHO sanctions. 2021–2027. Sanction Clauses*, https://www.dgecho-partners-helpdesk.eu/sanctions/sanction-clauses.

efforts' even by humanitarian NGOs. It also obviously applies to bene-ficiaries of development aid projects channelled through DG INTPA or DG NEAR.

Interpreting conditional clauses—references to reasonable efforts and measures—in grant agreements is not easy in practice, especially in cases of organizations working in conflict situations and with local organiza-tions. As explained in a toolkit developed for supporting organizational decision-making (NRC, 2018b), there is a clear of spill-over effect built in the system, as counterterrorism clauses may "flow down or across a large number of organizations and sub-contractors, if official donors or their first-level contracts (aid agencies or NGOs) may consider including similar clauses" into sub-contracts. The experiences described in the NRC-toolkit correspond to and also illustrate the notion 'chain of security', a metaphor describing how individual transactions—deemed "indicators of suspi-cion" or "evidence of wrongdoing"—become links in a chain serving security-related purposes (De Goede, 2018, 35).

The impact of EU conditional funding can be illustrated by Pales-tinian concerns[5] too. When first implemented, it was unclear for the local NGO community whether the obligation formulated in the EU condi-tional clause (1.5.bis article) "applies towards natural persons who are not listed but are a part of [terrorist] organisation [listed on the EU restric-tive measures list], either formally or informally". Hence, if a local NGO is a(n) (in)direct beneficiary of an EU grant contract, a broad interpreta-tion of the clause may lead to the termination of the contract (BADIL, 2021). As a side effect of conditional funding, local NGOs can be easily marginalized or (self-)excluded from international cooperations, if they are not capable or willing to prove zero contacts with listed or designated persons as indicated by Palestinian experiences (El Taraboulsi-McCarthy, 2018, 6).

Discussing the impact of the US legislations would require a separate book, but the matter of compliance is further complicated if the US is involved as a donor in any of the operations of a European NGO. It requires all NGOs—regardless of the jurisdiction where they are regis-tered—that are *seeking* or obtaining funding from aid agencies, such as

---

[5] How screening is done by the EU as in international organization is not subject to this book, but the following documents confirm that the European Commission (or audit companies on behalf of it) screens Palestinian beneficiaries against sanctions lists by using a screening tool (World Check in 2013), see EU ECA (2013) and EU COM (2023).

the USAID under grants and cooperative agreements to provide a certification regarding support to terrorists (USAID, 2021, 4). In practice it means that any aid organizations benefiting from US funding sign the ATC (anti-terrorism certificate) with the following content (cited by Eckert, 2022, 442):

> The Recipient, to the best of its current knowledge, did not provide, within the previous *ten years*, and will take all reasonable steps to ensure that it does not and will not knowingly provide, material support or resources to any individual or entity that commits, *attempts to* commit, advocates, facilitates, or participates in terrorist acts, or has committed, attempted to commit, facilitated, or participated in terrorist acts.

This definition, in line with UNSC resolutions, not only requires (European, Global South) aid organizations to take responsibility for its contractual and non-contractual transactions both *ex ante* and *ex post*, but also to be 'fortune tellers' detecting the intentions of their local partners.[6] It also "interprets the category of 'terrorist' much more broadly than lists of counterterrorism and sanctions laws" usually do, and prompts that NGOs are required to screen not only against lists containing the names of designated individuals (and entities)—but basically "anyone that fits the US' interpretation" (Eckert, 2022, 450).

Reasonable Efforts Expected from Aid Organizations

As demonstrated by earlier research "intelligence and data-driven predictive technologies are used in compliance to profile, rate and evaluate external threats, creating (semi-) automated dossiers on suppliers, clients, customers, assigning risk scores" (Kuldova, 2022, 133). While the development and use of legal-regulatory compliance technologies, also known as Reg-Tech, is usually attributed to actors in the business sector (Arner et al., 2019), aid organizations have also contributed to the normalization of risk-based thinking. Their role and motivations, however, have been rather ambivalent, if not ambiguous. First and foremost, it should be acknowledged that aid organizations with human rights and humanitarian

---

[6] NCHS/PRIO workshop, Oslo, September 23, 2022.

profiles have fought against their mindless co-optation into counterterrorism activities for many years.[7] An important achievement has been more sensitive wording in funding agreements, including the 'exceptions' regulations, the aim of which is to protect principled humanitarian action, and final beneficiaries themselves.

Yet, while a recent UN resolution (UNSCR 2664/2022) has come as a 'relief' to humanitarian organizations by affirming that neither the payment or funds, nor the provision of services (aid) by (humanitarian) aid organizations constitutes a violation of the assets freeze measures, the UN has imposed on sanctioned individuals, paragraph 3 (on p. 3) prompts that the 'exemption' does not apply to the expected risk-mitigation measures with the Security Council requesting that:

> *providers* relying on paragraph 1 *use reasonable efforts* to minimize the accrual of any benefits prohibited by sanctions, whether as a result of direct or indirect provision or diversion, to individuals or entities designated by this Council or any of its Committees, including *by strengthening risk management and due diligence strategies and processes.* (text in italics highlighted by the author)

While humanitarian beneficiaries may not be screened and humanitarian organizations may not be held liable for making funds to sanctioned individuals, humanitarian organizations are not exempted from demonstrating and implementing 'reasonable efforts'. Such efforts and measures belong to the realm of risk-management with solutions offered by the compliance industry (Arner et al., 2019; Kuldova, 2022). Reasonable efforts implemented originally by corporations and financial institutions encompass a broad range of actions, procedures and digital tools, such as listing, ethical guidelines, corporate due diligence (CDD) policies and the so-called know your customer (KYC) procedures. Screening is part of the KYC-procedure.

---

[7] See, for example, the toolkit offered by the Norwegian Research Council (NRC) (https://www.nrc.no/toolkit/principled-humanitarian-action-managing-counterterrorism-risks/), reports and guidelines published by the *International Review of the Red Cross* (https://international-review.icrc.org/reviews/irrc-no-916-917-counterterrorism-sanctions-and-war), the US-based Charity & Security Network (https://charityandsecurity.org/) or the European Center for Not-for Profit Law Stichting (ECLN, https://ecnl.org/focus-areas/security-and-counter-terrorism).

Risk management is a widely accepted (Arner et al., 2019), but also criticized approach (Kuldova, 2022)—in governmental, corporate, military and as screening also demonstrates even in civil society spaces—that combines various rationalities and technologies of risk to make (the otherwise non-predictable) life more predictable by offering expert (data-based) knowledge. Over the years, aid organizations also subscribed to regulatory arguments—or they were forced to accept arguments by regulatory and market-driven means—that security risks and threats can be predicted and prevented by reasonable efforts. The implementation of various remote management practices, such as profiling (Duroch & Neuman, 2021) or 'tacit engagement' (Akal, 2022) can also be seen as serving legitimate organizational-operational concerns and interests (Hayes, 2017, 28–29).

Their common purpose is to prevent or mitigate various risks experienced in the Global South. These risks may threaten organizational survival or the lives of their staff. Hence, various techniques have been developed and used to assess the potential risks by means of a qualitative assessment of people via surveillance, by profiling and categorizing individuals to different risk groups (Aradau, 2004, 267) supported by a wide range of technologies serving legal, regulatory and financial compliance (Arner et al., 2019). And while they may also be deployed to serve alternative purposes, for example, preventing the recruitment of sexual offenders, the "pursuit of terrorist monies depends on the deployment of preemptive decisions and speculative techniques that have their genealogy in financial practices" in the domain of (international) charity too (De Goede, 2012, 21).

Listing has played a role in the emergence of financial surveillance by banks and other financial institutions—the main actors in charge of money transfers and financial transactions—that are required to implement the regulations of Financial Action Task Force (FATF). FATF is an intergovernmental body that sets international standards, the original aim of which has been to prevent illegal activities originally in the field of global money laundering.[8] As a policy-making body, the FATF has been working to generate the necessary political will to bring about national legislative and

---

[8] Setting international standards the aim of which is to prevent illegal activities in the field of global money laundering and terrorist financing, FATF has 39 members (states, Norway included and the European Commission), an observer member, 9 associate members and 23 observer organizations (for example, the Interpol, competent UN

regulatory reforms also in the context of terrorist financing since 2001 (Hayes, 2012, 8–15; 2017; Rébé, 2020, UN SR HR/CT, 2023, 64–66). As a result, aid organizations with international transactions are not only directly subjected to various international, European and domestic laws, and indirectly via funding agreements, but also to reasonable efforts (risk assessment and 'de-risking') implemented by banks and financial institutions regulated by FATF-standards (Anwar et al., 2022; Hayes, 2012, 15–19; També, 2021). However, while risk assessments are inevitable for ensuring a necessary, proportionate CFT measures in line with both FATF-standards and international human rights law, they are "rarely undertaken with sufficient regularity, specificity, and public consultation" (UN SR HR/CT, 2023, 64).

Aid organizations are not only passive objects of governmental or financial surveillance and risk assessments (see also in in Chapter 5), but they have also 'learnt a lot' from banks (screening aid organizations as customers), public authorities and governmental agencies (screening various individuals). Indeed, listing and related FATF-standards on AML/CFT have widely influenced how security is interpreted and works within the domain of donations and giving. While some aid organizations cooperate with private actors' that are motivated to 'aidwash' their surveillance technologies in the Global South (Martin, 2023), many others, especially, larger NGOs conduct screening in-house for legal-regulatory compliance or other legitimate interests which may go beyond sanctions and counterterrorism (Hayes, 2017, 28–29), for example, preventing the recruitment of sexual offenders or making transactions with convicted criminals.

Mapping various risk mitigation measures implemented by NGOs, Muhomed et al. (2021) found that their due diligence (CDD-policies and practices) has become increasingly professionalized. Expertise, however, has its price. Although screening is only one among the many reasonable efforts the purpose of which is risk-mitigation, it is apparently the most secretive one usually done by legal or HR (human resources) departments at headquarters of aid organizations (Muhomed et al., 2021, 26–31, see Chapter 4). As screening is preceded or complemented by "an extensive review of the documentation provided by in-country teams", it is a

organizations, such as the UN Counter-Terrorism Committee Executive Directorate, the World Bank, OECD), https://www.fatf-gafi.org/about/.

costly procedure (Muhomed et al., 2021, 31) regardless of the cost of the technical tool involved.

Conclusion

The obligation of implementing reasonable efforts, such as CDD-policies and KYC-procedures, screening included, is not without dilemmas. One the one hand the interpretation of the given clauses is not always obvious to European or local INGOs[9] (NRC, 2018b). Indeed, what prevention and 'reasonable measures' mean is rarely specified in grant agreements (Gillard, 2021a, 47); rather, it is either discussed and negotiated between the given donor and the NGO considering the humanitarian implications (Gillard, 2021b, 523, 526–528; NRC, 2018b) or left to the market, which offers various compliance technologies and tools (Arner et al., 2019; Kuldova, 2022) as it is to be further explored focusing on the aid industry in the next chapters. On the other hand, a "lot of confusion" exists about the real rationale for screening, whether screening individuals and local partner organizations prevents the misuse of funds.[10] Regardless of the dilemmas, screening cannot be done without personal data, and if personal data involved, the matter of transparency and right to information deserves attention.

References

Akal, A. B. (2022). *Tacit Engagement as a Form of Remote Management: Risk Aversity in the Face of Sanctions Regimes*. NCHS paper. Retrieved October 22, 2023, from https://www.humanitarianstudies.no/resource/tacit-engagement-as-a-form-of-remote-management-risk-aversity-in-the-face-of-sanctions-regimes/

Amelung, N., Rafaela, G., & Machado, H. (2021). *Modes of Bio-Bordering*. Palgrave Macmillan.

Amicelle, A. (2011). Towards a 'New' Political Anatomy of Financial Surveillance. *Security Dialogue, 42*(2), 161–178. https://doi.org/10.1177/096701 0611401472

[9] Interview with a leader and data protection officer, NL advocacy organization [2], Zoom, 12 February 2021.

[10] Interview with an advisor working at a Norwegian NGO [3], Zoom, 8 January 2021.

Amicelle, A., & Favarel-Garrigues, G. (2012). Financial Surveillance: Who Cares. *Journal of Cultural Economy, 5*(1), 105–124. https://doi.org/10.1080/175 30350.2012.640560

Amnesty Internationalm. (2020). *AI Report 2020/2021: The State of the World's Human Rights.* Retrieved May 20, 2022, from https://reliefweb.int/sites/reliefweb.int/files/resources/POL1032022021ENGLISH.PDF

Anwar, T., Wesseling, M., & Soares, R. R. (2022). *New Tech, Perpetual Challenges. How Emerging Technologies for Financial Compliance are Impacting the Nonprofit Sector.* European Center for Not-for-Profit Law. Retrieved October 22, 2023, from https://ecnl.org/sites/default/files/2022-09/ECNL%20F INTECH%20Report.pdf

Aradau, C. (2004). The Perverse Politics of Four-Letter Words: Risk and Pity in the Securitisation of Human Trafficking. *Millennium, 33*(2), 251–278. https://doi.org/10.1177/03058298040330020101

Arner, D. W., Barberis, J. N., & Buckley, R. P. (Eds.). (2019). *The REGTECH Book: The Financial Technology Handbook for Investors. Entrepreneurs and Visionaries in Regulation* (ISBN: 978-1-119-36217-3). Wiley.

BADIL. (2021). *European Union Conditional Funding: Its Illegality and Political Implications* (BADIL Position Paper). Retrieved November 18, 2022, from https://www.badil.org/cached_uploads/view/2021/04/20/eur opeanunionconditionalfunding-positionpaper-april2020-1618905422.pdf

Bauman, Z. (1991). *Modernity and Ambivalence.* Polity Press.

Bloodgood, E. A., & Tremblay-Boire, J. (2011). International NGOs and National Regulation in an Age of Terrorism. *VOLUNTAS: International Journal of Voluntary and Nonprofit Organizations, 22*(1), 142–173. https://doi.org/10.1007/s11266-010-9148-2

Bossong, R., & Carrapico, H. (2016). *EU Borders and Shifting Internal Security. Technology, Externalization and Accountability.* Springer.

Buzan, B., Wæver, O., & de Wilde, J. (1998). *Security: A New Framework for Analysis.* Lynne Rienner.

De Goede, M. (2012). *Speculative Security: The Politics of Pursuing Terrorist Monies.* University of Minnesota Press.

De Goede, M. (2018). The Chain of Security. *Review of International Studies, 44*(1), 24–42. https://doi.org/10.1017/S026021051700035

De Goede, M., & Sullivan, G. (2016). The Politics of Security Lists. *Environment and Planning D: Society and Space, 34*(1), 67–88. https://doi.org/10.1177/0263775815599309

Duffield, M. (2001). *Global Governance and the New Wars: The Merging of Development and Security.* Zed Books.

Duffield, M. (2007). *Development, Security and Unending War: Governing the World of Peoples.* Polity Press.

Duroch, F., & Neuman, M. (2021). *Should We Discriminate in Order to Act? Profiling: A Necessary but Debated Practice.* HPN paper. Retrieved October 22, 2023, from https://odihpn.org/publication/should-we-discriminate-in-order-to-act-profiling-a-necessary-but-debated-practice/

Eckert, S. (2022). Counterterrorism, Sanctions and Financial Access Challenges: Course Corrections to Safeguard Humanitarian Action. *International Review of the Red Cross, 103*(916–917), 415–458. https://international-review.icrc.org/articles/counterterrorism-sanctions-and-financial-access-challenges-916#footnote81_27rk033

El Taraboulsi-McCarthy, S. (2018). *A Humanitarian Sector in Debt. Counter-Terrorism, Bank De-risking and Financial Access for NGOs in the West Bank and Gaza.* Overseas Development Institute (ODI, UK). https://odi.org/en/publications/a-humanitarian-sector-in-debt-counter-terrorism-bank-de-risking-and-financial-access-for-ngos-in-the-west-bank-and-gaza/

EU (European Union). (2005). *Directive 2005/60/EC of the European Parliament and of the Council of 26 October 2005 on the Prevention of the Use of the Financial System for the Purpose of Money Laundering and Terrorist Financing.* Retrieved April 13, 2023, from https://eur-lex.europa.eu/legal-content/EN/TXT/PDF/?uri=CELEX:32005L0060

EU (European Union). (2017). *Directive (Eu) 2017/541 of the European Parliament and of the Council of 15 March 2017 on Combating Terrorism and Replacing Council Framework Decision 2002/475/JHA and Amending Council Decision 2005/671/JHA.* European Union. Retrieved September 14, 2023, from https://eur-lex.europa.eu/legal-content/EN/TXT/?uri=celex%3A32017L0541

EU (European Union). (2020). *ANNEX II. General Conditions Applicable to EU-Financed Grant Contracts for External Actions* (version: version 2021.1, e3h2, e3h2_gencond_en.pdf). Retrieved October 31, 2020, from the practical guide on contract procedures for European Union external action (PRAG): https://wikis.ec.europa.eu/display/ExactExternalWiki/Annexes and https://ec.europa.eu/europeaid/prag/document.do?nodeNumber=1

EU COM. (2023, November 21). *Review of Ongoing Financial Assistance for Palestine.* Communication to the Commission: C(2023) 8300 final, Strasbourg. https://neighbourhood-enlargement.ec.europa.eu/system/files/2023-11/Communication%20to%20the%20Commission%20on%20the%20review%20of%20ongoing%20financial%20assistance%20for%20Palestine.pdf

EU EC (European Union European Commission). (2022). *Commission Guidance Note on the Provision of Humanitarian Aid in Compliance with EU Restrictive Measures.* https://finance.ec.europa.eu/system/files/2022-07/220630-humanitarian-aid-guidance-note_en.pdf

EU ECA. (2013). *European Union Direct Financial Support to the Palestinian Authority* (Special Report No. 14). European Court of Auditors. https://www.eca.europa.eu/lists/ecadocuments/sr13_14/sr13_14_en.pdf

EU GDPR (European Union General Data Protection Regulation). (2016). *Regulation 2016/679 of the European Parliament and of the Council of 27 April 2016 on the Protection of Natural Persons with Regard to the Processing of Personal Data and on the Free Movement of Such Data.* Retrieved April 13, 2023, from https://eur-lex.europa.eu/eli/reg/2016/679/oj

Fassin, D. (2007). Humanitarianism as a Politics of Life. *Public Culture, 19*(3), 499–520. https://doi.org/10.1215/08992363-2007-007

FATF (Financial Action Task Force). (2001). *Special Recommendation VIII (SR VIII)—Recommendation 8 (Measures to Prevent the Misuse of Non-Profit Organisations).* For the current version see FATF (2015).

FATF (Financial Action Task Force). (2014). *Risk of Terrorist Abuse in Non-Profit Organisations.* Retrieved 13 June, 2021, from https://www.fatf-gafi.org/media/fatf/documents/reports/Risk-of-terrorist-abuse-in-non-profit-organisations.pdf

FATF (Financial Action Task Force). (2015). *Best Practices Paper on Combating the Abuse of Non-Profit Organisations.* FATF Recommendation 8. Retrieved April 8, 2022, from https://www.fatf-gafi.org/en/publications/Financialinclusionandnpoissues/Bpp-combating-abuse-npo.html

FATF (Financial Action Task Force). (2016). *Guidance for a Risk-Based Approach: Money or Value Transfer Services.* Retrieved October 23, 2022, from https://www.fatf-gafi.org/publications/fatfrecommendations/documents/rba-money-or-value-transfer.html

Federer, J. P. (2022). The Politics of Proscription and Peacemaking: Implications of Labelling Armed Groups as Terrorists and Extremists. *Journal of Intervention and Statebuilding, 17*(2), 207–213. https://doi.org/10.1080/17502977.2022.2107361

Gillard, E. (2021a). *IHL and the Humanitarian Impact of Counterterrorism Measures and Santions. Unintended Ill Effects of Well-Intended Measures.* Chatham House Report. Retrieved April 28, 2022, from https://www.chathamhouse.org/2021/09/ihl-and-humanitarian-impact-counterterrorism-measures-and-sanctions/04-funding-agreements

Gillard, E. (2021b). Screening of Final Beneficiaries—A Red Line in Humanitarian Operations. An Emerging Concern in Development Work. *International Review of the Red Cross, 103*(916–917), 517–537. https://international-review.icrc.org/articles/screening-of-final-beneficiaries-a-red-line-in-humanitarian-operations-916

Hayes, B. (2012). The Surveillance-Industrial Complex. In K. Ball, K. D. Haggerty, & D. Lyon (Eds.), *Routledge Handbook of Surveillance Studies* (pp. 167–175). Routledge. https://doi.org/10.4324/9780203814949.ch2_2_c

Hayes, B. (2017). *The Impact of International Counter-Terrorism on Civil Society Organisations: Understanding the Role of the Financial Action Task Force*. Bread for the World. Retrieved March 23, 2021, from http://efc.issuelab.org/resources/27481/27481.pdf

Heath-Kelly, C., & Gruber, B. (2023). *Vulnerability. Governing the Social Through Security Politics*. Manchaster University Press.

Helgesson, K. S., & Mörth, U. (2019). Instruments of Securitization and Resisting Subjects: For-Profit Professionals in the Finance-Security Nexus. *Security Dialogue, 50*(3), 257–274. https://doi.org/10.1177/0967010619835655

Hosein, G., & Nyst, C. (2013). *Aiding Surveillance: An Exploration of How Development and Humanitarian Aid Initiatives Are Enabling Surveillance in Developing Countries*. Privacy International. Retrieved March 8, 2023, from https://privacyinternational.org/sites/default/files/2017-12/Aiding%20Surveillance.pdf

Howell, J. (2014). The Securitisation of INGOs Post-9/11. *Conflict, Security and Development, 14*(2), 151–179. https://doi.org/10.1080/14678802.2014.903692

Howell, J., & Lind, J. (2009). *Counter-Terrorism, Aid and Civil Society: Before and After the War on Terror*. Palgrave Macmillan.

Jackson, P. (Ed.). (2015a). *Handbook of International Security and Development*. Routledge.

Jackson, R. (2015b). The Epistemological Crisis of Counterterrorism. *Critical Studies on Terrorism, 8*(3), 33–54. https://doi.org/10.1080/17539153.2015.1009762

Jarvis, L. (2019). Terrorism, Counter-Terrorism, and Critique: Opportunities, Examples, and Implications. *Critical Studies on Terrorism, 12*(2), 339–358. https://doi.org/10.1080/17539153.2019.1575607

Kaunert, C., & Léonard, S. (2019). The Collective Securitization of Terrorism in the European Union. *West European Politics, 42*(2), 261–277. https://doi.org/10.1080/01402382.2018.1510194

Kaunert, C., & Léonard, S. (2021). Collective Securitization and Crisification of EU Policy Change: Two Decades of EU Counterterrorism Policy. *Global Affairs, 7*(5), 687–693. https://doi.org/10.1080/23340460.2021.2002098

Kuldova, T. Ø. (2022). *Compliance-Industrial Complex: The Operating System of a Pre-Crime Society*. Palgrave Macmillan.

Lazell, M., & Petrikova. I. (2020). Is Development Aid Securitized? Evidence from a Cross-Country Examination of Aid Commitment. *Development Policy Review, 38*(3), 323–343. https://doi.org/10.1111/dpr.12426

Lyon, D. (2007). *Surveillance Studies: An Overview.* Polity Press.

Martin, A. (2023). Aidwashing Surveillance: Critiquing the Corporate Exploitation of Humanitarian Crises. *Surveillance & Society, 21*(1), 96–102. https://doi.org/10.24908/ss.v21i1.16266

Mackintosh, K., & Duplat, P. (2013). *Study of the Impact of Donor Counter-Terrorism Measures on Principled Humanitarian Action.* United Nations Office for the Coordination of Humanitarian Affairs (OCHA) and Norwegian Refugee Council (NRC). https://www.nrc.no/globalassets/pdf/reports/study-of-the-impact-of-donor-counterterrorism-measures-on-principled-humanitarian-action.pdf

Minella, C. M. (2019). Counter-Terrorism Resolutions and Listing of Terrorists and Their Organizations by the United Nations. In E. Shor & S. Hoadley (Eds.), *International Human Rights and Counter-Terrorism* (pp. 31–53). Springer.

Muhomed, S., Puri, J., Stickler, H., & Sugand, D. (2021). *NGOs' Due Diligence and Risk Mititagion: A Holistic Approach.* London School of Economics and Political Science and The Charity and Security Network. Retrieved September 13, 2023, from https://charityandsecurity.org/wp-content/uploads/2021/04/NGOs-Due-Diligence-and-Risk-Mitigation.pdf

NRC (Norwegian Refugee Council). (2018a). *Principles Under Pressure: The Impact of Counterterrorism Measures and Preventing/Countering Violent Extremism on Principled Humanitarian Action.* Retrieved March 13, 2021, from https://reliefweb.int/sites/reliefweb.int/files/resources/nrc-principles_under_pressure-report-screen.pdf

NRC (Norwegian Refugee Council). (2018b). *Understanding Conditional Clauses.* Retrieved March 13, 2021, from https://www.nrc.no/shorthand/stories/understanding-counterterrorism-clauses/index.html and https://www.nrc.no/globalassets/pdf/reports/toolkit/nrc_toolkit_03_reviewing-counterterrorism-clauses.pdf

OECD DAC (Organisation for Economic Co-operation and Development, Development Assistance Committee). (2023). *ODA Levels in 2022—Preliminary Data. Detailed Summary Note. Table 3.* OECD. https://www.oecd.org/dac/financing-sustainable-development/ODA-2022-summary.pdf

O'Leary, E. (2021). Politics and Principles: The Impact of Counterterrorism Measures and Sanctions on Principled Humanitarian Action. *International Review of the Red Cross, 103*(916–917), 459–477. https://doi.org/10.1017/S1816383121000357

Overton, J., & Murray, W. E. (2021). *Aid and Development.* Routledge.

Perkowiski, N. (2021). *Humanitarianism, Human Rights and Security. The Case of Frontex.* Routledge.

Rébé, N. (2020). *Counter-Terrorism Financing: International Best Practices and the Law.* Brill.

Sullivan, G. (2020). *The Law of the List.* Cambridge University Press.

També, N. (2021). *Unintended Consequences of AML/CFT regulation: the challenges of banking non-profit organisations.* European Center for Not-for-Profit Law. Retrieved October 22, 2023, from https://ecnl.org/publications/uni ntended-consequences-amlcft-regulation-challenges-banking-non-profit-org anisations

UN SR HR/CT. (2019). *Impact of measures to address terrorism and violent extremism on civic space and the rights of civil society actors and human rights defenders: report of the Special Rapporteur on the Promotion and Protection of Human Rights and Fundamental Freedoms while Countering Terrorism,* A/HRC/40/52. Geneva: UN Human Rights Council. Retrieved June 8, 2022, from https://documents-dds-ny.un.org/doc/UNDOC/GEN/G19/ 057/59/PDF/G1905759.pdf?OpenElement

UN SR HR/CT. (2023). *Global study on the impact of counter-terrorism on civil society and civic space.* Geneva: UN Human Rights Council. Retrieved August 8, 2023, https://defendcivicspace.com/wp-content/uploads/2023/ 06/SRCT_GlobalStudy.pdf

UNSC (United Nations Security Council). (2001). *S/RES/1373. Adopted by the Security Council at Its 4385th Meeting, on 28 September 2001.* Retrieved April 17, 2023, from https://www.unodc.org/pdf/crime/terrorism/res_1373_e nglish.pdf

UNSC (United Nations Security Council). (2017). *S/RES/2396. Adopted by the Security Council at Its 8148th Meeting, on 21 December 2017.* Retrieved April 17, 2023, from https://documents-dds-ny.un.org/doc/UNDOC/GEN/ N17/460/25/PDF/N1746025.pdf?OpenElement

UNSC (United Nations Security Council). (2022). *S/RES/2664. Adopted by the Security Council at Its 9214th Meeting, on 9 December 2022.* Retrieved April 17, 2023, from http://unscr.com/en/resolutions/doc/2664

USAID. (2021). *ADS Chapter 319 Partner Vetting.* New Edition Date: 01/ 15/2021 Responsible Office: M/MPBP File Name: 319_011521. USAID. Retrieved October 24, 2023, from https://www.usaid.gov/sites/default/ files/2023-07/319.pdf

Vaughn, J. (2009). The Unlikely Securitizer: Humanitarian Organizations and the Securitization of Indistinctiveness. *Security Dialogue, 40*(3), 263–285. https://doi.org/10.1177/0967010609336194

Watson, S. (2009). The 'Human' as Referent Object? Humanitarianism as Securitization. *Security Dialogue, 42*(1), 3–20. https://doi.org/10.1177/096701 0610393549

Watson, S., & Burles, R. (2018). Regulating NGO Funding: Securitizing the Political. *International Relations, 32*(4), 430–448. https://doi.org/10.1177/0047117818782604

Ziv, O., & Abraham, Y. (2022). Israel's New Secret Document Still Fails to Tie Palestinian INGOs to 'Terrorism'. *+972 Magazine*. Retrieved March 8, 2022, from https://www.972mag.com/israel-document-palestinian-ngos/

CHAPTER 3

Screening as Data Processing Operation

Abstract The purpose of this chapter is to introduce the territorial and material scope of GDPR, to conceptualize screening as a data processing operation, to introduce the related notification obligations prescribed by the EUs General Data Protection Regulation 2016/679 (GDPR), and to map how EU/EEA-registered NGOs notify their data subjects about screening. To do so it is needed, as a minimum, to review what personal data is collected and processed during screening; how screening can be unpacked as a series of data processing operation, what is the typical legal bases for collecting personal data and what is to be communicated to data subjects—provided that restrictions do not apply. Sources selected for analysis equally included legal instruments and academic sources in the field of law and social science. Findings indicate that if screening is communicated to data subjects, it is communicated vaguely and selectively, while publicly available privacy notices are rarely used for such purpose.

Keywords EU GDPR · Screening as data processing operation · Transparency · Right to information

While aid organizations supporting individuals from the Global South or operating in countries in the Global South are concerned with the advancement of human rights regardless of their profiles (humanitarian, development, human rights advocacy, mixed), the protection of human rights is to be considered even in the context of counterterrorism (Tzanou, 2017). As the right to privacy, private life[1] and personal data protection[2] are human rights, just as the right to information and transparency (Klareen, 2013; Vrabec, 2021), insights from privacy and data protection studies are helpful to explore the meaning and function of the principle of transparency and the right to information with regard to screening. Therefore, the purpose of this chapter is to recall the territorial and material scope of the General Data Protection Regulation 2016/679 (EU GDPR, 2016) and to analyse screening in light of its relevant provisions by focusing on the following questions: how (under what conditions: purpose and legal basis) can screening be conceptualized as a data processing operation? What does the principle of transparency and the right to information mean in the GDPR? How do NGOs registered in the European Union communicate screening to data subjects?

With regard to EU/EEA jurisdictions, the core instrument regulating data protection, and as part of that, the principle of transparency and related right to information is the GDPR. Being a regulation, it has

---

[1] The right to respect for private life can be found in Article 8(1) of the European Convention on Human Rights; Charter of Fundamental Rights of the EU (Article 7); Universal Declaration on Human Rights (Article 12) and International Convention on Civil and Political Rights (Article 17). Regional instruments: Organization of Islamic Conference (1990): Cairo Declaration on Human Rights in Islam (Article 18b, c); although the African Charter on Human and Peoples' Rights (1982) does not contain reference to privacy rights, the recently adopted African Declaration on Internet Rights and Freedoms, a Pan-African initiative, tries to address this issue with regards to the online space (https://africaninternetrights.org/en/about).

[2] The *EU Charter on Fundamental Rights* (EUCFR) distinguished the right to personal data protection (Article 8) from the right to privacy and private life (Article 7). Processing of personal data may, in particular circumstances, constitute an interference with the data subject's right to respect for private life as ruled by the ECtHR in various cases. Considering the importance of the CoE (Council of Europe) EctHR in interpreting privacy and personal data related issues, the CoE Convetion 108 deserves to be mentioned, even if its relationhip to the GDPR cannot be detailed here. Being an international instrument adopted in 1981, Convention 108 protects individuals with regard to processing of their personal data by private and public actors, including judiciary and law enforcement authorities (EU Handbook, 2018, 24–28). The OECD, the current membership of which is overlapping with that of the EU (donors), mentioned transparency among its privacy guidelines as early as 1980: https://habeasdatacolombia.uniandes.edu.co/wp-content/uploads/OECD_Privacy_Guidelines_1980.pdf.

general application and as such it is binding in its entirety and directly applicable in all Member States. Its status implies that the principles listed in Article 5—transparency included—are also legally binding. In addition to the regulation itself, recitals in the preamble of the GDPR were also used for analysis in this chapter. While recitals in EU law do not constitute the rule itself, they elaborate on the reasons for the operative provisions avoiding normative language and political argumentation. Guidelines issued by the European Data Protection Board (EDPB), or its predecessor (Article 29 Working Party) were also selected and scrutinized for relevant content. They detail the GDPR's territorial scope (EDPB, 3/2018), transparency (Article 29 WP, 2018) and data subject's rights: access to information (EDPB, 1/2022).

Acknowledging that the right to data protection is not an absolute human right, and as such it can be restricted in European Union too,[3] personal data enjoy protection—and deserves attention—for it is considered interrelated with other human rights by EU/EEA legislation, the European Court of Human Rights (ECtHR) and Court of Justice of the EU (CJEU) too. As the ECtHR's interpretation of Article 8 of the European Convention of Human Rights (ECHR) demonstrates "the protection of personal data are of fundamental importance to a person's enjoyment of his or her right to respect for private and family life"[4] (EU Handbook, 2018, 18–21; Psychogiopoulou, 2017).

European Aid Organizations in the Global South and the Scope of GDPR

Reflecting the importance it attributes to the protection of fundamental rights, the GDPR not only applies within the EU, but is also extended to the EU's external trade—and aid—relationships for its territorial scope (Bennett, 2018; Schmidt, 2022, 246). EU/EEA-registered NGOs, even if they implement projects in the Global South are bound by the GDPR (Franz et al., 2020; Gazi, 2020; Paragi, 2021) as long as their data processing operations fall under the scope of GDPR. The GDPR is the first data protection law to make specific reference, however vaguely, to

[3] *European Convention on Human Rights*, Article 8(2). The EU GDPR also allows members states to enact national legislation (Article 23) that may restrict data protection principles and data subjects' rights in certain cases and under certain conditions.

[4] ECtHR, *S and Marper v. The United Kingdom*, para 103.

humanitarian action without elaborating on the legal status of the data controllers (non-governmental, international (IOs), HOs enjoy special legal status).[5]

With reference to its territorial scope, Article 3(a) of the GDPR states that "the regulation applies to the processing of personal data in the context of the activities of an establishment of a controller or a processor in the Union, regardless of whether the processing takes place in the Union or not" (GDPR). The global significance of this article made the EDPB issue guidelines on the meaning of territorial scope (EDPB, 3/ 2018, 10) interpreting Article 3(a) in the following way:

> [A]ny personal data processing in the context of the activities of an establishment of a controller or processor in the Union would fall under the scope of the GDPR, regardless of the location or the nationality of the data subject whose personal data are being processed.

Citizenship does not make a difference: individuals in the Global South can be identified by their personal data (name, date of birth, etc.) the same way as if they were EU citizens in case of screening too. This approach is strengthened by Recital 14, which states that '[t]he protection afforded by this Regulation should apply to natural persons, whatever their nationality or place of residence, in relation to the processing of their personal data' (EDPB, 3/2018, 10). This implies that aid organizations (NGOs, business organizations or public agencies) that are registered within the EU/EEA but operate outside its borders (implementing aid projects, delivering services and related processing activities) are regulated by the GDPR. In other words, the GDPR applies even if an EU-based NGO processes the personal data of non-EU citizens and/or if it operates in the Global South[6] (Franz et al., 2020; Gazi, 2020; Paragi, 2021).

---

[5] Regarding the mandatory selection of a lawful basis of processing, some types of processing may serve both important grounds of public interest and the vital interests of the data subject as for instance when processing is necessary for humanitarian purposes (Recital 46); with regard to restrictions they can be imposed to protect the rights and freedoms of others, including social protection, public health and humanitarian purposes (Recital 73); and referring to data transfers to international organizations in humanitarian context (Recital 112) (Kuner & Marelli, 2020).

[6] It should also be briefly mentioned that if a project is financed from the EU budget and the EU institutions are project owners, a sister-regulation governing data protection within the EU institutions also applies (EUDPR, 2018).

With regard to the material scope, as Article 2(1) says, the GDPR "applies to the processing of personal data wholly or partly by automated means and to the processing other than by automated means of personal data which form part of a filing system or are intended to form part of a filing system". Article 2(2) lists exceptions, cases when the GDPR does not apply, namely, when the course of an activity (and related data processing operations) fall outside the scope of the Union law; when personal data are processed by Member States when carrying out activities in the context of provisions concerning the common foreign and security policy (the scope of Chapter 2 of Title V of the TEU); when personal data are processed by natural persons "in the course of a purely personal or household activity" and last but not least when competent authorities process personal data for the purposes of "the prevention, investigation, detection or prosecution of criminal offences or the execution of criminal penalties, including the safeguarding against and the prevention of threats to public security" (EU GDPR, 2016, Article 2). Considering these exceptions, it should be noted, that NGOs are legal entities (not natural persons) and not authorities in charge of criminal investigations, national or public security issues—even if their work and operations have been securitized in the context of counterterrorism.

Aid organizations collect and process the personal data of various categories of data subjects. Employees, board members, volunteers, activists, beneficiaries of aid projects or services, suppliers and partners are equally natural persons whose personal data, processed by NGOs, can be used to identity verification before a contract is signed, a transaction is made or a project is implemented. NGOs, however, may also use personal data to screen against sanctions and other watchlists which can be considered a data processing operation on its own.

SCREENING AS DATA PROCESSING OPERATION

Screening in practice is about running a search online, among others, that is, checking whether lists of personal data match various watchlists in a consolidated database (De Goede & Sullivan, 2016). Various commercial tools—described in Chapter 4—enable users, aid organizations included, to synchronize watchlist screening and navigate diverse and continuously changing sanctions, law enforcement regimes, financial crime compliance and anti-bribery requirements by providing access to a consolidated database of various lists.

Regardless of service providers, but using information from Lexis-Nexis' website for illustration screening implies users' access to results of "a thorough sequence of research, vetting and data compilation … provide[d in] robust databases of high-risk individuals and entities" (LexisNexis, 2021) which, for example, provides access to LexisNexis® WorldCompliance™ to its clients. The operation includes sharing personal data collected by NGOs with the service provider (for example, LexisNexis, Refinitiv/LSEG in case of World-Check or CSI in case of WatchDOG Elite[7]) by uploading names or files (lists containing personal data) to the cloud, running the search online to check if lists of personal data (names of natural persons) match various watchlists in a consolidated database, and storing the records in order to document compliance.[8]

To understand the matter of transparency and the notification obligations prescribed by GDPR, a typical NGO would need to consider as a minimum what screening means in the context of data protection law: what kinds of personal data are involved; to which extent screening fits the definition of data processing provided in GDPR; who defines the purposes of processing and, if data processors are used for screening, what is the relationship between the actors, and which legitimate basis is used for screening. Emphasizing that this chapter contributes to academic scholarship without the ambition to provide 'compliance advice' on the subject, the paragraphs below will approach these matters first by introducing the most relevant general rules (GRDR provisions) and then by applying that to screening.

Personal data in the GDPR. Data can be considered personal if they relate to an identified or identifiable person, defined as 'data subject' in Article 4(1) of EU GDPR (2016). To determine whether a natural person is identifiable, the controller should take into account 'all the means reasonably likely to be used' such as singling out, to identify the natural person directly or indirectly (Recital 26) in order to treat one

---

[7] World-Check was operated initially by Thomson-Reuters, now by Refinitiv/LSEG, https://solutions.refinitiv.com/LP=8110, CSI's WatchDogElite: https://www.csiweb.com/how-we-help/regulatory-compliance/sanctions-screening/.

[8] While the majority of suppliers are US-based, search results are usually stored in a database on AWS servers in Ireland, or elsewhere in Europe, if the NGO (as data controller) decides to store them.

person differently from another. If data about an identified (or identifiable) person is being processed, this person is called 'data subject'. EU law in general, the GDPR in particular treat these data subjects as 'beneficiaries of data protection rules' provided that they are living natural persons (Recital 27) (Article 29 Working Party, 2007, 22).

The definition of 'personal data' can be understood by breaking it down into its four constituent elements: (1) 'any information'; (2) 'relating to'; (3) 'identified or identifiable'; (4) 'natural person' (Bygrave & Tosoni, 2020a, 109–110). Not repeating scholarly analysis at length, any piece of information can be considered personal as long as it relates to[9] an identified or identifiable person regardless of the circumstances: it may concern private life, relations and correspondence with others, work-related or other professional activities and aspects of public life (EU Handbook, 2018, 86). The most obvious example of 'any information' is a person's name, but date and place of birth, email addresses, phone numbers, various ID numbers can also be used to single out individuals. The same applies to attributes—cookies, web traffic or other online surveillance tools monitoring online behaviour, habits and movement in the physical space—the extent to which these measures make it possible to identify a particular person (EU Handbook, 2018, 89). The combination of identifiers also qualifies as personal data.

Furthermore, the GDPR also distinguishes general personal data from special categories of personal data (Article 9, sensitive data), the processing of which calls for special protection. Data is considered special or sensitive if it reveals a person's ethnic or racial origin, political opinions, religious or other beliefs, membership in trade unions, genetic and biometric data (if processed for the purpose of identifying a person) as well as information concerning health or sexual life.

As for identifiability, when various measures for personal data protection are considered, the difference between 'identified' and 'identifiable' disappear (Bygrave & Tosoni, 2020a, 110–111; EU Handbook, 2018, 90). In other words, for the GDPR to be applicable, there is no need for actual identification: it is sufficient that the person concerned can potentially be identified by the data (information, attributes) collected

---

[9] In *Nowak* (Case C-434/16, para 35), cited by Bygrave and Tosoni (2020a, 110) the CJEU stated that the 'relate to' element 'is satisfied where the information, by reason of its content, purpose or effect, is linked to a particular person'.

and processed (Recital 26). Only when the personal data are successfully anonymized—that is, they are no longer personal data, and as a result—data protection legislation do not apply for their processing anymore.

Personal data processed in case of screening. Aid organizations collect and process the personal data of various categories of data subjects for various purposes. Employees, board members, volunteers, activists, beneficiaries of aid projects or services, suppliers, partners are equally natural persons. Organizations and NGOs may use their personal data to screen against various watchlists. Citizenship does not make a difference, but practical challenges may arise with regard to the transliteration of non-Latin names. Yet, a foreign name (spelled, for example, in Arabic) does not necessarily make the individual non-identifiable.

While a narrower set of personal data (name, date of birth) is needed for starting screening, the outcome of screening, presented in form of a file in case of alerts or (false) positive matches, contains a far more detailed set of information that can be related to the person (for the description of the process and the related tool, *see* Chapter 4). The outcome of the search provides integrated profiles in form of .html or .pdf file indicating the probability of the match. As a result, the following information can also be accessed by the NGO: (i) a detailed set of personal data, a photo included; (ii) a narrative description containing references to the sources of each pieces of information; (iii) a section on the reported addresses; (iv) a network of relationships indicating the type of relations: family members; associated others; related companies and organizations.[10] The outcome file also contains sensitive information (as defined in Article 9). These information types can be considered personal data following the GDPR (Bygrave & Tosoni, 2020a, 109–110) and relevant CJEU interpretations. It should also be noted that the tool presents only probabilities—the likelihood of match (for example, 60% or 80%)—in case of alerts. Therefore, it is not impossible that the user (the NGO) has access to profiles of multiple individuals that, in effect, do not match fully, only resemble the searched (sought ones) to some extent.

---

[10] And (v) an extensive list of sources, websites and documents, that were used by LexisNexis researchers to draw the profile. Interview with representative of LexisNexis, via Zoom, 20 May 2021. See also De Goede and Sullivan (2016).

In case of positive matches, the NGOs need to consider if the result is real or false positive hit and make decisions accordingly (on exclusion, terminating or not signing a contract, etc.). The absence of an alert or a false positive match indicates that the given person, identified by its personal data, is neither officially listed (as a terrorist, a sanctioned individual or a politically exposed person), nor appears in the ADVERSE MEDIA category (list) (*see* Chapter 4 for the features and functionality). Even in this case the NGO may be interested in documenting the clarity of the person by keeping the records, which also qualifies as a data processing operation.

Data processing operations in GDPR. The GDPR is aimed at regulating all or most stages of the data processing cycle, including registration, storage, retrieval and dissemination of personal data (Tosoni & Bygrave, 2020, 117). The legal understanding of data processing implies that any operation or set of operations performed on personal data is a data processing operation, regardless of the fact if it covers wholly or partly automated or non-automated, manual processing (EU GDPR 2016, Article 2(1), 4(2), Recital 15; (EU Handbook, 2018, 100).

Processing by automated means ('automated processing') refers to all processing done by means of computer technologies (Tosoni & Bygrave, 2020, 117). Article 4(2) lists various such activities, whereby the term 'such' "indicates that the list is by no means comprehensive or exclusive" (Tosoni & Bygrave, 2020, 117). Furthermore, the listed practices are also to be complemented by those provided in CJEU jurisprudence (Tosoni & Bygrave, 2020, 120). Accordingly, processing "may consist in one or a number of operations, each of which relates to one of the different stages that the processing of personal data may involve"[11] irrespective of its duration, the amount of data processed and the actual recording or storing of personal data (Tosoni & Bygrave, 2020, 117).

Screening as a data processing operation implies users' access to results of "a thorough sequence of research, vetting and data compilation … provide[d in] robust databases of high-risk individuals and entities" (LexisNexis, 2021).[12] This definition corresponds to terms used in Article

---

[11] *Fashion ID*, CJEU Case C-40/17, para 72.

[12] AI is not considered in this paper, but the customized solutions/subscriptions also enabled LexisNexis to develop and deploy simple, rule-based AI in order to increase

4(2) and in CJEU jurisprudence, such as collection, recording, structuring, storage, retrieval, consultation, use, disclosure, loading personal data on an internet page. While search may be run occasionally or regularly, these databases are cloud-based, multiple and integrated.

Consolidated databases, such as World-Check (provided by Refinitiv/ LSEG), CSI's WatchDOG Elite and LexisNexis® WorldCompliance™ data or other LexisNexis tools used for screening, are built by using browsers, that is "search engines exploring the internet automatically, constantly and systematically in search of the information which is published there", the result of which is "the disclosure of such information in the form of lists of search results" to users[13] (NGOs as data controllers). Looking at the technical description in Chapter 4, the content of the consolidated datasets slightly varies from provider to provider, but the problematic data gathering practices are common for the research teams of these companies work with open-source data, from sources otherwise publicly available (De Goede & Sullivan, 2016). This kind of data collection (esp. the PEP and ADVERSE MEDIA lists) goes well beyond from what is reasonable for flagging some as terrorist or a criminal convicted for financial offence.

Screening can also be considered a data processing operation the extent to which personal data are shared with the service provider during search and the operation is about running a search online, that is, checking if lists of personal data (of natural persons) match various watchlists in a consolidated database. While the majority of suppliers are US-based, if the EU-established controller (aid NGO) wants to save its search results— even if there is no alert, partial or full match—the data will be stored in a database and in form of files, for example, on Amazon Web Servers in Ireland. In other words, screening also implies storing in addition to other elements. This distinction carries relevance with regard to reasonable expectations too (see later), for merely storing data "relating to an individual's private life" constitutes data processing operation and an interference with the right to respect for private life even without the

---

efficiency in search. Interview with a former representative of LexisNexis, via Zoom, 20 May 2021.

[13] *Google Spain*, CJEU Case C-131/12, paras 26–31 (cited by Tosoni & Bygrave, 2020, 120).

subsequent use of stored data.[14] In case of alerts (positive matches), the 'manual' phase of screening follows: it depends on the internal policies and procedures of the aid NGO and on its organizational profile (humanitarian vs. development) what to do about an alert, that is, how to process the results further. As this non-exhaustive list of sub-operations prompts, each can be associated with distinct purposes, and as such, may require alternative legal basis (Table 3.1).

Consequently, if an NGO—for whatever purpose, on whatever legal basis and regardless of the complicated conceptual relationship between purposes and lawful grounds—(i) shares personal data (a person's name, date and place of birth) with an external vendor (ii) to search for positive matches in a cloud-based database containing consolidated watchlists, (iii) makes decisions in case of positive matches and (iv) stores the results of

Table 3.1 Components of screening as data processing operation

Purposes of data processing		Typical (sub)purposes	Lawful grounds (legal basis)
Overall	Screening: background check	To minimize various risks, to comply with legal obligations	Article 6 (any)
Element (i)	Uploading files with names	To search in the online database	Article 6 (any)
Element (ii)	Running the search	To find positive matches	Article 6 (any)
Element (iii)	Making decisions based on the results	(Not) to sign a contract, (not) to include beneficiaries in projects	Article 6 (any) Typical: 6(b), (c), (f)
Element (iv)	Storing search results	To document and demonstrate compliance	Article 6 (any) Typical: 6(b), (c)

[14] *Amman v Switzerland,* appl. no. 27798/95 (ECtHR, 16 February 2000), para 69; *S and Marper v. The United Kingdom,* appl. no. 30562/04 and 30566/04 (ECtHR, 4 December 2008) para 67; *Kopp v Switzerland,* app no. 23224/94 (ECtHR, 15 March 1998), paras 51–53. The listed cases concerned data storage by public authorities.

search for an (in)definite amount of time, the given set of data processing operations (labelled simply as 'screening') falls within the scope of the GDPR.

The controller, the processor and the purposes of processing in the GDPR. The role played by controllers and processors are defined in Article 4 (7) and (8). While controllers are "primary bearers of the obligations set by … law towards data subjects" (Bygrave & Tosoni, 2020b, 146) by determining the purposes and means of the processing of personal data, processors process personal data on behalf of the controller. Both the formal legal allocation of control and the factual control exercised should be considered with regard to the question who the data controller is (Bygrave & Tosoni, 2020b, 148). The data subject's perspective cannot be ignored either. According to the Article 29 WP, "the image given to data subjects and reasonable expectations of data subjects on the basis of this visibility" are equally relevant factors in determining the controller's status (Article 29 WP, 2010, 12). Furthermore, the CJEU also places weight on the effect that an entity's activity has on the privacy and data protection interests of data subject.[15]

Processors are entities legally separate from the controllers (Article 29 WP, 2010, 25). Emphasizing that the controller–processor relationship implies that the processor must follow ('obey') the instructions of the controller regarding the purposes and means of the processing (Article 28 and 29), providers of cloud services are typically processors for the purposes of data protection (Bygrave & Tosoni, 2020c, 158 and 160).

Tasks and responsibilities of controllers and processors are detailed in Articles 24–43, a detailed analysis of which is beyond the scope of this chapter. Cooperation with processors is the controller's responsibility the extent to which "the controller shall use only processors providing sufficient guarantees to implement appropriate technical and organisational measures in such a manner that processing will meet the requirements of this Regulation and ensure the protection of the rights of the data subject" (Article 28(1)). As further prescribed by Article 24 (1), the controller shall implement "appropriate technical and organizational measures to ensure and to be able to demonstrate that processing is performed in accordance with this Regulation" by (3) demonstrating

[15] *Google Spain*, CJEU Case C-131/12, paras 26–31 (cited by Tosoni & Bygrave, 2020, 120).

compliance with the obligations of the controllers. The "technical and organizational measures should be considered by considering the nature, scope, context and purposes of processing as well as the risks of varying likelihood and severity for the rights and freedoms of natural persons" (Article 24(1)) and by "ensuring data protection by design and by default" (Article 25). This latter implies that "the data protection principles are to be implemented in an effective manner ... in order to protect the rights of the data subjects" (Article 25(1)).

One of the most relevant principles is known as purpose limitation (Article 5(1)b) which prescribes that personal data can be "collected for [x] specified, explicit and [y] legitimate purposes and not further processed in a manner that is [z] incompatible with those purposes" (Bygrave, 2014, 153 and 155). This formulation—a cluster of three sub-principles marked by x, y, z—aims to ensure foreseeability in data processing outcomes: both the way in which personal data are processed and the results of processing should conform with the reasonable expectations of data subjects (Bygrave, 2014, 153 and 155).

Recalling Article 6(4) and Recital 50 in order to ascertain whether a purpose of further processing [screening] is compatible with the purpose for which the personal data are initially collected [for example, signing a contract], the controller should take into account, among others: any link between the original purposes and the purposes of the intended further processing; the context in which the personal data have been collected, in particular the reasonable expectations of data subjects based on their relationship with the controller as to their further use; the nature of the personal data; the consequences of the intended further processing for data subjects [such as exclusion or an employment position denied]. For example, as the ECtHR argued, information collected and stored (in connection with medical treatment) could not have been used for other purposes (examining compensation claims) without the consent (and as implied, knowledge) of the data subject.[16]

Controllers, processors and the purposes of data collection/processing in case of screening. The sampled privacy notices were so diverse in terms of depth and content that they cannot be really used in any reliable manner for analysing the purposes for which personal data are

---

[16] ECtHR, *M.S. v Sweden*, Appl. No. 20837/92, 27 August 1997, para 35.

collected by NGOs. Only supervisory authorities or courts could investigate properly the purposes for which aid NGOs process personal data, but recalling the findings of the online survey contractual obligations for screening (vetting, background check of individuals) was mentioned by 60% of the respondents ($n = 21$) as a purpose for data collection (Q10). When asked about the specific purposes of collecting personal data for meeting donor requirements in a follow-up question (Q15c), 60% of the respondents (21 of 35 respondents) agreed with the statement that they collect personal data for 'contractual obligations required by donors (background check, vetting or screening of individuals expected by our donors)'; six respondents indicated that this question was not applicable in their case, while 8 organizations (22.8%) claimed that they did not collect personal data for such purposes. This finding not only confirms earlier reports (NRC, 2018, 24; VOICE, 2021), but also indicate that NGOs are data controllers determining the purposes of processing.

Considering the nature of relationship between a typical NGO as user and the provider of the screening tool (the anonymized CompliancePartner), its *Data Protection Compliance* notice (CompliancePartner, 20yy-e) and legal notice at the bottom of each profile (CompliancePartner, 20yy-d) may also be used to determine the roles:

> the information contained in th[e] profile[s] is derived from public sources such as government and industry global watch lists and published news articles. [CompliancePartner] is not the source of the data and is not responsible for the content of third party sources. [CompliancePartner] does not determine any positive or negative risks associated with the profiled entity. These decisions are solely determined by [the] clients [such as aid NGOs, international organizations] as mandated by with their applicable regulatory obligations.

It can be reasonably inferred from this formulation, even without access to the data processing agreements between aid organizations and the vendors or other documents (terms and conditions) that the former is the legal entity that actually exercises control over the data processing. The supplier of the tech tool (Refinitive/LSEG in case of World-Check, LexisNexis, CSI, or the anonymized CompliancePartner) is the processor undertaking processing of personal data following the controller's instructions.

With regard to 'control', decisions concerning the purposes, purpose limitation included, (whom to screen, against what lists, how often, by which sampling logic and on what legal basis) are results of internal considerations and policies of aid organizations, NGOs included. Varying from organization to organization, these 'due diligence' decisions depend on international standards and on the legal nature of the relationship between the aid NGO and the individuals, among others. Employees and volunteers are usually screened differently than suppliers or board members of local partner organizations. Those disposing over 10–15,000 EUR/USD per transaction (either as managers in charge of payments or suppliers with contracts) are screened more frequently, even on a weekly basis.[17] Common is the general objective, but the differences may equally concern both the legal basis (*see* later) and the frequency of data processing operation (once or regularly/repetitively).[18]

The lawfulness of processing and legal basis in light of purposes. Following Chapter II (Principles) of the GDPR, especially the principle of lawfulness, fairness and transparency (Article 5(1)), the possible lawful grounds of data processing[19] (Article 6) and the conditions for processing sensitive data (Article 9) are to be considered. Every processing activity—screening included—requires the selection of a legal basis (Article 6(1) and Article 9(2)) which is to be documented before the data controller starts to process personal data. Furthermore, any legally sound ('lawful') processing of personal data necessitates fulfilling all of the core principles for processing personal data too (Article 5(1)) beyond the selection of any legal basis (Kotschy, 2020, 327).

Data controllers can collect personal data for a wide range of purposes provided that they can select a legal basis—from an exhaustive, final, but hierarchically not ranked list (Article 6(1))—take and demonstrate

---

[17] For example, following the FATF (2016, 12) recommendations actors (originally banks, FSPs) engaged in money transfers are required to implement preventive measures … before they (i) establish business relations; (ii) in case of those carrying out occasional transactions above the applicable designated threshold (USD/EUR 15,000) (…); or (iii) there is a suspicion of money laundering or terrorist financing.

[18] Interviews and NCHS/PRIO workshop, Oslo, September 23, 2022.

[19] The list corresponds to the general rules for lawful limitations on fundamental rights set out in Article 52(1) Charter of Fundamental Rights of the European Union and Article 8(2) European Convention on Human Rights.

responsibility for the processing by complying with the regulation (Article 6(4) included). They, however, must keep in mind that "the processing of personal data for purposes other than those for which the personal data were initially collected should be allowed only where the processing is compatible with the purposes for which the personal data were initially collected"; in this a case, "no legal basis separate from that which allowed the collection of the personal data is required" (Recital 50). If the original and the 'further' purpose are not compatible, different legal basis needs to be selected.

Legal basis in practice: screening. Aid NGOs collect and process personal data for various purposes with various legal basis, such as signing a supplier contract (Article 6b), signing a labour contract (Article 6b), complying with AML/CFT laws and/or conditional clauses in funding agreements (Article 6c), delivering aid (legal basis: Article 6a, 6d, 6e or 6f) or other organizational considerations (legal basis: Article 6f). The very same personal data—with or without the knowledge of data subjects—can be used for screening too, which (if the purpose is separate) may require the selection of a distinct legal basis (see Table 3.2).

A crucial question concerns if screening can be considered a 'specified, explicit and legitimate [original] purpose' for which personal data are collected or it is collected for other purposes and is further processed in a manner that is incompatible with the original purposes. Recalling the interviews and the workshop, aid organizations do not do 'screening for screening', it is rather a means of serving other ends. Therefore, Article 6(b), (c) or (f) are the most common legal grounds selected for the purpose of screening, but how NGOs define, distinguish and document the purposes and related legitimate basis in practice could not be verified in absence of access to internal documentation.

Considering the content of various list-categories provided, for example, by LexisNexis according to its website[20] (enforcement, PEP, ADVERSE MEDIA, SANCTIONS, see also Chapter 4), the consolidated SANCTIONS list is the only category (e.g. purpose of data processing) screening against which can be based on legal obligation (Article 6(c)) by citing counterterrorism laws and conditional clauses. Screening against the remaining lists (law enforcement, PEP, ADVERSE MEDIA) requires the selection of different legal basis (most likely Article 6b or 6f) in light

---

[20] https://risk.lexisnexis.com/products/worldcompliance-data, see 'Profiles relating to'.

Table 3.2 Publicly available privacy notices containing clear information on screening as of November 2022

International Medical Corps (IMC) Croatia	https://internationalmedicalcorps.hr/	To comply with anti-money laundering, terrorism and sanctions laws and regulations, there are times when we need to confirm (or reconfirm) the name, date of birth, address and other details of our donors and business partners (including their directors, officers, board members, owners, shareholders, authorised representatives and affiliates and their circumstances). We may need to do this whether you are applying to be a new donor or business partner or have been one for some time. *This information may be shared with third-party service providers for this purpose*
Norwegian Refugee Council (NRC)	https://www.nrc.no/globalassets/graphics/nrcpeople/privacy-notice-for-recruitment.pdf	PN addressed for employees (p. 1, footnote 1): "In accordance with core humanitarian principles, NRC implements a range of safeguards *to prevent or reduce the possibility of humanitarian aid falling into the wrong hands. This includes in particular those individuals and groups who are subject to sanctions imposed by the United Nations Security Council and other applicable sanctions lists. As part of this process, NRC may screen the details of the successful candidate for a position against these sanctions lists*"

(continued)

Table 3.2 (continued)

| Plan International UK | https://plan-uk.org/terms-conditions/privacy-notices | PN addressed to employees: "it is necessary to carry out *criminal records checks* to ensure that individuals are permitted to undertake the role in question"; general PN: "5. Ethical *screening* … To do this we sometimes use profiling and *screening methods* so that we can better understand our supporters and potential supporters … we may carry out *background checks* … on donors and potential donors or check donations to help protect the charity from abuse, fraud and/or money laundering and/or terrorist financing" |

of the original purpose (preparing or signing a contract, for example, or preventing hiring a convicted criminal).

Even if the purpose for which the personal data are collected and the corresponding legal basis may vary, if personal data are used for screening without data subjects' knowledge, not only their right to information may be violated, but their right to private life may also be compromised (Klareen, 2013; Vrabec, 2021). Therefore, it is necessary to assess objectively prior to screening if there are less intrusive means than screening that can realistically be implemented to prepare or perform the (labour or supplier) contract (Article 6b). The same applies to consent (Article 6a) even if this legal basis is used less frequently by aid organizations. A single consent "giving HOs *carte blanche* to use beneficiary data however they see fit, with no further consultation of the data subject, clearly breaches fundamental data protection principles" (Hayes, 2017, 196). Therefore, the key legal test with regard to the selection of legal basis is whether further processing (screening in our case) is compatible with the documented purposes for which the personal data were initially collected, which latter is not unrelated to the reasonable expectations of the data subjects either (*see in* Chapter 4).

To sum up, as personal data are involved, screening can be considered a data processing operation following the definition provided, for example, in Article 4(2) of GDPR. The process of screening described above corresponds to the terms used in GDPR Article 4(2) and in CJEU jurisprudence to describe processing operations, such as collection, recording, structuring, storage, retrieval, consultation, use, disclosure, loading personal data on an internet page. While search may be run occasionally or regularly, these databases are cloud-based, multiple and integrated. Screening can also be considered a data processing operation to the extent to which personal data are shared with the service provider during search to check if lists of personal data (of natural persons) match various watchlists in a consolidated database or when NGOs store results of screening for compliance purposes. Therefore, if an aid NGO—for whatever purpose and on whatever legal basis—(i) shares personal data (a person's name, date and place of birth) with an external service provider (ii) to search for positive matches in a database containing consolidated watchlists, (iii) stores the results of search for a(n) (in)definite amount of time and (iv) makes decisions based on the results, the given set of data processing operations (labelled simply as 'screening') falls within the scope of the GDPR.

Transparency and Right to Information in the GDPR

The GDPR requires controllers to render the data processing transparent to data subjects, as access and information rights represent integral components of privacy and other fundamental rights (Polčák, 2018, 405). In other words, transparency is a precondition for exercising the right to information—just as the right to information is the precondition for exercising other rights enshrined in the GDPR (Vrabec, 2021, 64). If data subjects are not provided information on the fact and purposes of (potential) screening, they can neither raise questions and claim their rights, nor consider the consequences of this operation either. As the relationship between the data subjects and the aid organization is voluntary (at least theoretically), the information provided to them is crucial. Individuals may or may not enter or remain in contractual (or other) relationship with the given aid organization, if they are aware of being screened.

Principles governing data processing and protection are listed in GDPR Article 5. The six (seven) principles—(1) lawfulness, fairness, transparency; purpose limitation; data minimization; data accuracy; storage limitation; integrity and confidentiality and (2) accountability (not discussed in this chapter)—govern how personal data should be processed and protected by data controllers and processors.

Focusing only on the first set of overlapping principles presented in Article 5(1)a, it prescribes that personal data shall be processed "lawfully, fairly and in a transparent manner in relation to the data subject ('lawfulness, fairness and transparency')". Lawfulness and fairness were explicitly mentioned in earlier legislation concerning data protection too (Directive 95/46/EC), and their meaning has not changed with the adoption of GDPR in 2016. The third element in Article 5(1)a, transparency, however, is a new component, at least in the EU data protection framework, complementing the first two principles.

Looking at the components of Article 5(a) one by one, lawfulness of processing means that personal data can be processed only if authorized by law. In other words, those processing personal data are required to follow the GDPR (as a rule of thumb) for ensuring adequate data protection by selecting a lawful basis for processing (Article 6: consent obtained from the data subject; necessity to enter a contract; legal obligation; vital interests of the data subject; performing a task for public interest; legitimate interests of the controller or a third party). Furthermore, data processing also needs to be in line with other EU legislation and domestic laws. Rights enshrined in the GDPR can be restricted recalling that "the right to the protection of personal data is not an absolute right; it must be considered in relation to its function in society and be balanced against other fundamental rights ..." (Recital 4).

The fairness principle governs the relationship between the controller and the data subject by ensuring that processing operations are "not performed in secret" and data subjects are "aware of the potential risks" (EU Handbook, 2018, 118).[21] The principle of fairness already appeared in the Directive 95/46/EC (preceding the GDPR) as the prohibition of secrecy and the requirement of comprehensive information.[22] It also implies that "natural persons should be made aware of risks, rules, safeguards and rights in relation to the processing of personal data and how to exercise their rights in relation to such processing" (Recital 39 and 60). Furthermore, fairness also implies that "data controllers must take some account of the reasonable expectations of data subjects" which carries "direct consequences for the purposes" for which data may be processed (Bygrave, 2014, 146). In other words the principle of 'fairness' and fair processing likely requires that the data subject should be consulted (Bygrave, 2014, 153 and 155).

---

[21] While secrecy in the context of national security and surveillance is to be distinguished from 'professional secrecy' conceptually, both can limit or restrict individuals' rights, even the transparency principle (EU Handbook, 2018, 71) as long as such measures are in line with the legal conditions of restrictions. Professional secrecy is interpreted a "special ethical duty that incurs a legal obligation inherent in certain professions and functions, which are based on faith and trust", for example, medical context, lawyer-client privilege, financial sector (EU Handbook, 2018, 69).

[22] Recital 38 to Directive 95/46/EC; see also CJEU, *Smaranda Bara* C-201/14 (1 October 2015), para 34, which says that "[i]t follows that the requirement of fair processing of personal data laid down in Article 6 of Directive 95/46 requires a public administrative body to inform the data subjects of the transfer of those data to another public administrative body for the purpose of their processing by the latter in its capacity as recipient of those data". Non-profit organizations are not public bodies, but states should ensure that private actors also respect the law.

The third component, transparency, establishes—among others—an obligation for the controller to ensure that the data subjects are informed about how their data is used (Recital 39 and 60) and for what purposes their data is processed (EDPB, 2/2019, 8). The application of this principle cannot be limited to a single event, a single act (providing only certain information), a single piece of information or a particular means or form used for communicated information. The rationale behind transparency is to enable data subjects to understand, and if necessary, challenge those processes, by empowering data subjects to hold data controllers and processors accountable and to exercise control over their personal data (Article 29 WP, 2018, 4 and 5). As argued by the EDPB, transparency "empowers data subjects to hold data controllers and processors accountable and to exercise control over their personal data by, for example, providing or withdrawing informed consent" (Article 29 WP, 2018, 5). Regardless of the legal basis of a given data processing operation and for being a principle, transparency is prescribed, that is, to be applied in general—and not only in cases when the legal basis of processing is consent.

As implied, the relationship between transparency and fairness is two-way or mutual (Article 29 WP, 2018, 4). Fairness and transparency together concern the ways and method (of communication vis-a-vis the data subjects) and the content of the information (provided to them). While fairness is about the provision of complete information by the data controller, transparency has more to do with the content and quality of the information. On the one hand, fairness may ensure transparency as a proportionality safeguard (Article 29 WP, 2018, 5), especially in cases of power imbalance between the controller and the data subject. On the other hand, 'fair processing means [implies] transparency of processing, especially vis-à-vis data subjects' by implying that 'data have not been obtained nor otherwise processed through unfair means, by deception or without the data subject's knowledge' (de Terwangne, 2018, 314). These principles explicitly appear in the articles describing data subjects' rights: "the controller shall … provide the data subject with the … information necessary to ensure *fair* and *transparent* processing" (Article 13(2) and 14(2)).

The principle of transparency is supported and advanced by other elements in the GDPR. Rights of the data subjects are too complex to be discussed here comprehensively, but it should be noted that transparency encompasses all of them. Transparency with regard to data processing and data protection is proportional to the strengths of individual rights: more transparency (from the perspective of the data subject) entails stronger rights. The most relevant legal content is detailed in GDPR Article 12, 13–14 and 15; Recitals 11, 58, 59, 60, 63, 166 (Polčák, 2018, 398–420). As expressed by Article 12(1) too, while compliance with the transparency principle is a precondition for exercising rights, the right to information is also deemed to be the precondition for other rights enshrined in the GDPR (Vrabec, 2021). In the framework of data subject rights, Article 12 lays down the requirements for appropriate measures to be adopted by the controller when providing the information (in line with Article 13 and 14) and also for communications referred to in Article 15–22 and 34 GDPR.

The controller shall take appropriate measures to provide any information referred to in Articles 13 and 14 (see Annex) and any communication under Articles 15 to 22 and 34 relating to processing the data subject in a "concise, transparent, intelligible and easily accessible form, using clear and plain language" (Recital 58). Without having general information on data processing operations, including personal data and/or access to specific information on data processing involving one's personal data—such as screening—there is no knowing and understanding which is further needed for claiming rights.

As far as the content and ways of communication (disclosing information about the essence of the use of data and related data processing operations) are concerned, the following main elements (of Article 13 and 14) require consideration by aid NGOs as data controllers as a minimum: the content of the information, the timing of providing information, the appropriate ways of providing information and the right to lodge a complaint. The GDPR implies an obligation requiring the NGOs (data controllers) to comply with the transparency and fairness obligations proactively—unless restrictions or exceptions apply.

While transparency is listed among the rights of the data subjects (in Article 12), privacy notices are not mentioned in the GDPR as a modality of communications. Yet, the privacy notice (data protection notice, privacy policy, privacy statement or fair processing notice) is seen as one of the most efficient measures to provide information (Article 29 WP, 2018, 13) to data subjects—either on websites of organizations, or in alternative channels—at least from the perspective of legal compliance.

Transparency and Right to Information in Practice: Communicating Screening

Repeating the description of methods in the Introduction (Chapter 1), interviews, a workshop and publicly available privacy notices (PNs) were used to understand how data subjects are notified about screening by aid organizations. As for the privacy notices, it should be emphasized that they are not mentioned in the GDPR as a modality of communications. Yet, even if they are heavily criticized for being incomprehensible regardless of jurisdictions (Becher & Benoliel, 2021; Zarsky, 2022, 1461–1464), they form an important component, if not equivalent of, privacy policies. Such policies and/or notices are nevertheless important for they remain the "single most important [written] source of information for users" attempting to learn how companies collect, use and share their personal data (Zarsky, 2022, 1462). Regardless of their importance—ignored by data subjects in many cases—organizations, aid NGOs included, share information about their data processing operations in privacy notices in different ways. Some of them consider this document in minimalist terms (addressing only users of their websites), others notify data subjects in a more comprehensive manner, providing information about all sorts of data processing operations conducted with personal data.

Keeping the above in mind, PNs posted on websites were selected for their accessibility. They were used as proxies (the second-best alternative to ethnographic data) assuming that if screening can be conceptualized as a data protection operation, data subjects (individuals screened regardless of the nature of their relationship with the aid organization) have right to know about it. The accessibility of these written documents also ensured comparison across organizations. While PNs were scrutinized for any reference to screening, terms such as (ethical) screening, vetting, background check, due diligence, fraud prevention and AML/CFT were deemed 'direct' evidence. Indirect formulation was also considered for the extent to which screening may have been inferred from other wording.

Considering that there are thousands of NGOs registered in the EU/EEA, NGOs were selected based on their VOICE membership[23] ($n = 88$) as well as on a random basis ($n = 5$) so that

---

[23] VOICE stands for Voluntary Organisations in Cooperation in Emergencies and it is the largest European humanitarian NGO network promoting efficient and effective humanitarian aid worldwide since 1992, *see* https://voiceeu.org/.

larger actors present in multiple areas with a diverse profile and employee pool were part of the sample. All in all, the content of 92 publicly available privacy notices were assessed for evidence on screening (usually under the subthemes derived from GDPR: purposes of processing, legitimate interest, data transfer to third parties as data processors) in Spring 2021 first and later on in November 2022. It should also be noted that revising privacy notices, merging or splitting them is a dynamic, ongoing process. Therefore, changes may have occurred in some cases since the data was collected. Furthermore, some organizations provide public access to multiple privacy notices, others may have a version for external use (on their websites) and other PNs are available for internal use only.

As screening is only one among the many data processing operations conducted by an aid NGO, a comprehensive analysis of publicly available privacy notices was not the intention of this paper. Yet, a few general observations are necessary before notification with regard to screening is scrutinized. First, privacy notices of aid organizations are mostly addressed to European audiences—in national languages, sometimes with translations also available in English. The target audience is composed first and foremost of website visitors, social media users, newsletter subscribers (typical categories data subjects addressed in almost all privacy notices), followed by individual donors, employees, volunteers, job applicants or candidates.[24] Transaction partners (suppliers, consultants) in the Global South and beneficiaries of aid programmes and projects are sometimes listed,[25] but it is not typical at all. An exceptionally clear reference to Global South individuals can be found in the privacy notice of *People in Need* (Czech Republic), which mentioned 'data on aid recipients' as a separate (5) category:

---

[24] As in the case of most German NGOs in the sample; the Jesuite Refugee Service (Italy) also has a very detailed 'web privacy notice': https://jrseurope.org/en/privacy-policy/. Others, for example, War Child Holland, claims that the privacy statement is addressed "for all individuals, companies and organisations involved in our work. This includes individual donors, large and small institutional donors, partner organisations implementing our work and *people who participate in our projects* or research ... [with regards to those that have different kinds of relations to the NGO, separate PNs are used] our privacy statement does *not* address the processing of employee, intern, consultant or volunteer data, which is covered by other internal privacy documents and agreements" https://www.warchildholland.org/yourprivacy/.

[25] See, for example, CARE NL: https://www.carenederland.org/privacy-statement.

In cases where we provide humanitarian aid to certain persons in the Czech Republic or abroad (in order to save lives, alleviate hardship and help victims of disasters or crises get back on their feet) or development aid (to help people in their efforts to break out of poverty and further develop) it is usually necessary in the interest of aid effectiveness, but also its reporting to donors to collect the personal data of aid recipients. The processing time is usually limited by the project implementation time and further by the time set by the donor or based on the nature of the specific project.

Privacy notices posted on NGO websites were primarily scrutinized for the civil sector usually treats the right to information and the principle of transparency as values to be promoted not only in their interactions with their donors, the public authorities both in the donor and recipient states and their beneficiaries, but also in privacy notices.[26] Yet, findings indicate that reference to counterterrorism, reasonable efforts or screening as a data processing operation in the publicly available privacy notice is invisible to the general public. EU-registeredaid NGOs, with rare exceptions, almost never communicate the practice of screening to data subjects in such PNs.

Among the NGOs whose publicly available privacy notices were analysed for their content in Spring 2021 and November 2022, only three (or four) privacy notices mentioned screening explicitly as a purpose of data collection: the (recruitment/employment) privacy notices of NRC and PLAN UK; PLAN's general privacy notice and the privacy notice of the Croatian International Medical Corps (Table 3.2). None of them linked purpose with a legal basis (Article 6(1)), but two of them made references to working with an external service provider.

Eight other organizations used a formulation which might be indicative of them collecting personal data for the purpose of screening, but the language is not clear and concise enough to draw conclusions. The privacy notices of *War Child Holland* and *Goal Global* (Ireland) may also be cited as examples of communicating data processing probably for the

---

[26] For example, Mercy Corps (NL) promises in its Data Protection Statement that when it records personal information it will "[b]e transparent about the use to which it is put"; Cesci (Italy) assures the reader that "[s]ince its creation, Cesvi has decided to inspire its action to the values of transparency, quality and safety". Links to the PNs are available by google search or upon request.

purpose of screening and/or compliance with AML/CFT law as distinct from other purposes.[27]

Considering the transparency principle and the notification obligations prescribed by GDPR, a typical NGO would need to consider when drafting a privacy notice, among others, how personal data is involved in the case of screening, what screening means as a data processing operation; who defines the purposes of processing and, if data processors are used for conducting screening (related also to the matter of data transfers), what is the relationship between the controller and the processor, and which legitimate basis is used for screening.

The explanations for missing information on screening vary and require further research. However, it is worthwhile to recall that privacy notices are widely criticized both by data subjects and legal scholars for being 'unreadable and uninterpretable', for being 'too long, unstructured' or too 'noisy' in terms of content in absence of proper standards (Becher & Benoliel, 2021). If privacy notices are not read, it is irrelevant—from the perspective of the non-reader—if the information is provided in a manner that complies with the GDPR, legal or scholarly advice. While the recent WhatsApp-decision of the Irish data protection authority (DPC, 2021) established that privacy notices must be detailed—with far more detail being given than is currently typical—and must be easily accessible (without use of multiple linked documents, which may be hard to find and assimilate), it does not solve the problem of length. Those not reading— or being discouraged by purely seeing the length of any text—will not be helped by a well-structured text either. But this circumstance does not eliminate the data controllers' (aid NGOs) obligation (manifested in the principle of transparency among others) to notify the data subjects.

Assuming that communication channels other than privacy notices posted on websites may also be a GDPR-friendly solution, guidelines on information provided orally can be considered relevant (Article 29 WP, 2018, 13):

---

[27] War Child Holland lists 22 purposes, two of which (#14 and #15) prompting that data need for preparing a contract and for signing it are collected and processed on different legal basis: «14: To see if we can accept you as a partner or supplier [background check, watchlist screening – if at all]; 15: to enable the completion of an agreement with you as a company or supplier [signing the contract]», https://www.warchildholland.org/yourprivacy/. In case of Goal Global (Ireland) the purpose and legal basis is not only directly linked, but the collection of personal data (for AML, CFT) is also mentioned as a separate DP operation (https://www.goalglobal.org/privacy/).

where a data controller has chosen to provide information to a data subject orally, or a data subject requests the provision of oral information or communications, WP29's position is that the data controller should allow the *data subject to re-listen to pre-recorded messages*. This is imperative where the request for oral information relates to visually impaired data subjects or other data subjects who may have difficulty in accessing or understanding information in written format.

No evidence confirms the use of pre-recorded messages by the sampled NGOs. A further problem with providing information orally is that it does not look feasible considering the scope of screening. When tens of thousands of personal data records are screened on a weekly or monthly basis, when hundreds of new suppliers or employees are screened before the contract signed and later on, by the time contracts are terminated, providing information orally—in a 'concise, transparent, intelligible and easily accessible form and using clear and plain language'—looks even more time-consuming than screening itself.

How and when information on screening is provided likely depends on the nature of the relationship between the NGO and the perceived (digital) literacy of the individuals, not so much on the documented legitimate basis. As both privacy rights and surveillance in employment contexts are much better scrutinized and regulated in OECD countries (Nouwt et al., 2005) than in case of individuals living in experimental Global South settings (Sandvik et al., 2017), labour contracts usually contain a clause on screening. Consequently, those who have a contractual relationship (as employee or supplier) or are in charge of money transfers over internationally set standards are notified about screening when they sign the contract.[28] These contracts usually contain a clause making references to screening as a respondent on behalf of a "small-to-medium size NGO, working across the globe, focusing on human rights, labour rights and women's rights" illustrate[29]:

> In each specific agreement (either a labour contact or partner agreement) the purpose of the screenings is mentioned. In our Policy Framework, it is also elaborated.

---

[28] NCHS/PRIO workshop, Oslo, September 23, 2022.

[29] Second questionnaire, filled out July 20, 2023.

However, even when information is provided on screening (in the form of a contract or in form of an oral message accompanying a contract), details are usually provided orally and in generic terms even in case of a labour or supplier contract with a clause making references to screening.[30] Practices likely vary from organization to organization, however, and maybe also within organizations with multiple branches in multiple jurisdictions.

Those individuals whose relationship with NGOs are less strictly regulated in legal terms or by legal means, for example, there is no contract signed, are usually not provided with information.[31] Volunteers, consultants, beneficiaries of development projects or beneficiaries of CVA (cash and voucher) assistance—that might (also) be screened as clients by the external financial service providers (FSPs) based on the lists provided by NGOs in the Global South—are not necessarily made aware of screening regardless of how the legal basis (public interest, vital interest, legal obligation) may be documented by the aid organization.

Taking the example of FSPs, they are external partners (and data processors in the context of data protection) that facilitate the implementation of cash and voucher assistance (CVA) projects, for example, by issuing debit cards to beneficiaries in cooperation with humanitarian organizations. These FSPs receiving lists of names from humanitarian organizations might conduct screening by considering the individuals also as (potential) clients and not simply humanitarian beneficiaries.[32] Yet, aid organizations struggle to notify the data subjects about such implicit outsourcing of screening,[33] even if it is recommended by the International Federation of Red Cross and Red Crescent Societies in its guidance addressed to cash practitioners (IFRC, 2021, 23–25):

> Inform beneficiaries and explain the KYC requirements or at minimum include these requirements in the privacy notice that could be consulted at any time.

If beneficiaries are to be informed about such data transfers to FSPs in privacy notices, privacy notices should also be used to inform data subjects

---

[30] NCHS/PRIO workshop, Oslo, September 23, 2022.

[31] NCHS/PRIO workshop, Oslo, September 23, 2022.

[32] Workshop, September 23, 2022.

[33] Workshop, September 23, 2022.

about screening by NGOs themselves. Although PNs posted on website hardly ensure transparency in this regard, it should be acknowledged that NGOs usually draft multiple privacy notices—some of them publicly available, others used only internally—and not all of them are available for public scrutiny (or research purposes).

Contrary to the abundance of such notices and data protection guidelines prepared by and for larger humanitarian organizations (Franz et al., 2020; Kuner & Marelli, 2020), little reliable information (written source) is available about the notification procedures of NGOs with regard to screening. Therefore, the content of information that they share about screening cannot be assessed either. While the findings clearly demonstrate that aid organizations prefer not speaking much about screening in general, the abundance of relations (between individuals and particular NGOs) makes it almost impossible to explore in a scientifically reliable manner how individuals—that are notified about being screened—are provided information on the purpose and legitimate basis of screening, the frequency of screening or the substance of data transfers.

Possible Restrictions and Alternative Ways of Communicating Screening

Are aid organizations allowed to withhold information on screening or minimize what they disclose? Considering the distinction made between transparency as an idea and as a legal principle, there is no straightforward reply. It depends on how the type of aid organization (NGO or an international organization enjoying special legal status), how they interpret transparency in light of various legal sources permitting exemptions (for example in the context of national security, counterterrorism) on the one hand and their own internal ethical standards or branding policies on the other hand. As for the former, counterterrorism and other laws regulating public order and national security in the UK, France, Germany, the Netherlands, Sweden and Norway in Europe—the US and Canada outside it—merit special attention for these are the countries with the largest aid budgets and most extensive funding schemes. As for the latter, self-imposed ethical considerations also matter, because the NGO sector in general, aid organizations in particular, are traditionally distrustful towards (over-)regulation. Their criticisms towards financial surveillance by their banks illustrate it well (see Chapter 5).

Yet, as long as screening is a data processing operation, the GDPR applies for aid organizations registered in the EU/EEA. The regulation, however, allows certain exemptions and restrictions. Although a detailed discussion is not possible here for that would require selecting a jurisdiction, it should be noted that restrictions concerning *principles*—such as transparency, fairness, lawfulness prescribed by the GDPR—are strict. They are allowed only to the extent they (i) correspond with rights and obligations provided in Article 12 to 22 and (ii-1) only if exemptions and restrictions are provided for at EU or national level by law, (ii-2) pursue a legitimate aim and (ii-3) can be considered proportionate and necessary in a democratic society—at the same time (EU Handbook, 2018, 116). In line with this, Article 23 allows Member States (or the EU) to legislate for further restrictions on the scope of the data subjects' rights in relation to transparency and the substantive data subjects' rights provided that fundamental rights are not compromised, and restrictions are necessary and proportionate to safeguard one or more of the ten objectives set out in Article 23.1(a) to (j) (Article 29 WP, 2018, 33).

Data subjects' rights—enshrined in GDPR—are mostly restricted in the context of law enforcement and matters related to national security and counterterrorism by states or public authorities. The objectives and conditions justifying restrictions are listed in Article 23: national security; defence; public security; criminal prevention and enforcement; other important objectives of general public interest of the Union or of a Member State, e.g. financial or economic interests; the prevention, investigation, detection and prosecution of breaches of ethics for regulated professions; a monitoring, inspection or regulatory function connected, even occasionally, to the exercise of official authority in the cases referenced in points (a) to (e) and (g); and the protection of the data subject or the rights and freedoms of others. Article 23(2) lists the provisions (subject to restrictions) which should be legislated, such as the purposes of processing, categories of personal data, the nature of restrictions, etc. Recital 73 further specifies that restrictions may be imposed by Union or Member State law.

However, even if restrictions apply in some member states, "the domestic law must be sufficiently clear in its terms to give individuals an adequate indication of the circumstances and conditions under which controllers are empowered to resort to any such restrictions … and … it is indeed essential that legislative measures, which seek to restrict the scope of data subjects' rights or of controllers' obligations, are foreseeable for the data subjects" (EDPB, 10/2020, 8). In other words, even if aid NGOs might be allowed to restrict data subjects' rights—information on being screened—individuals should understand the "circumstances in and conditions under" which controllers withhold information. Furthermore, there should be a legislative measure referred to in Article 23(1) containing specific provisions that prescribe or allow such restrictions: the controller is expected to inform data subjects that they are relying on such a national legislative restriction to the exercise of data subject rights, or to the transparency obligation in line with Article 23(2)h.

Recalling that transparency is not only a legal principle in the context of human rights and data protection law, but also a general idea that influences power relations, actors in the non-profit sector may consider certain due diligence practices and strategies implemented by for-profit actors, such as banks or lawyers (Helgesson & Mörth, 2019). These practices not only include the collection and verification of client information (when a bank account is opened) and the monitoring of client transactions, but also the content and ways of communication with clients about the AML/CFT measures. Taking the website of DNB, the largest commercial bank in Norway, as an example, the bank not only makes relevant information available on its website,[34] but also a disclaimer stating that "the bank is neither an investigator nor a judge, but we monitor and report suspicious transactions to the police. In this area, we have a duty of confidentiality, which means that we do not inform our customers or others about what we do". Such practices may not be considered fair by those being victims of financial surveillance, but (would be) clients are at least allowed to know what they can expect from banks before opening a bank account or transferring money to a 'high risk' country.

CONCLUSIONS

This chapter conceptualized screening as a data processing operation and focused on the principle of transparency and right to information. Regardless of the oral versus written form of notification, the concerned data subjects seem to be kept behind a 'veil of ignorance' (a term borrowed

---

[34] *Anti-money laundering, anti-corruption and international sanctions*: https://www. dnb.no/en/about-us/csr/Financial-crime/aml.html and *KYC/AML in DNB*: https:// www.dnb.no/en/about-us/kyc-aml-in-dnb.html.

from Rawls 1971) by aid organizations. As findings indicate, the majority is rarely (made) aware of the fact that their personal data, collected for purposes such as signing a contract or participating in an event, may also be checked against sanctions and enforcement lists, and as part of this process, potentially disclosed to third parties.[35] Data transfers can be particularly sensitive for multiple actors may have vested interest in and access to the screening lists of NGOs, such as (i) donors looking for evidence on NGO-compliance during various phases of the project cycle; (ii) authorities in aid recipient countries that may be interested in such lists for political reasons; (iii) the U.S.-based suppliers that not only provide access to the screening databases in exchange of subscription fee, but also gain access to the NGOs' lists (the latter is likely used for 'feeding' or 'training' the consolidated databases to increase the number of searchable profiles) and also (iv) external partners of aid organizations, such as financial service providers (FSPs) facilitating CVA-projects.

Obviously, the broader context in which aid organizations work in the Global South, especially in humanitarian and conflict settings entail ethical questions beyond GDPR-compliance. An apparent challenge for NGOs is to navigate among their mission (providing assistance to vulnerable populations by considering not only human rights, but also local norms and values in a manner that does not undermine trust and their credibility), their mandate (ensuring that donor funds are processed within the given timeframes and in line with the project purposes), organizational interests (not hiring sexual offenders or those potentially involved in human trafficking), other legal compliance requirements in the context of AML/CFT (ensuring that their private donors, suppliers, partners and intended beneficiaries are *bona fide* entities) and data protection laws (fulfilling data subjects' rights by providing minimum information on screening). However, it is precisely the opacity—the opposite of transparency—characterizing the communication on screening that raises the question whether it can also be considered surveillance.

---

[35] Interview with an advisor working at a Norwegian NGO, Teams, 4 May 2021; NCHS/PRIO workshop, Oslo, September 23, 2022.

References

Legal Sources (Case Law: ECtHR and CJEU)

- *M.S. v Sweden*, appl. no. 20837/92; 27 August 1997 (paras 35 and 67).
- *Kopp v Switzerland*, appl. no. 23224/94; 15 March 1998 (paras 51–55).
- *Amman v Switzerland*, appl. no. 27798/95; 16 February 2000 (para 69).
- *S and Marper v. The United Kingdom*, appl. no 30562/04 and 30566/04; 4 December 2008 (para 41 and 67).
- *Google Spain v Agencia Española de Protección de Datos (AEPD) and Mario Costeja González*, Case C-131/12. Judgment of CJEU, 13 May 2014.
- *Smaranda Bara* and Others v Casa Naţională de Asigurări de Sănătate and Others, C-201/14. Judgement of the CJEU, 1 October 2015.
- *Peter Nowak v Data Protection Commissioner*, Case C-434/16. Judgment of the CJEU, 20 December 2017.
- *Fashion ID GmbH & Co. KG v Verbraucherzentrale NRW e. V.*, Case C-40/17. Judgment of CJEU, 29 July 2019.

Article 29 WP (Article 29 Working Party). (2007, June 20). *Opinion 4/2007 on the Concept of Personal Data* (WP 136). Retrieved September 20, 2022, from https://ec.europa.eu/justice/article-29/documentation/opinion-recommendation/files/2007/wp136_en.pdf

Article 29 WP (Article 29 Working Party). (2010). *Opinion 01/2010 on the Concepts of "Controller" and "Processor"*. Retrieved September 20, 2022, from https://ec.europa.eu/justice/article-29/documentation/opinion-recommendation/files/2010/wp169_en.pdf

Article 29 WP (Article 29 Working Party). (2018). *Guidelines on Transparency Under Regulation 2016/679*. Retrieved September 20, 2022, from https://ec.europa.eu/newsroom/article29/items/622227

Becher, S. I., & Benoliel U. (2021). Law in Books and Law in Action: The Readability of Privacy Policies and the GDPR. In K. Mathis & A. Tor (Eds.), *Consumer Law and Economics. Economic Analysis of Law in European Legal Scholarship* (Vol. 9, pp. 179–204). Springer. https://doi.org/10.1007/978-3-030-49028-7_9

Bennett, C. J. (2018). The European General Data Protection Regulation: An Instrument for the Globalization of Privacy Standards? *Information Polity, 23*(2), 239–246. https://doi.org/10.3233/IP-180002

Bygrave, L. A. (2014). Core Principles of Data Privacy Law. In *Data Privacy Law: An International Perspective* (Online ed., pp. 145–168). Oxford Academic. Retrieved October 13, 2022, from https://doi.org/10.1093/acprof:oso/9780199675555.003.0005

Bygrave, L. A., & Tosoni, L. (2020a). Article 4(1). Personal Data. In Christopher Kuner and others (eds),*The EU General Data Protection Regulation (GDPR):*

A Commentary New York: Oxford Academic, online edn), pp. 103–115), https://doi.org/10.1093/oso/9780198826491.003.0007

Bygrave, L. A., & Tosoni, L. (2020b). Article 4(7). Controller. In Christopher Kuner and others (eds), *The EU General Data Protection Regulation (GDPR): A Commentary*. New York: online edn, Oxford Academic, pp. 145–156. https://doi.org/10.1093/oso/9780198826491.003.0013

Bygrave, L. A., & Tosoni, L. (2020c). Article 4(8) Processor. In Christopher Kuner and others (eds), *The EU General Data Protection Regulation (GDPR): A Commentary*. New York: online edn, Oxford Academic, pp. 157–162. https://doi.org/10.1093/oso/9780198826491.003.0014

De Goede, M., & Sullivan, G. (2016). The politics of security lists. *Environment and Planning D: Society and Space, 34*(1), 67–88. https://doi.org/10.1177/0263775815599309

de Terwangne, C. (2018). Principles (Articles 5–11) Article 5. Principles Relating to Processing of Personal Data. In C. Kuner, L. A. Bygrave, C. Docksey, & L. Drechsler (Eds.), *The EU General Data Protection Regulation (GDPR): A Commentary* (Oxford Academic, Online ed., pp. 309–320). Oxford University Press. https://doi.org/10.1093/oso/9780198826491.003.0034

DPC (Data Protection Commission, Ireland). (2021). *Whatsapp. Data Protection Commission, In the Matter of the General Data Protection Regulation.* DPC Inquiry Reference: IN-18-12-2, 2021. Retrieved September 15, 2022, from https://edpb.europa.eu/system/files/2021-09/dpc_final_decision_red acted_for_issue_to_edpb_01-09-21_en.pdf

EDPB (European Data Protection Board). (3/2018). *Guidelines 3/2018 on the Territorial Scope of the GDPR (Article 3)*. Version 2.1. https://edpb_guidelines_3_2018_territorial_scope_after_public_consultation_en_1.pdf (europa.eu)

EDPB (European Data Protection Board). (2/2019). *Guidelines 2/2019 on the Processing of Personal Data Under Article 6(1)(b) GDPR in the Context of the Provision of Online Services to Data Subjects*. Version 2.0. https://edpb.europa.eu/sites/default/files/files/file1/edpb_guidelines-art_6-1-b-adopted_after_public_consultation_en.pdf

EDPB (European Data Protection Board. (10/2020). *Guidelines 10/2020 on Restrictions Under Article 23 GDPR*. https://edpb.europa.eu/our-work-tools/our-documents/guidelines/guidelines-102020-restrictions-under-art icle-23-gdpr_en

EDPB (European Data Protection Board). (1/2022). *Guidelines 01/2022 on Data Subject Rights—Right of Access*. https://edpb.europa.eu/our-work-tools/documents/public-consultations/2022/guidelines-012022-data-sub ject-rights-right_en

EUDPR (2018) Regulation (EU) 2018/1725 of the European Parliament and of the Council of 23 October 2018 on the protection of natural persons with regard to the processing of personal data by the Union institutions, bodies, offices and agencies and on the free movement of such data, and repealing Regulation (EC) No 45/2001 and Decision No 1247/2002/EC. Retrieved 13 May, 2024 from https://eur-lex.europa.eu/legal-content/en/TXT/?uri= CELEX:32018R1725

EU (European Union) Handbook. (2018). *Handbook on European Data Protection Law*. European Commission and FRA. https://fra.europa.eu/en/public ation/2018/handbook-european-data-protection-law-2018-edition

EU GDPR (European Union General Data Protection Regulation). (2016). *Regulation 2016/679 of the European Parliament and of the Council of 27 April 2016 on the Protection of Natural Persons with Regard to the Processing of Personal Data and on the Free Movement of Such Data*. Retrieved April 8, 2022, from https://eur-lex.europa.eu/eli/reg/2016/679/oj

FATF (Financial Action Task Force). (2016). *Guidance for a Risk-Based Approach: Money or Value Transfer Services*. Retrieved October 23, 2022, from https://www.fatf-gafi.org/publications/fatfrecommendations/docume nts/rba-money-or-value-transfer.html

Franz, V., Hannah, L., & Hayes, B. (2020). *Civil Society Organizations and General Data Protection Regulation Compliance Challenges, Opportunities, and Best Practice*. Brussels: Open Society Foundation. Retrieved April 18, 2022, from https://www.opensocietyfoundations.org/publications/civil-soc iety-organizations-and-general-data-protection-regulation-compliance

Gazi, T. (2020). Data to the Rescue: How Humanitarian Aid Organizations Should Collect Information Based on the GDPR. *International Journal Humanitarian Action, 5*(9), 1–7. https://doi.org/10.1186/s41018-020-00078-0

Hayes, B. (2017). *The Impact of International Counter-Terrorism on Civil Society Organisations: Understanding the Role of the Financial Action Task Force*. Bread for the World. Retrieved May 8, 2022, from http://efc.issuelab.org/resources/27481/27481.pdf

Helgesson, K. S., & Mörth, U. (2019). Instruments of Securitization and Resisting Subjects: For-Profit Professionals in the Finance–Security Nexus. *Security Dialogue, 50*(3), 257–274. https://doi.org/10.1177/096701061 9835655

IFRC (International Federation of Red Cross). (2021). *Practical Guidance for Data Protection in Cash and Voucher Assistance*. https://www.ifrc.org/doc ument/practical-guidance-data-protection-cash-and-voucher-assistance

Klareen, J. (2013). The Human Right to Information and Transparency. In A. Bianchi & A. Peters (Eds.), *Transparency in International Law* (pp. 223–238). Cambridge University Press.

Kotschy, W. (2020). Article 6: Lawfulness of Processing. In C. Kuner, L. A. Bygrave, C. Docksey, & L. Drechsler (Eds.), *The EU General Data Protection*

Regulation (GDPR): A Commentary (Oxford Academic, Online ed., pp. 71–76). Oxford University Press.

Kuner, C., & Marelli, M. (Eds.). (2020). *Handbook on Data Protection in Humanitarian Action* (2nd ed.). ICRC—Brussels Privacy Hub. Retrieved March 3, 2022, from https://www.icrc.org/en/data-protection-humanitarian-action-handbook

LexisNexis. (2021). *LexisNexis® WorldCompliance^{TM} Data*. Retrieved March 12, 2022, from https://risk.lexisnexis.com/global/en/products/worldcompliance-data

NRC (Norwegian Refugee Council) (2018). Principles Under Pressure: *the Impact of Counterterrorism Measures and Preventing/Countering Violent Extremism on Principled Humanitarian Action*. Retrieved March 13, 2021, from https://reliefweb.int/sites/reliefweb.int/files/resources/nrc-principles_under_pressure-report-screen.pdf

Nouwt, S., de Vires, B. R., & Prins, C. (Eds.) (2005). *Reasonable Expectations of Privacy? Eleven Country Reports in Camera Surveillance and Workplace Privacy*. T. M. C. Asser

Paragi, B. (2021). Digital4development? European Data Protection in the Global South. *Third World Quarterly, 42*(2), 254–273. https://doi.org/10.1080/01436597.2020.1811961

Polčák, R. (2018). Rights of the Data Subject (Articles 12–23) Section 1 Transparency and Modalities Article 12. Transparent Information, Communication and Modalities for the Exercise of the Rights of the Data Subject. In C. Kuner, L. A. Bygrave, C. Docksey, & L. Drechsler (Eds.), *The EU General Data Protection Regulation (GDPR): A Commentary* (Oxford Academic, Online ed., pp. 397–412). Oxford University Press. https://doi.org/10.1093/oso/9780198826491.003.0042

Psychogiopoulou, E. (2017). The European Court of Human Rights, Privacy and Data Protection in the Digital Era. In E. Psychogiopoulou & M. Brkan (Eds.), *Courts, Privacy and Data Protection in the Digital Environment* (pp. 32–63). Edward Elgar.

Sandvik, K. B., Jacobsen, K. L. & McDonald, S. M. (2017). Do Not Harm: A Taxonomy of the Challenges of Humanitarian Experimentation. *International Review of the Red Cross, 99*(1), 319–344. https://doi.org/10.1017/S18163 8311700042X

Schmidt, J. (2022). The European Union and the Promotion of Values in Its External Relations—The Case of Data Protection. In J. Lee & A. Darbellay (Eds.), *Data Governance in AI, FinTech and Legal Tech* (pp. 238–262). Edward Elgar Tech.

Tosoni, L., & Bygrave, L. A. (2020). Article 4(2). Processing. In C. Kuner, L. A. Bygrave, C. Docksey, & L. Drechsler (Eds.), *The EU General Data*

Protection Regulation (GDPR): A Commentary (Oxford Academic, Online ed., pp. 116–123). Oxford University Press.

Tzanou, M. (2017). *The Fundamental Right to Data Protection: Normative Value in the Context of Counter-Terrorism Surveillance.* Hart Publishing.

VOICE (Voluntary Organisations in Cooperation in Emergencies). (2021). *Adding to the Evidence the Impacts of Sanctions and Restrictive Measures on Humanitarian Action* (VOICE Survey Report). Retrieved January 20, 2022, from https://voiceeu.org/search?q=adding+to+the+evidence

Vrabec, H. U. (2021). The Right to Information. In *Data Subject Rights Under the GDPR* (Oxford Academic, Online ed., pp. 64–101). Oxford University Press. https://doi.org/10.1093/oso/9780198868422.003.0004

Zarsky, T. (2022). Serious Notice: A Celebration, Discussion, and Recognition of Joel Reidenberg's Work on Privacy Notices and Disclosures. *Fordham Law Review, 90*(4), 1457–1487. Available at SSRN: https://ssrn.com/abstract=4050682

CHAPTER 4

Screening and/or Surveillance?

Abstract Surveillance in the context of aid work originally refers to control over procedures, supplies and people, which is deemed necessary for providing recognition and services. It is widely considered an inalienable, albeit criticized, part of care provision. International aid organizations, however, also screen individuals following either conditional clauses in funding agreements in the context of counterterrorism or pursuing other organizational interests. While this opaque practice has raised concerns both in humanitarian and development circles, it is much less known how screening is implemented and if it can be construed as (harmful) surveillance. Therefore, this chapter introduces a screening tool as a core empirical part to discuss the surveillance dimension characterizing aid work. As findings indicate, surveillance tools can help aid organizations to navigate the complexity of sanctions and enforcement lists, ensure legal compliance and demonstrate accountability towards donors. However, recognition, support, contracting, employment—either in the humanitarian or the development context—increasingly depend on how NGOs categorize individuals before screening and how they make decisions based on the results. The chapter at least as much contributes to earlier research by including screening in the conceptualization of (counter)surveillance in aid work, than raises questions meriting further research.

© The Author(s), under exclusive license to Springer Nature   99
Switzerland AG 2024
B. Paragi, *Screening by International Aid Organizations Operating
in the Global South*, https://doi.org/10.1007/978-3-031-54165-0_4

Keywords Screening as surveillance · Watchlist database · Surveillance tools · Transparent subjects · Risks of generosity

The scope of surveillance studies is too broad to be summarized here (Ball et al., 2012; Lyon, 2007), but its nexus with privacy studies on the one hand (Goold & Neyland, 2009; Skinner-Thompson, 2022) and with IR and security studies on the other hand, makes it necessary to include relevant dimensions into the analysis. One of its most relevant subfields, international financial surveillance, has enjoyed academic attention for more than a decade due to the controversial politics of listing in the context of counterterrorism (De Goede, 2012; De Goede & Sullivan, 2016; Minella, 2019; Sullivan, 2020); the involvement of private actors, financial institutions, lawyers and corporations in securitization and AML/CFT activities (Amicelle, 2011; Amicelle & Favarel-Garrigues, 2012; De Goede, 2018; Helgesson & Mörth, 2019); and the emergence of the reg-tech and fin-tech industry serving, among others, compliance with counterterrorism regulations (Arner et al., 2016; Hanley-Giersch, 2019) and undermining politics (Kuldova, 2022). While international NGOs are known targets of financial surveillance in exchange for access to banking services (Hayes, 2012; També, 2021), their engagement in/with surveillance-like activities, however, is much less highlighted or somehow mischaracterized.

Surveillance in the aid industry is widely seen as an inalienable, albeit criticized, dimension of recognition and care provision (Weitzberg et al., 2021). Terms such as digital humanitarianism (Duffield, 2016), financial humanitarianism (Tazzioli, 2019), surveillance humanitarianism (Latoreno, 2019), humanitarian dataveillance (Sandvik, 2020) and surveillance funded by foreign donors in Global South countries (Hosein & Nyst, 2013; Martin, 2023) equally express the controversial manner in which aid organizations engage with private actors, technologies and data. As digital innovations, especially in humanitarian fields, are not without harmful consequences (Sandvik et al., 2017), increasing attention has been paid to the blurred borders of control and care (Fast & Jacobsen, 2019; Paragi & Altamimi, 2022) and those of recognition and surveillance (Weitzberg et al., 2021). While the term 'surveillance' has also been used to describe how the digital refugee body—or the refugee's digital body—is constantly surveilled and reassembled through the digital footprints of displacement data for humanitarian and commercial-financial purposes (Lemberg-Pedersen & Haioty, 2020), aid organizations also seem to monitor and govern their subjects within their domains by conducting screening.

Therefore, to contribute to earlier research, the purpose of this chapter is to extend the understanding of surveillance in the context of aid work by exploring how screening conducted by INGOs, HOs and increasingly by NGDOs too can be interpreted within the conceptual framework of (critical) surveillance studies. Surveillance in this latter domain means "a focused, systematic and routine attention to personal details for purposes of influence, management, protection or direction" (Lyon, 2007, 14) and of governing populations' activities (Haggerty, 2009, 278). It usually involves "relations of power in which watchers are privileged", where the watched may also play a role by participation (Lyon, 2007, 15).

Insights from surveillance studies are helpful to understand screening because security listing—making lists of terrorist organizations, sanctioned individuals, etc.—is generally seen as a "relatively simple technology distinct from the more dynamic and processual security techniques grounded in machine learning and algorithmic analysis" by critical security scholars (Sullivan, 2020, 117). And although "the sounding alert of the watch list—a disciplinary form of security risk management—is rarely heard", partially because other technologies are considered more risky (Amoore, 2013, 89–90 cited by Sullivan, 2020, 117), making decisions based on access to consolidated databases is not without risks either—especially, if those screening individuals are non-governmental actors that otherwise subjects to extensive governmental and financial surveillance with all of its consequences on the shrinking civil space in the contemporary context of counterterrorism (UN SR HR/CT, 2019, 2023).

The traditional sites of surveillance—military, governmental, employment, police and crime control, consumer spaces (Lyon, 2007, 25–45)—as well as their sister- and sub-spaces, have not only received widespread scholarly attention but have also been increasingly scrutinized in the context of privacy and personal data protection. The civil space, however, is usually included in the analysis in two main cases: when INGOs and national NGOs are targets of governmental or financial surveillance, and when they advocate for human rights to prevent harmful surveillance, in many cases by implementing counter-surveillance measures as Chapter 5 will demonstrate.

To explore how aid organizations are made 'watchers'—how they provide "focused, systematic and routine attention to personal details" (Lyon, 2007, 14)—the third research question (Considering the opacity around screening, can the latter be conceptualized as a form of surveillance?) formulated in the Introduction can be answered by scrutinizing how screening is conducted and how technology (a compliance tool supplied by private vendors) work from empirical perspective.

The most important themes of surveillance, along which different sites of surveillance can be compared, include rationalization, technology, sorting, knowledgeability and urgency (Lyon, 2007, 26–27). It must be noted that the term 'technology' is used with a somewhat different connotations in this chapter than by Sullivan (2020) whose work focused on the law and politics of listing. While Sullivan (2020, 55) conceptualized sanctions and terrorist lists "as technologies of power and administrative rule" and "simple ordering techniques", the focus in our case is on a specific technology or a tool (the consolidated database) by means of which the lists themselves become easily accessible to users, INGOs (aid organizations) included. The power relations between the watchers and the watched in the context of screening will be approached by approximating reasonable expectations of the 'ignorant' watched. As findings of this chapter indicate screening strengthens and normalizes otherwise existing hierarchies between watcher and watched, but it may rather be an unintended side effect, sort of collateral damage, than a calculated purpose. The reasons and the context—alongside the matter of counter-surveillance—will be discussed in the following Chapter 5.

RATIONALIZATION AND URGENCY

Screening is rationalized by legal compliance and risk mitigation by aid organizations doing screening, noting, that legal non-compliance may also be seen as a risk. Screening as a risk-mitigating measure might also be considered alongside other, so-called remote management practices, such as tacit engagement (Akal, 2022) and profiling (Duroch & Neuman, 2021) the purpose of which is ensuring the (physical, bodily) security of international staff or other organizational interests, such as presence in the field, operability or project implementation. While the reasons for screening may vary from context to context, risks can be overlapping even if development INGOs work under different conditions than HOs and IOs, which usually justify their actions by 'emergency' situations. Hiring a politically exposed person (PEP; for a definition, see Gilligan, 2009), a sexual offender or a convicted criminal, using donor money for a project that benefits a sanctioned person, can equally carry legal, financial or reputational risk.

Screening may mitigate such risks, engagement with individuals or entities (terrorist organizations) that are either listed or can be suspected with involvement in terrorism or a terrorist organization, provided that both the needed tool/technology and expertise is available to an aid NGO. As screening is about examining something or somebody to detect a fault in order to prevent harmful effects, this practice is more controversial in the context of counterterrorism or national security (passenger screening by airlines, customer screening by banks, or screening by NGOs) than in medical contexts because societal or political faults are more contested than medical or biological equivalents (see Introduction, Chapter 1). Yet, there are common features, such as, producing transparent bodies or subjects by combining expertise with law and technology during decision-making. Law plays a crucial role in legitimizing efforts to force transparency on individuals, which can be equally problematic in democratic and authoritarian settings the extent to which it normalizes open/legible behaviour and criminalizes secrets and secretive behaviours (Adams, 2020, 69–73). Furthermore, as argued by Sullivan (2020, 73), as preempting global terrorism has increasingly come to rely on relevant security expertise, the politics of listing has been shaped by the seemingly innocent and apolitical, such as legal or technical questions of list administration and implementation. Such expertise "allows diverse, localised threats to be identified, stripped of their specificity and globally rescaled without modifying their internal properties" (Sullivan, 2020, 83). As a result of these global processes, aid organizations are not allowed to trust their own experience and local knowledge based on their embeddedness. Rather, they are increasingly required, partially due to their size and growing distance from the problems they aspire to cure (Akal, 2022), to rely on 'expert knowers' and technologies offering expert knowledge to distinguish the normal from the not normal. Recalling Bauman (1991, 213), it is "the experts who set the standards of normality. However these standards are set, they leave outside a solid chunk of reality which, by the fact of being left outside, turns into an anomaly requiring treatment". It is even more so in the era of digitalization when realities (narratives, stories, qualitative information) that cannot be easily recorded in databases are increasingly neglected.

One of the most delicate dimensions of listing concerns the preventative or preventive function of lists. One does not have to be a convicted criminal, sanctioned individual or listed terrorist, suspicion is sufficient in many cases. As a result, national security agencies frequently "retain their ability to disrupt the lives of terrorist suspects in their jurisdictions using whatever national tools are at their disposal" (Sullivan, 2020, 83). As there are hundreds of international and domestic (sanctions, terrorists, other) lists, expertise plays a significant role in determining whether listed (designated, sanctioned) persons or organizations merit attention, if not exclusion, in practice. Delisting is challenging even in the case of international sanctions lists (Minella, 2019; Sullivan, 2020) and does not even help in cases when individuals remain listed on domestic sanctions or terrorist lists.

Aid organizations, however, are not 'funded' to doubt or map the truth behind a listed person or organization, but to implement projects in a lawful and cost-effective manner that is also in line with norms (for example, humanitarian principles). When decisions on screening are considered, the context determining an aid organization's room of manoeuvring—the official donors it works with, the jurisdictions of its operations, its financial autonomy, the contracts it signed with or without conditional clauses, the nature of relationship between the aid NGO and the given community or individual—is at least as decisive than expertise concerning the biographical profile of the concerned (listed) person or entity.

As preventing the use of donor money for illicit purposes is in the best interest of any implementing actor, the inclusion of conditional clauses in funding agreements has become a norm (EU, 2020; NRC, 2018b). When NGOs receive funding from official donors, financial and legal compliance may also be enforced by funding agreements as demonstrated in Chapter 2. By signing the donor contract, an NGO becomes responsible not only for the aid project it implements but also for complying with legal conditions in the context of counterterrorism or AML. Conditional clauses rarely prescribe screening per se, but the expectation is implied in their wording according to experiences.[1]

Screening as a 'reasonable effort' means that larger aid organizations use personal data collected from a wide range of individuals, as shown

---

[1] Workshop, September 23, 2022.

in Chapter 3, to check if the names can be found on any watchlist. In the case of screening, one of the 'faults' is transferring donor money to individuals that are either criminalized (by law enforcement actors), securitized (listed on a sanctions list or designated as a terrorist) or simply considered a legal or reputational hazard (a convicted sexual offender, for example). As a result, regular screening may enable aid organizations to distinguish persons with 'normal' backgrounds from those engaged in 'suspicious' activities based on their biographical profile available in consolidated databases. Recalling Dean (1999, 189) and Aradau (2004), access to information not only enables humanitarian organizations and potentially also NGDOs to identify, assess and potentially mitigate risks based on the biographical profiles of individuals constructed by research teams of suppliers, but also facilitates the governing of the subjects being (supported, employed, contracted, etc.) in the 'empire of humanity'.

As indicated by the results of the online survey—the purpose of which was to explore experiences and dilemmas with GDPR compliance (see Chapter 1)—contractual obligations for screening (vetting, background checks of individuals) were mentioned by 60% of the respondents ($n = 21$) as a purpose for data collection (Q10: "What are the main purposes of collecting and processing personal data of local (non-European) data subjects at your organization (as data controller) in the context of project implementation?"). When asked about the specific purposes of collecting personal data for meeting donor requirements in a follow-up question (Q15c), 60% of the respondents (21 of 35 INGOs) confirmed that they collect personal data for "contractual obligations required by donors (background check, vetting or screening of individuals expected by our donors)"; six respondents indicated that this question was not applicable in their case; while eight organizations (22.8%) claimed that they did not collect personal data for such purposes. While the sample of this small survey was by no means representative to the entire population on European aid organizations, the majority of larger (humanitarian) organizations that participated in earlier surveys (NRC, 2018a, 24; VOICE, 2021) acknowledged using external supplier or vendor for screening. Smaller NGOs usually use free versions of datasets and screen only against specific US lists (Muhomed et al., 2021, 31).

Little is known about urgency and frequency, but screening is mostly done at large scale and it is a constant activity pursued on a regular basis. Regarding frequency, screening may be conducted in various ways (for various purposes) occasionally or regularly. Screening is usually done—a search is run—not only on individual basis before a contract is signed, but at regular intervals. Muhomed et al. (2021, 30) found that there are NGOs screening all employees across their operations, all of their suppliers, individual board members of partner organizations and their partners' sub-contractors and suppliers too. Or, as a legal advisor at a Norwegian NGO elaborated[2]:

> We usually ask for personal data before a contract is signed or when an event is organized. As part of the preparation, we check if an individual is listed by using [OMITTED]. While we do such checks continuously, by verifying the identity and background of hundreds of people annually.

What 'continuously' mean may vary from organization to organization, but two responses of the second online (follow-up) questionnaire (mentioned in the Introduction) indicated that screening is done at least twice a year. Citing the words of the representative of a medium size INGO with presence in 38 countries and working in several sectors[3]:

> We screen often, but how often depends on risk—Syria screens more often than a country program in South-East Asia—at least every 6 months or earlier if there is a contract renewal. ... In case of a false positive you first have to establish that it indeed is a false positive, with good argumentation. When that is done, the argumentation is checked by compliance [officer] who approves the false positive.

Acknowledging that considerable opacity prevails around screening in the NGO-sector too (VOICE, 2021, 13), only estimations are available regarding the scope of the matter. For example, the Norwegian Refugee Council conducted 7053 searches for screening partner staff, suppliers and employees only in the Middle East in 2018 (Charny, 2019). It may be reasonably inferred that humanitarian organizations with special legal

---

[2] Interview with an advisor working at a Norwegian NGO [8], Zoom, 4 May and 14 June 2021.

[3] The form was filled out anonymously on June 26, 2023; the other respondent (filling out the form on July 9, 2023) introduced this organization in the following manner: "[o]ur organization is involved in longer-term development interventions as well as humanitarian aid, including emergency response. Development work concentrates mainly in Africa, central Asia and south-east Asia".

status or international aid organizations with thousands of employees, transactions and beneficiaries run tens of thousands of searches each year, an amount which also follows from the business models of the commercial actors supplying the product. Companies are charged per number of units screened, whereby the cost increases by the number of 'false positives' which require extra checks at least in case of World-Check (Muhomed et al., 2021, 31). If the probability of match is higher than 80%, NGOs need to invest more to figure out if the alert is real or not (Muhomed et al., 2021, 31). In case of alerts expertise is crucial because false positive cases can be settled 'with good argumentation' in administrative terms.

It has also been acknowledged that many organizations purposely over-apply donor compliance requirements and screen all individuals (potential employees, contractors, suppliers and partners, beneficiaries)[4] rather than just those who pass a certain spending threshold in an effort to ensure they do not omit an entity from the process inadvertently (NRC, 2018a, 24). Therefore, being a 'large scale' data processing operation, screening obviously poses high risk for data subjects' rights by GDPR-standards.[5]

Technology, Expertise and Sorting

Screening, if done manually, requires a lot of work. As legal-regulatory requirements of international and domestic sanctions law have become increasingly complex, commercial actors have started to consolidate the different lists into searchable products by offering digitalized solutions to their customers. As also mentioned briefly in Chapter 2, these products and services were originally developed for or by financial service providers (FSPs) being under legal obligation to implement customer due diligence procedures, such as know-your-customer (De Goede & Sullivan, 2016; Kuldova, 2022, 129–140; Shabibi & Bryant, 2016). As bank clients, NGOs are also subject to screening (També, 2021; *see also* Chapter 5).

The technology. Screening is about running a search online, among others, that is, checking whether lists of names (personal data) match various watchlists in the consolidated database. The most popular tech

---

[4] Workshop, September 23, 2022.

[5] Article 35 (data protection impact assessments) and Article 37 (the requirement for appointing a data protection officer) is not discussed in this book (not even in Chapter 3).

solutions available on the market are FinScan, LexisNexis (WorldCompliance™ Data, Bridger Insight, other tools), CSI's WatchDOG Elite, Visual Compliance System (VOICE, 2021, 13), and World-Check which was acquired by Refinitiv/LSEG from Thomson Reuters (De Goede & Sullivan, 2016). Recalling, for example, the website of LexisNexis (2021), these tools enable users, aid organizations included, to synchronize watchlist screening and navigate continuously shifting sanctions, financial crime compliance, and anti-bribery requirements. While the World-Check database included 1.2 million records in 2009 (De Goede & Sullivan, 2016, 77), LexisNexis offered access to almost 5 million global 'risk profiles' covering individuals, organizations, businesses and vessels from 240 countries and territories in 2022 according to its website.[6] These profiles are sold to customers (users) for profit.

Acknowledging that legal entities can also be screened depending on the settings, but focusing only on individuals here, basic personal data (names, place and birth of date) is usually obtained from the concerned persons by users. Such personal data is needed for establishing a match with the profiles available in the databases. The concerned individuals may or may not be aware that their data is being used for screening. Screening is usually automated, that is, not names one by one, but lists of names are uploaded in batches in the system. Once the search is run by a compliance officer, the system controls the data against the integrated database, which is a result of a "thorough sequence of research, vetting and data compilation" (LexisNexis, 2021). The customized solutions/subscriptions also enabled some vendors to develop and deploy simple, rule-based artificial intelligence to increase efficiency in search.[7]

---

[6] The company offers various solutions for its clients: https://risk.lexisnexis.com/global/en/products/worldcompliance-data.

[7] Interview with the representative of LexisNexis, Zoom, May 20, 2021. What AI means in case of screening has not been explored. Images (photos of individuals) may potentially be available to users, such as NGOs, in copies of ID-documents, for example; international organizations (such as UNHCR, ICRC) also collect and dispose over biometric data. In principle, such data could be matched with the screening database as long as biometric data (photos) may also be available in the system, but such feature is likely not available. Various lists would likely perform differently in case of biometrics matching. While lists of convicted criminals (Interpol lists, etc.) or politically exposed persons usually contain profiles with photos, designated terrorists or sanctioned individuals cannot be identified this way, simply for their photos or images are not necessarily available to authorities. To my best knowledge, only textual data can be searched in the system by using the keyboard to record (type) names or other data.

Visibility, a further crucial component of surveillance, is ensured by watch lists in case of lists and screening tools. The lists can be grouped roughly into two sets based on the origin of the data. The first set contains lists that are available publicly on official governmental websites and integrated by LexisNexis® WorldCompliance™ Data or other tools according to the following categories in the database (LexisNexis, 2021)[8]:

- SANCTIONS category: information on individuals and organizations from targeted sanctions lists worldwide. Both national and international sanctions lists are included.
- ASSOCIATED ENTITY category: information about family members and associates of sanctioned entities, when the associated entity is mentioned in targeted sanctions lists.
- LAW ENFORCEMENT category: information on criminal offences based on materials published by official government agencies (courts, tax authorities, law enforcement agencies) and international organizations, among others. Individuals on such lists are not designated as sanctioned (terrorists), but they can be convicted criminals.
- PEP category: information about individuals who occupy a senior prominent public function; adhering to FATF global standards, the database may also contain information on family members and partners of PEPs.
- SOE (sovereign owned entities) category: information about entities that are majority or minority owned by governments around the world.

The subcategories in the second set (ADVERSE MEDIA) is based on open source information. Such categories are not unique to LexisNexis even if the labels (names of list categories) may slightly vary from vendor

---

[8] Vendors share long documents with their customers that detail the content of each category. Another source contains the titles and sources (websites) of sanctions and enforcement lists—by country and international organization—that are integrated in tools, such as LexisNexis® WorldCompliance™ Data. The latter is updated every day following the changes in the list. See also the official website for a description of each category: https://risk.lexisnexis.com/global/en/products/worldcompliance-data. Interview with a former representative of LexisNexis, Zoom, 20 May 2021 and email exchange with CompliancePartner (March 20–27, 20YY).

to vendor. To illustrate what screening means and how it works, CP-WatchList-Tech is used in the following paragraphs. Both the company and product names are anonymized as indicated in Chapter 1 too and bibliographical data of written sources (version year and page numbers) are also encrypted.

Focusing first on the two most important categories, SANCTIONS contains all the sanctions (CompliancePartner, 20yy-b, 20–51), while ENFORCEMENT synthetizes all the enforcement sources (CompliancePartner, 20yy-b, 52–376) that the tool provided by CompliancePartner generates from official governmental sources (websites). For example, while there are 24 lists in the SANCTIONS lists category managed by various US authorities (CompliancePartner, 20yy-b, 47–51), the items listed in ENFORCEMENT category take almost 70 pages in case of the US (CompliancePartner, 20yy-b, 297–368). In case of Israel there are lists from three governmental agencies (Israeli Governmental Advertising Agency, the terrorism list edited by the Ministry of Defence and a list provided by the Ministry of Finance on enemy organizations) in the SANCTIONS part of the database (CompliancePartner, 20yy-b) and seven other lists edited by other authorities (Bank of Israel and its Sanctions Committee; the Israel Antitrust Authority; Israeli Intelligence and Terrorism Information Center; Israel Military Advocate General; Israel Ministry of Environmental Protection; Israel Police) in the ENFORCEMENT lists category (CompliancePartner, 20yy-b). Taking Norway as a third example it did not have separate sanctions list to be included in the SANCTIONS category in 20yy, while the sources of the ENFORCEMENT category included six lists edited by authorities (Authority for Investigation and Prosecution of Economic and Environmental Crime; Financial Supervisory Authority; Norges Bank Observation and Exclusion of Companies; Norwegian Gaming Authority—Pyramid Schemes; Norwegian Gaming Authority—Unlicensed Gambling Operators; Norwegian Gaming Authority—Decisions). For example, if someone (a Norwegian citizen or organization) is officially placed on a law enforcement list by the Norwegian Gaming Authority, his or her name will be available to any user (for example, a German aid NGO) subscribing to the screening tool (CP-WatchList-Tech or similar tools).

It also applies to the third main category (second set of sources) which is composed of publicly available news, feeds or social media appearances that are systematically gathered by the researcher teams of vendors. Hoewever, The ADVERSE MEDIA category, seen as perhaps the most problematic, contains personal information about identifiable individuals that can be linked to illicit activities based on open source information, news that is published by news media sources or in social media in dozens of languages (CompliancePartner, 20yy-a, 14). Actually, the content of this category is so rich that it takes about 20 pages and 48 different sub-categories to read all those sorts of crimes and harms listed in an alphabetical order that may be included into the profiles starting from 'aircraft hijacking' and 'antitrust violations' through 'piracy', 'pornography', 'securities fraud' and 'smuggling to war crimes', 'terrorism', 'wire fraud' and 'weapons of mass destruction' (CompliancePartner, 20yy-a, 15–30). In other words, one does not have to be a real terrorist designated following an international (UN) sanctions list to appear in the database. One may appear—with a personal profile—in the database of the screening tool based purely on the information available on websites or social media posts.

The 'terrorism' sub-category within ADVERSE MEDIA, described on two pages, deserves particular attention because it complements the official SANCTIONS and ENFORCEMENT lists. Recognizing "the complexity of identifying terrorist activities and the individuals or groups that perpetrate these acts", CompliancePartner uses the following core criteria to identify terrorist acts beyond official terrorist lists: the use of physical or coercive violence; the use of these acts is to instal fear; the use of these means to effect government or international organization policies or actions; that further certain political or social causes; the acts are perpetrated by individuals or organized groups (CompliancePartner, 20yy-a, 33). Further criteria are provided to identify groups that are involved in terrorist acts and individuals that are involved (CompliancePartner, 20yy-a, 34). Terrorism acts are understood broadly including lone wolf attacks and acts that are legally classified as domestic extremism (in the USA) but excluding 'incidents that do not include a political or social motivation and that do not intend to affect the policies or actions of government or international organizations' and 'incidents that are motivated by domestic violence or personal grudges or vendettas' (CompliancePartner, 20yy-a, 34–35). In other words, organizations and individuals not associated with financial crimes or terrorist organizations are also listed which is problematic in cases of other, similar tools too. Recalling De Goede and Sullivan (2016, 78) on World-Check:

> Inclusion in the World-Check database is based on open-source information research performed by multi-lingual teams around the world. In this process, web-based sources, public indictment records, newspaper articles and other publicly available information of very diverse quality – including blogs, news sites and online photographs – are reviewed for possible connections to financial crime, narcotics trafficking, money laundering, gambling and internet fraud [and] those types of things.

Observations characterizing World-Check and CP-WatchList-Tech also apply to other products (tools, databases) offered by other vendors. How information is gathered within the ADVERSE MEDIA category by the researcher teams is unclear both to subscribing users (NGOs) and to individuals (screened by NGOs), who may or may not be aware of being on such lists (Hayes, 2017, 28). As these US-based service providers are supervised neither by financial nor by data protection authorities in the EU,[9] the quality of information available—sold—to their customers cannot be controlled either. It explains not only the importance of expertise (from practitioner perspectives), but perhaps also why the entire matter is undercommunicated.

All in all, consolidated databases join the family of those technologies that offer profiles with a criteria of profiling being opaque to the persons whose data is used for such purposes (Lyon, 2007, 179–197). It obviously may entail negative impacts—discrimination, prejudice, stereotypes, bias, exclusion—that may or may not be counterbalanced by human involvement and expertise.

Expertise and sorting. Commercially available tools are used to make screening and, as an expected result of that, sorting—of individuals from those that do not deserve contacts with or benefits from aid organizations because they are or seem to mean a risk—more efficient. Regarding expertise within aid organizations, which is needed for making informed decisions, customer due diligence (CDD) assessments are usually composed of two stages (initial assessment and extended assessment), with the latter stage conducted by compliance officers working at the legal and/or HR department at headquarters (Muhomed et al., 2021, 28–31). Even the largest aid organizations do not have more than one or two officers in charge of regulatory compliance and

---

[9] Interview with a representative of LexisNexis, Zoom, 20 May 2021.

screening.[10] Therefore, the procedural-technical part is usually a confidential matter, which is not so much known to the general staff, not even in head offices.[11] Screening tools are not only used to make the process of screening simpler and more efficient (by minimizing working hours), but also to mitigate potential discrimination. It implies that most aid organizations do mass screening by treating everyone with 'categorical suspicion'—following Marx (2005) who distinguished five types of suspicion (categorical, personalized, behavioural, protectional and locational)—instead of screening only certain individuals in a targeted manner. Acknowledging that practices likely vary across organizations, there seems to be a trade-off between quantity and quality. This trade-off implies a sort of trap: either everyone is regularly screened (to avoid discrimination and to increase efficiency) or only certain individuals are selected for screening (which may compromise the efficiency of sorting or lead to discrimination as a result of mistaken human judgement).

Having logged into the online system, the user (authorized staff of a given aid organization) may also record identifiers (personal data: name, date of birth, etc.) in a field ('single search'), or upload lists of such data ('multiple search'). Settings can be made regarding the type of entity (individual, organization) and categories (SANCTIONS, ENFORCEMENT, ADVERSE MEDIA, PEP, etc.), types, sources and countries (CompliancePartner, 20yy-c).

The result of the submitted search is a value indicating probability that can be grouped roughly into three main sets: negative (in most cases), positive (an alert with X probability) or false positive (it is also an alert). To illustrate the procedure in case of false positive matches by the experiences of an advisor working with CSI's WATCHDOG Elite[12]:

> If [it is] a false positive, [the country programme officers] have to write comments in the software (CSI WatchDog) where they argue for the reasoning of the false positive. It could be the wrong name, date of birth or even gender. It could also be an identical name, but that listed person [whose profile is presented by the tool] has a personal history that

---

[10] The interviews and the workshop equally confirm this observation. Data protection officers are in charge of all personal data-related (compliance) matters, not only screening.

[11] Interview with an project advisor at a Norwegian NGO, Oslo, October 22, 2021.

[12] Second questionnaire filled out by a medium-size INGO with presence in 38 countries; June 26, 2023.

doesn't fit with our screened person's. When the comments are written, Compliance [officer] approved[s] the false positive in the software.

As illustrated by the formulation above, an organization needs to consider if the result is real or a false positive hit and make sorting-related decisions (on exclusion, not engaging in a contract, etc.) accordingly in case of alerts. The search result, however, always depends on the settings. It is usually a matter of organizational consideration which of the above-listed categories (which types of data) and countries are included in the FULL file or associated files. As indicated by the discussion with practitioners, individuals may be screened against certain lists—law enforcement lists, for example—by some aid organizations, but not by others. In principle, the user can also exclude a country if it distrusts its sanctions lists. For example, recalling the story of the Palestinian NGOs introduced in Chapter 2, the names of the listed organizations or individuals associated with them will likely come up as an alert (positive hit) if the aid organization searches against their names either in the SANCTIONS list,[13] or in the ADVERSE MEDIA category (CompliancePartner, 20yy-a, 34–35).[14] If a humanitarian organization or development NGO does not trust the Israeli lists, or it does not consider them relevant for whatever reason, any of them can be excluded; certain lists (Russian, Chinese) are indeed excluded in many cases for various considerations.[15] Not only the alert, but obviously sorting itself—the result of which may be exclusion—depends on the settings and the extent to which the aid organization can select which categories, types or countries to search against.

The absence of a positive (or false positive) match indicates that the given person, identified by their personal data, is not listed as a terrorist or a PEP. Even in this case, the aid organizations may be interested in documenting the absence of persons from the lists by keeping some of their personal data for reporting or compliance purposes. The internal policies and procedures of the NGO and its organizational profile (humanitarian vs. development), as well as the expertise and experience accumulated by their compliance officers or legal advisors will always determine what it

---

[13] In the case of Israel the relevant governmental websites are https://www.mod.gov.il/Defence-and-Security/Fighting_terrorism/Pages/default.aspx and https://nbCFT.mod.gov.il/he/Announcements/Pages/nbCFTDownloads.aspx.

[14] Workshop, September 23, 2022.

[15] Workshop, September 23, 2022.

does about an alert and how it further processes the results (Muhomed et al., 2021, 26–31).

While a narrow set of personal data (name, place and date of birth) is needed for conducting screening, the outcome of screening, presented in the form of a file in case of alerts and (false) positive matches, contains a far more detailed set of information that can be related to the person as confirmed by various sources[16] (CompliancePartner, 20yy-c). Recalling-repeating Chapter 3, in case of a (false) positive hit, the outcome is in the form of an integrated biographical profile containing the following information: (i) a detailed set of personal data, photo included; (ii) a narrative description containing references to the sources of each piece of information; (iii) a section on the reported addresses; (iv) a network of relationships indicating the type of relations: family members, associated others, related companies and organizations and (v) a reference list of sources (websites, documents) behind the information provided in the profile (CompliancePartner, 20yy-c).

Aid organizations, depending on their legal status, profile, contractual and legal obligations or legitimate interests, may equally screen beneficiaries and local suppliers, employees and volunteers, but true alerts—positive matches—are said to be rare (VOICE, 2021, 12–14). Acknowledging that little is known about the real impacts of decisions based on screening, the theoretical risk of sorting is discrimination or exclusion without explanation—not only of humanitarian beneficiaries (Gillard, 2021b; O'Leary, 2022, 466), but also of—employers and job seekers, transactions partners on grounds that may be unclear or invisible to the concerned individuals. Considering that decisions are increasing reliant upon digital(ized) information about real-life individual, that is, on the data-double or the virtual self (Lyon, 2007, 55), further research is needed to see how aid organizations—both NGOs and international organizations with special legal status—conduct screening and how compliance officers handle 'suspicious' cases, and as a result of that, how they govern their relations with the concerned (screened) individuals. Inasmuch as the results of screening (positive hits, alerts) are not communicated to the concerned individuals—the same way as it is done in the context of medical screening when individual patients are referred to specialists that interpret the results and potentially provide treatment—the surveillance logic seems to be valid.

---

[16] Also confirmed by the interview with representative of LexisNexis, Zoom, May 20, 2021.

Knowledgeability and Reasonable Expectations

The next component needed for conceptualizing screening as surveillance is *knowledgeability* and (un)willing "participation on the part of those who[se] are under scrutiny" (Lyon, 2007, 27). Expectations and knowledge on screening—on its substance, purposes, legal basis, the involvement of third-party actors and the consequences of decisions based on positive matches—not only determine how surveillance works but also affects human rights. Regarding the documentation requirements associated with funding agreements signed with donor countries, record-keeping carries relevance because merely storing data "relating to an individual's private life" constitutes a data processing operation. As such it is considered an interference with the right to respect for private life even without the subsequent use of stored data.[17]

Expectations are shaped by what individuals (are allowed to) know about the processing operations concerning their personal data. Recalling Chapter 3 and relevant provisions of the GDPR (Article 5(1), Article 12, 13–14 and Recital 39), it should be transparent to natural persons that personal data concerning them are being collected, used, consulted or otherwise processed and to what extent such personal data are or will be processed or, if applicable, further processed. The obligation of fairness, transparency and lawfulness (Article 5(1)) is to be read in line with the interpretations of the European Court of Human Rights regarding the extent to which individuals' expectations or assumptions concerning the use and processing of their personal data are to be considered when decisions are made about the use of their data (see Paragi, 2023).

If a humanitarian or other aid organization consider itself not well-positioned enough to negotiate the terms of the contract with a donor (see Chapter 2), the only solution is to refrain from submitting a proposal for a call or signing a funding agreement with an official donor expecting screening (NRC, 2018b). Such organizational decisions, however, are rarely discussed with concerned individuals:

---

[17] *Amman v Switzerland,* appl. no. 27798/95 (ECtHR, 16 February 2000), para 69; *S and Marper v. The United Kingdom,* appl. no. 30562/04 and 30566/04 (ECtHR, 4 December 2008) para 67; *Kopp v Switzerland,* app no. 23224/94 (ECtHR, 15 March 1998), paras 51–53. The listed cases concerned data storage by public authorities.

We [as a humanitarian organization] try not to screen our beneficiaries, but we do not really consult this matter with them before making decisions ... we say to our donors that screening [of beneficiaries in case of humanitarian projects] is an absolute red line, but we do not ask the local people about it. Maybe, they would not mind being screened if it was the price to be paid for the cash assistance or any other project that we, as an organization, reject for the sake of principled humanitarian action.[18]

As noted elsewhere, the willingness to intervene in someone else's life without her/his consent[19] is not only the hallmark of paternalism—at least from liberal perspectives—but has been historically typical in name of care in humanitarian contexts (Barnett, 2002, 35). However, while some Global South individuals may not mind being screened as a precondition for, or sharing personal data in exchange for, aid, others reject the idea of conditional funding—signing any contract with Northern donors, INGOs included, with conditions—for cultural or political reasons. Recent Palestinian NGO objections formulated against EU conditions (restrictive measures, conditional clauses in grant agreements, screening and vetting) illustrate that the price of funding (being treated as a risk by default) can be considered too high by locals interpreting their own lives in a context alternative to (counter)terrorism. EU conditions are deemed unfair and unacceptable because they are perceived as undermining the Palestinian right to self-determination and defending Israeli security interests (BADIL, 2021).

Yet, surveillance—monitoring workers in a recruitment and employment context (Nouwt et al., 2005), customers or consumers in a commercial context (Zuboff, 2019), clients by financial institutions (Amicelle, 2011; Amicelle & Favarel-Garrigues, 2012)—has been normalized worldwide (Ball et al., 2012). Being surveilled by the police or secret service may also be considered 'normal' even when someone has not committed

---

[18] Interview with an advisor working at a regional office of a Norwegian NGO [8b], 3 November 2021.

[19] It must be acknowledged that 'informed consent' is not only a legal term, but also a social-cultural construct. Obtaining a written—informed—consent is equally difficult for aid organizations and social scientists in certain communities/contexts for this measure, reminding to a written agreement, is considered culturally 'alien' or inappropriate (indicating distrust) regardless of its purpose: to protect the participants' rights. Gusterson, H. (2009). Ethnographic Research. In A. Klotz & D. Prakash (Eds.), *Qualitative Methods in International Relations*. Palgrave.

a crime in such non-democratic settings where aid projects are usually implemented. And even if data extraction, techno-colonialism (Madianou, 2019) and surveillance funded by aid or implemented in cooperation with aid organizations are known in academic and practitioner circles (Hosein & Nyst, 2013; Martin, 2023), screening by aid INGOs is neither intuitive nor well known.

Knowledge and expectations depend on the context. Aid organizations, especially humanitarian organizations (are allowed to) operate in the Global South on the premise that they provide help to individuals or communities (Chatterjee, 2004). How individuals relate to an aid organization is shaped by the local cultural and political setting; the aid organization's mandate, core activities and its image as communicated on websites or in their interactions with locals, conveying solidarity and altruism; the relationship between resource-rich international aid organizations and local individuals (characterized by strong power imbalances); and other factors. Yet, getting/giving help in the form of charity aid or hospitality is rarely considered pure altruism by beneficiaries and recipients (Chatty, 2017; Mauss, 2002; Pyyhtinen, 2014). On the contrary, reciprocity (the obligation to return what was given) is perceived and conceptualized as a constitutive part of contemporary aid relations in both development and humanitarian contexts too (Fassin, 2007; Furia, 2015; Hattori, 2001; Paragi, 2017). Personal data are by no means the exception, not even in humanitarian contexts. As argued by Sandvik (2019), certain digital humanitarian services and goods represent a new form of 'gifting' from beneficiaries to humanitarian actors and their partner whereby the real (return) gift is the beneficiary data. Therefore, what individuals as data subjects (are allowed to) know about the purposes of and ways in which their personal data are used shape their expectations.

As aid images are conceptually far from surveillance imaginaries, it is unlikely that individuals would reasonably assume that aid organizations 'assess' individuals not only by considering their needs or (in employment or supplier contracts) merits, vulnerability and resilience capacities, but also by checking their personal data against a database to sort the risky from the reliable. The use of third-party service providers for screening or sharing personal data of beneficiaries with FSPs that may screen them before they provide CVA (IFRC, 2021, 23–25) should also be considered as an activity *beyond* the reasonable expectation of the data subjects.

To sum up, expectations, not least reasonable expectations, about mass screening conducted by aid organizations in any context likely do not exist. Even if personal data is requested by aid organizations, it is not intuitive that it is systematically and routinely checked against various watchlists by actors who are otherwise interested in providing a living in the form of employment, supplier contract, cash assistance, in-kind aid or access to an event. While screening is far from 'normal' from the perspective of the watched, and even if humanitarian organizations are critical of donors' expectation of their participation in AML/CFT (Eckert, 2022; O'Leary, 2022), their compliance teams gather information by screening not only about designated persons (terrorists, sanctioned individuals) but also about individuals that may mean other kinds of potential risk to them. While there are usually no (donor) contractual obligations to do it, implementing organizations are interested in preventing the recruitment of sexual offenders or people that committed fraud or were involved in human trafficking, which are criminal offences, not terrorist crime. Screening in such cases is for due diligence as "it is the NGO's legitimate interest to know if a (would-be) supplier committed a criminal offence or did not paid tax".[20]

Yet, as it was emphasized in Chapter 3, "operations done with personal data [of Global South individuals too, by EU/EEA-registered INGOs] … [should be] within the reasonable expectations of the data subject" (cited by de Terwangne, 2018, 313), precisely because of the power imbalances between the controller (watcher) and the data subject (watched). Imbalances can be mitigated only if adequate information is provided in an adequate manner. To put the related themes of knowledgeability and reasonable expectations into perspective (somewhat ironically)—following Aradau (2004)—individuals ('at risk') can only conceptualize themselves 'as risk' threatening the aid organization provided that they are notified about being screened. It is not impossible that in certain cases the dual act of listing and screening makes the individual 'as risk' and not the way around.

Screening as Surveillance Serving Security

Surveillance in the context of aid work has mostly been interpreted as being in a dialectical relationship with recognition, where the latter (providing increasingly digitalized care to people) is inherently linked with

---

[20] Workshop, September 23, 2022.

the former (exercising control over data describing identities, traits, needs, movements of people and humanitarian goods) (Fast & Jacobsen, 2019; Jacobsen, 2015; Paragi & Altamimi, 2022; Weitzberg et al., 2021).

Screening as surveillance. As the analysis presented above indicate, screening is not simply a commercial tool of legal-regulatory compliance (Kuldova, 2022), but it can also be interpreted as surveillance following Lyon (2007, 26–27), inasmuch as surveillance involves the process of screening, namely, identifying individuals that meet the criteria of various lists. Surveillance by aid organizations is directed at determining if changing (or new) risk factors—individuals or local partner organizations—are emerging which may impact their operation or work environment, reputation or credibility and legal-regulatory compliance. During this process aid organizations resort on screening, a unique combination of technology and expertise, to identify individuals and organizations that were deemed or designated 'dangerous' by official security, governmental or international agencies making the original lists and by service providers consolidating the hundreds of lists in integrated databases. However, it is not simply machines (and their coding, algorithms) which makes surveillance delicate, but searchability itself (Lessing, 1999, 151 cited by Lyon, 2007, 100–101). Systematic monitoring of watchlists and their consolidation into databases by commercial actors yield searchable records that not only makes 'profiling' and categorization possible by 'remote control' (from headquarters of aid organizations in European/Northern capitals), but also raises questions with regard to manipulation, equal opportunities and human rights in general.

Screening is standardized and reasoned by legal-regulatory compliance or organizational interests and is organized by the use of tech tools. Its purpose is to categorize people according to the security risk they may pose to the aid organization, that is, to sort out—exclude—potentially risky individuals from any transaction while as little information as possible is provided on screening in line with surveillance logics. Recalling that the involvement of third parties (vendors providing access to consolidated databases) has been critically discussed in the context of financial surveillance (Amicelle & Favarel-Garrigues, 2012; De Goede & Sullivan, 2016), similarities are detectable and include both internal weaknesses (the quality of data) and the external dimension of screening (how it is regulated and prescribed).

The quality of the data. When humanitarian and other aid organizations do screening, compliance officers make decisions based on information available in the consolidated databases of screening tools and their experiences accumulated (expertise). Even if they can exclude certain lists through settings, individual donors, would-be suppliers, participants of events and beneficiaries—just like sanctioned individuals, listed terrorists and leaders of armed groups—are represented by, if not reduced to, their personal data (digital bodies, data doubles). Narratives provided by individuals might be listened to in some cases, but they cannot be considered at large scale. Considering that decisions depend on the 'quality' of the personal data, the content of consolidated databases is decisive. While official sanctions lists (available on governmental websites) are identical to sanctions lists provided in the consolidated databases (errors included), the latter also contain alternative categories of lists (PEP; ADVERSE MEDIA), the content of which is the result of institutionalized or professionalized social surveillance by research teams of vendors.

Social surveillance originally referred to "an ongoing inquiry that constitutes information gathering by people about their peers, made salient by the social digitization normalized by social media ... encompass[ing] using social media sites to broadcast information, survey[ing] content created by others, and regulating one's own content based on perceptions of the audience" (Marwick, 2012, 397). In the case of consolidated watchlists, this content is edited by the research teams managing the screening databases based on news articles and media appearances available online (De Goede & Sullivan, 2016, 77). Making decisions based on this content has created complications for compliance officers at banks (Amicelle & Favarel-Garrigues, 2012, 112; Malakoutikhah, 2020). Legal advisors and compliance officers at INGOs face similar dilemmas.

The fact that (knowing the) data (the digital double) is increasingly considered more important than (knowing the) real person (the story and narrative behind a digitalized person/body) characterizes not only the contemporary compliance industry (Arner et al., 2016; Kuldova, 2022), but also seems relevant in the case of aid organizations. If so, errors are bound to occur because personal data are by no means identical to the person itself and such lists do not necessarily offer comprehensive knowledge on the context and background of listing (in the case of 5 million profiles, the probability of error is high). Yet an individual's trajectory and profile, if interpreted against a given social-political context, might lead to understandings and decisions alternative to what is supported by (false) alerts as the case of the six Palestinian NGOs likely demonstrate.

The costs and benefits of ambiguous regulation. The civil society sector demonstrates ambivalent attitudes towards regulation, even if "accountability is the price to be paid (if price it is) for the freedom to exercise power and authority in a democratic society" (Edwards, 2006, ix). Not operating in sterile democratic settings, aid organizations suffer the consequences of too extensive financial surveillance and political oversight. Therefore, they are obviously interested minimizing the impacts of regulation for two main reasons. On the one hand, regulation constrains flexible responses needed in emergency situations and may also hinder effective humanitarian responses in dangerous and unpredictable environments. On the other hand, resistance to regulation contributes to the perpetuation of the myth that humanitarianism "is altruism when it is actually self-monitored against non-enforceable standards for which nobody is held accountable" (Sattler, 2023).

Fitting this logic, screening procedures by aid organizations are self-regulated at least as much as KYC procedures of financial institutions were ten years ago (Amicelle, 2011). As a result, expert knowledge also becomes self-reproduced (as noted by Bauman, 1991, 121–220). Self-regulation, however, also represents a particular kind of interventionism (by states, IOs) in which key concepts are autonomy and responsibility as experiences from the financial sector demonstrate (Amicelle, 2011, 166). Indirect—hidden or covert—interventionism "does not impose rigid measures but promotes techniques of self-regulation that provide autonomy while simultaneously delegating responsibility and 'risks' in relation to the translation and implementation of abstract rules" in the financial sector (Amicelle, 2011, 166).

Legal-regulatory compliance has also become simultaneously self-regulated and self-enforced in aid domains too. Firstly, aid organizations voluntarily subscribe to commercially available solutions and tools to demonstrate 'reasonable efforts' or the implementation of such measures. Secondly, just as compliance officers working in banks distinguish "between at-risk sectors of activity [and] the geographical zones which they believe are particularly exposed to money-laundering practices" (Amicelle & Favarel-Garrigues, 2012, 113), aid organizations' legal advisors include or exclude individuals on the one hand and watchlists on the other hand in line with their own expertise, values and organizational norms. This generates a feeling, the burden of responsibility, that explains perceptions,[21] such as that they are expected to do the 'dirty work' while donors "are 'put at ease' by [INGOs'] use of screening procedures (and software)" (VOICE, 2021, 13). These non-profit perceptions resonate to some extent with the perceptions of lawyers who also experience AML/CFT regulation as invasive and hegemonic with regard to certain norms guiding their relations with their clients, such as confidentiality and professional secrecy. However, while such actors may resist being proactive in relation to security threats in spite of delegated powers and obligations (Helgesson & Mörth, 2019), further research would be needed to explore the manoeuvring room of NGO advisors vis-à-vis their donors or their boards.

The NRC's counterterrorism toolkit available for other aid organizations reveals certain bargaining power (NRC, 2018b), but this power is a matter of human, legal, financial resources that smaller INGOs or local NGOs cannot necessarily afford while navigating between donors and tenders. Subpages with the title *Definitions and scope of terminology* and *Processes for understanding and addressing counterterrorism clauses* offer advice how to recognize references to screening/vetting in funding agreements and strategies to re-negotiate terms. However, as authors of the toolkit (NRC, 2018b) note:

> regardless of the text of the partnership agreement, the organisation and those signing it will be subject to the laws of the donor state and should therefore ensure they are aware of the obligations these impose.

All in all, while screening is deemed to conflict with humanitarian principles, ineffective considering the low rate of true positive matches, and entailing too high subscription fees and reputational risks (Newhouse, 2021; VOICE, 2021, 12–14), perceived inconveniences are likely to be outweighed by the benefits. Given the extent to which the number of aid organizations cooperating with service providers is increasing (Gillard, 2021b), the sector is contributing to the normalization of risk-based thinking and regulation. It does so either by accepting regulatory arguments that security threats (e.g. terrorism) can be prevented by reasonable measures, or by responding to organizational challenges (abuse of the aid

[21] Workshop, September 23, 2022.

sector by sexual offenders, local security threats) experienced during aid implementation in the Global South (see next Chapter).

Conclusions

While dilemmas stemming from screening as a normalized securitized activity are acknowledged by practitioners (NRC, 2018a; VOICE, 2021), the problem is usually framed as a compliance issue in the context of counterterrorism/PVE regulations or a matter jeopardizing principled humanitarian action in the context of international humanitarian law (Eckert, 2022; O'Leary, 2022). Acknowledging that little is known about how international aid organizations—either NGOs or international humanitarian organizations—make decisions internally (whom to screen, against which watchlists exactly, by which settings, when and how often and last but not least how they make decisions in case of alerts, that is, suspicious cases), the securitization argument deserves further research to understand how hierarchies and power imbalances—between aid organizations and individuals; between the Global North and Global South—are strengthened by screening, that is, to see the probability of exclusion. Preventing the exclusion of beneficiaries (Gillard, 2021a, 2021b), however, is only part of the problem associated with screening as the next chapter will demonstrate.

References

Adams, R. (2020). *Transparency. New Trajectories in Law*. Routledge.

Akal, A. B. (2022). *Tacit Engagement as a Form of Remote Management: Risk Aversity in the Face of Sanctions Regimes* (NCHS Paper). Retrieved November 8, 2022, from https://www.humanitarianstudies.no/resource/tacit-engagement-as-a-form-of-remote-management-risk-aversity-in-the-face-of-sanctions-regimes/

Amicelle, A. (2011). Towards a 'New' Political Anatomy of Financial Surveillance. *Security Dialogue, 42*(2), 161–178. https://doi.org/10.1177/0967010611401472

Amicelle, A., & Favarel-Garrigues, G. (2012). Financial Surveillance: Who Cares. *Journal of Cultural Economy, 5*(1), 105–124. https://doi.org/10.1080/17530350.2012.640560

Amoore, L. (2013). *The Politics of Possibility: Risk and Security Beyond Probability*. Duke University Press.

Aradau, C. (2004). The Perverse Politics of Four-Letter Words: Risk and Pity in the Securitisation of Human Trafficking. *Millennium, 33*(2), 251–278. https://doi.org/10.1177/03058298040330020101

Arner, D. W., Barberis, J. N., & Buckley, R. P. (2016). The Emergence of Regtech 2.0: From Know Your Customer to Know Your Data. *Journal of Financial Transformation, 44*(79), 17–63. https://doi.org/10.2139/ssrn.3044280

BADIL. (2021). *European Union Conditional Funding: Its Illegality and Political Implications* (BADIL Position Paper). Retrieved November 18, 2022, from https://www.badil.org/cached_uploads/view/2021/04/20/eur opeanunionconditionalfunding-positionpaper-april2020-1618905422.pdf

Ball, K., Haggerty, D., & Lyon, D. (Eds.). (2012). *Routledge Handbook of Surveillance Studies*. Routledge.

Barnett, M. (2002). *Empire of Humanity*. Cornell University Press.

Bauman, Z. (1991). *Modernity and Ambivalence*. Polity Press.

Charny, J. R. (2019). *Counter-Terrorism and Humanitarian Action: The Perils of Zero Tolerance. Commentary*. War on the Rocks. Retrieved October 14, 2022, from https://warontherocks.com/2019/03/counter-terrorism-and-humanitarian-action-the-perils-of-zero-tolerance/

Chatterjee, D. K. (2004). *The Ethics of Assistance: Morality and the Distant Needy*. Cambridge University Press.

Chatty, D. (2017, March 14). The Duty to Be Generous (Karam): Alternatives to Rights-Based Asylum in the Middle East. Lecture on Africa, Asia and the Middle East. *Journal of the British Academy, 5*, 177–199. https://doi.org/10.5871/jba/005.177

CompliancePartner. (20yy-a, March 27). *Categories for* CP-WatchList-Tech. Email Attachment Sent to the Author of This Paper by CompliancePartner.

CompliancePartner. (20yy-b, March 27). *Data Sources for* CP-WatchList-Tech. Email Attachment Sent to the Author of This Paper by an Officer at CompliancePartner.

CompliancePartner. (20yy-c, March 27). *Sample Profile: [Name Omitted]*. Email Attachment Sent to the Author of This Paper by an Officer at CompliancePartner.

CompliancePartner. (20yy-d, March 27). *Data Protection Compliance, Version November 20YY*. Email Attachment Sent to the Author of This Paper by an Officer at CompliancePartner.

Dean, M. (1999). *Governmentality: Power and Rule in Modern Society*. Sage.

De Goede, M. (2012). *Speculative Security: The Politics of Pursuing Terrorist Monies*. University of Minnesota Press.

De Goede, M. (2018). The Chain of Security. *Review of International Studies, 44*(1), 24–42. https://doi.org/10.1017/S026021051700035

De Goede, M., & Sullivan, G. (2016). The Politics of Security Lists. *Environment and Planning D: Society and Space, 34*(1), 67–88. https://doi.org/10.1177/0263775815599309

de Terwangne, C. (2018). Principles (Articles 5–11) Article 5. Principles Relating to Processing of Personal Data. In C. Kuner, L. A. Bygrave, C. Docksey, & L. Drechsler (Eds.), *The EU General Data Protection Regulation (GDPR): A Commentary* (Oxford Academic, Online ed., pp. 309–320). Oxford University Press. https://doi.org/10.1093/oso/9780198826491.003.0034

Duffield, M. (2016). The Resilience of the Ruins: Towards a Critique of Digital Humanitarianism. *Resilience, 4*(3), 147–165. https://doi.org/10.1080/21693293.2016.1153772

Duroch, F., & Neuman, M. (2021). *Should We Discriminate in Order to Act? Profiling: A Necessary but Debated Practice* (HPN Paper). Retrieved April 8, 2022, from https://odihpn.org/publication/should-we-discriminate-in-order-to-act-profiling-a-necessary-but-debated-practice/

Eckert, S. (2022). Counterterrorism, Sanctions and Financial Access Challenges: Course Corrections to Safeguard Humanitarian Action. *International Review of the Red Cross, 103*(916–917), 415–458. https://international-review.icrc.org/articles/counterterrorism-sanctions-and-financial-access-challenges-916#footnote81_27rk033

Edwards, M. (2006). Foreford. In L. Jordan & P. Van Tujil (Eds.), *NGO Accountability. Politics, Principles and Innovations* (pp. vii–ix). Earthscan.

EU (European Union). (2020). *ANNEX II. General Conditions Applicable to EU-Financed Grant Contracts for External Actions* (version: August 2020, 3h2_gencond_en). c from the Practical Guide on Contract Procedures for European Union External Action (PRAG): https://ec.europa.eu/europeaid/prag/document.do?nodeNumber=1

Fassin, D. (2007). Humanitarianism as a Politics of Life. *Public Culture, 19*(3), 499–520. https://doi.org/10.1215/08992363-2007-007

Fast, L., & Jacobsen, K. L. (2019). Rethinking Access: How Humanitarian Technology Blurs Control and Care. *Disasters, 43*(S2), S151–S168. https://doi.org/10.1111/disa.12333

Furia, A. (2015). *The Foreign Aid Regime: Gift-Giving, States and Global Dis/Order*. Palgrave.

Gillard, E. (2021a). *IHL and the Humanitarian Impact of Counterterrorism Measures and Sanctions. Unintended Ill Effects of Well-Intended Measures*. Chatham House Report. Retrieved April 28, 2022, from https://www.chathamhouse.org/2021/09/ihl-and-humanitarian-impact-counterterrorism-measures-and-sanctions/04-funding-agreements

Gillard, E. (2021b). Screening of Final Beneficiaries—A Red Line in Humanitarian Operations. An Emerging Concern in Development Work.

International Review of the Red Cross, 103(916–917), 517–537. https://int ernational-review.icrc.org/articles/screening-of-final-beneficiaries-a-red-line-in-humanitarian-operations-916

Gilligan, G. (2009). PEEPing at PEPs. *Journal of Financial Crime, 16*(2), 137–143. https://doi.org/10.1108/13590790910951812

Goold, B. J., & Neyland, D. (2009). *New Directions in Surveillance and Privacy.* Routledge.

Guinane, K. (2021). *The Alarming Rise of Lawfare to Suppress Civil Society: The Case of Palestine and Israel.* The Charity & Security Network. Retrieved September 15.

Gusterson, H. (2009). Ethnographic Research. In A. Klotz & D. Prakash (Eds.), *Qualitative Methods in International Relations* (pp. 93–113). Palgrave.

Haggerty, K. (2009). Methodology as a Knife Fight: The Process, Politics and Paradox of Evaluating Surveillance. *Critical Criminology, 17*(4), 277–291. https://doi.org/10.1007/s10612-009-9083-y

Hanley-Giersch, J. (2019). RegTech and Financial Crime Prevention. In D. W. Arner, J. N. Barberis, & R. P. Buckley (Eds.), *The REGTECH Book: The Financial Technology Handbook for Investors. Entrepreneurs and Visionaries in Regulation* (Online ed.). Wiley. https://doi.org/10.1002/978111936219 7.ch4

Hattori, T. (2001). Reconceptualizing Foreign Aid. *Review of International Political Economy, 8*(4), 633–660. https://doi.org/10.1080/096922901100 77610

Hayes, B. (2012). Counter-Terrorism, "Policy Laundering," and the FATF: Legalizing Surveillance, Regulating Civil Society. *The International Journal of Not-for-Profit Law, 12*(1–2), 1–40. https://www.icnl.org/resources/res earch/ijnl/1-introduction-2

Hayes, B. (2017). *The Impact of International Counter-Terrorism on Civil Society Organisations: Understanding the Role of the Financial Action Task Force.* Bread for the World. Retrieved May 8, 2022, from http://efc.issuelab.org/resources/27481/27481.pdf

Helgesson, K. S., & Mörth, U. (2019). Instruments of Securitization and Resisting Subjects: For-Profit Professionals in the Finance-Security Nexus. *Security Dialogue, 50*(3), 257–274. https://doi.org/10.1177/096701061 9835655

Hosein, G., & Nyst, C. (2013). *Aiding Surveillance: An Exploration of How Development and Humanitarian Aid Initiatives are Enabling Surveillance in Developing Countries.* Privacy International. Retrieved March 8, 2023, from https://privacyinternational.org/sites/default/files/2017-12/Aiding% 20Surveillance.pdf

IFRC (International Federation of Red Cross). (2021). *Practical Guidance for Data Protection in Cash and Voucher Assistance.* Retrieved May 8,

2022, from https://www.ifrc.org/document/practical-guidance-data-protec tion-cash-and-voucher-assistance

Jacobsen, K. L. (2015). *The Politics of Humanitarian Technology: Good Intentions, Unintended Consequences and Insecurity*. Routledge.

Kuldova, T. Ø. (2022). *Compliance-Industrial Complex the Operating System of a Pre-Crime Society*. Palgrave Macmillan.

Lemberg-Pedersen, M., & Haioty, E. (2020). Re-assembling the Surveillable Refugee Body in the Era of Data-Craving. *Citizenship Studies, 24*(5), 607–624. https://doi.org/10.1080/13621025.2020.1784641

Latoreno, M. (2019, July 11). Stop Surveillance Humanitarianism. *New York Times*. https://www.nytimes.com/2019/07/11/opinion/data-humanitarian-aid.html

LexisNexis. (2021). *LexisNexis® WorldCompliance^{TM} Data*. Retrieved March 12, 2022, from https://risk.lexisnexis.com/global/en/products/worldcompliance-data

Lyon, D. (2007). *Surveillance Studies: An Overview*. Polity Press.

Madianou, M. (2019). Technocolonialism: Digital Innovation and Data Practices in the Humanitarian Response to Refugee Crises. *Social Media + Society, 5*(3), 1–13. https://doi.org/10.1177/2056305119863146

Malakoutikhah, Z. (2020). Financial Exclusion as a Consequence of Counter-Terrorism Financing. *Journal of Financial Crime, 27*(2), 663–682. https://doi.org/10.1108/JFC-09-2019-0121

Martin, A. (2023). Aidwashing Surveillance: Critiquing the Corporate Exploitation of Humanitarian Crises. *Surveillance & Society, 21*(1), 96–102. https://doi.org/10.24908/ss.v21i1.16266

Marwick, A. E. (2012). The Public Domain: Surveillance in Everyday Life. *Surveillance & Society, 9*(4), 378–393. https://doi.org/10.24908/ss.v9i4.4342

Marx, G. T. (2005). Seeing Hazily, But Not Darkly, Through the Lens: Some Recent Empirical Studies of Surveillance Technologies. *Law and Social Inquiry, 30*(2), 339–399. https://doi.org/10.1111/j.1747-4469.2005.tb01016.x

Mauss, M. (2002). *The Gift: The Form and Reason for Exchange in Archaic Societies*. Routledge. (Original work published 1925)

Minella, C. M. (2019). Counter-Terrorism Resolutions and Listing of Terrorists and Their Organizations by the United Nations. In E. Shor & S. Hoadley (Eds.), *International Human Rights and Counter-Terrorism* (pp. 31–53). Springer.

Muhomed, S., Puri, J., Stickler, H., & Sugand, D. (2021). *NGOs' Due Diligence and Risk Mititagion: A Holistic Approach*. London: London School of Economics and Political Science-Washington: The Charity and Security

Network. Retrieved September 13, 2023 from https://charityandsecurity. org/wp-content/uploads/2021/04/NGOs-Due-Diligence-and-Risk-Mitiga tion.pdf

Newhouse, N. (2021). *Screening Recipients of Humanitarian Cash and Voucher Assistance: Necessary Precaution or Wasted Resources?* Blog post, Calp Network. Retrieved April 18, 2022, from https://www.calpnetwork.org/ blog/screening-recipients-of-humanitarian-cash-and-voucher-assistance-necess ary-precaution-or-wasted-resources/

Nouwt, S., de Vires, B. R., & Prins, C. (Eds.). (2005). *Reasonable Expectations of Privacy? Eleven Country Reports in Camera Surveillance and Workplace Privacy.* T. M. C. Asser.

NRC (Norwegian Refugee Council). (2018a). *Principles Under Pressure: The Impact of Counterterrorism Measures and Preventing/Countering Violent Extremism on Principled Humanitarian Action.* Retrieved March 13, 2021, from https://reliefweb.int/sites/reliefweb.int/files/resources/nrc-principles_ under_pressure-report-screen.pdf

NRC (Norwegian Refugee Council). (2018b). *Understanding Conditional Clauses.* Retrieved March 13, 2021, from https://www.nrc.no/shorthand/ stories/understanding-counterterrorism-clauses/index.html and https:// www.nrc.no/globalassets/pdf/reports/toolkit/nrc_toolkit_03_reviewing-cou nterterrorism-clauses.pdf

O'Leary, E. (2022). Politics and Principles: The Impact of Counterterrorism Measures and Sanctions on Principled Humanitarian Action. *International Review of the Red Cross, 103*(916–917), 459–477. https://doi.org/10.1017/ S1816383121000357

Paragi, B. (2017). Contemporary Gifts. Solidarity, Compassion, Equality, Sacrifice and Reciprocity from the Perspective of NGOs. *Current Anthropology, 58*(3), 317—339. https://www.journals.uchicago.edu/doi/abs/10. 1086/692086

Paragi, B. (2023). *Opacity or Transparency? Screening by NGOs in the Context of Aid Work* (NCHS-Paper). Norwegian Centre for Humanitarian Studies. Retrieved July 18, 2023, from https://www.humanitarianstudies.no/ resource/opacity-or-transparency-screening-by-ngos-in-the-context-of-aid-work/

Paragi, B. (2024). The Art of Screening: Reasonable Efforts and Measures at the Nexus of Aid Work and Counterterrorism. *Surveillance & Society, 22*(2), 138–159.

Paragi, B., & Altamimi, A. (2022). Caring Control or Controlling Care? Double Bind Facilitated by Biometrics Between UNHCR and Syrian Refugees in Jordan. *Society and Economy, 44*(2), 206–231. https://doi.org/10.1556/ 204.2021.00027

Pyyhtinen, O. (2014). *The Gift and Its Paradoxes.* Ashgate.

Sandvik, K. B. (2019). Making Wearables in Aid: Digital Bodies, Data and Gifts. *Journal of Humanitarian Affairs, 1*(3), 33–41.

Sandvik, K. B. (2020). Wearables for Something Good: Aid, Dataveillance and the Production of Children's Digital Bodies. *Information, Communication & Society, 23*(14), 2014–2029. https://doi.org/10.1080/1369118X.2020.175 3797

Sandvik, K. B., Jacobsen, K. L., & McDonald, S. M. (2017). Do Not Harm: A Taxonomy of the Challenges of Humanitarian Experimentation. *International Review of the Red Cross, 99*(1), 319–344. https://doi.org/10.1017/S18163 8311700042X

Sattler, M. (2023). Five Ways the Aid System Can Improve Its Accountability to Affected People. *The New Humanitarian.* https://www.thenewhumanitarian. org/opinion/2023/04/05/ways-aid-system-can-improve-its-accountability

Shabibi, N., & Bryant, B. (2016). *VICE News Reveals the Terrorism Blacklist Secretly Wielding Power over the Lives of Millions.* VICE News. Retrieved January 20, 2022, from https://www.vice.com/en/article/pa4mgz/vice-news-reveals-the-terrorism-blacklist-secretly-wielding-power-over-the-lives-of-millions

Skinner-Thompson, S. (2022). Introduction: Privacy Studies, Surveillance Law. *Surveillance & Society, 20*(3), 294–296. https://doi.org/10.24908/ss.v20i3. 15774

Sullivan, G. (2020). *The Law of the List. UN Counterterrorism Sanctions and the Politics of Global Security Law.* Cambridge University Press.

També, N. (2021). *Unintended Consequences of AML/CFT Regulation: The Challenges of Banking Non-Profit Organisations.* European Center for Not-for-Profit Law. Retrieved September 1, 2023, from https://ecnl.org/public ations/unintended-consequences-amlcft-regulation-challenges-banking-non-profit-organisations

Tazzioli, M. (2019). Refugees' Debit Cards, Subjectivities, and Data Circuits: Financial-Humanitarianism in the Greek Migration Laboratory. *International Political Sociology, 13*(4), 392–408.

UN SR HR/CT. (2019). *Impact of Measures to Address Terrorism and Violent Extremism on Civic Space and the Rights of Civil Society Actors and Human Rights Defenders: Report of the Special Rapporteur on the Promotion and Protection of Human Rights and Fundamental Freedoms While Countering Terrorism* (A/HRC/40/52). UN Human Rights Council. Retrieved June 8, 2022, from https://documents-dds-ny.un.org/doc/UNDOC/GEN/G19/ 057/59/PDF/G1905759.pdf?OpenElement

UN SR HR/CT. (2023). *Global Study on the Impact of Counter-Terrorism on Civil Society and Civic Space.* UN Human Rights Council. Retrieved August 8, 2023, from https://defendcivicspace.com/wp-content/uploads/ 2023/06/SRCT_GlobalStudy.pdf

VOICE (Voluntary Organisations in Cooperation in Emergencies). (2021). *Adding to the Evidence the Impacts of Sanctions and Restrictive Measures on Humanitarian Action*. VOICE Survey Report. Retrieved January 20, 2022, from https://voiceeu.org/search?q=adding+to+the+evidence

Weitzberg, K., Cheesman, M., Martin, A., & Schoemaker, E. (2021). Between Surveillance and Recognition: Rethinking Digital Identity in Aid. *Big Data & Society, 8*(1), 1–8. https://doi.org/10.1177/20539517211006744

Zuboff, S. (2019). *The Age of Surveillance Capitalism*. PublicAffairs.

CHAPTER 5

The Politics of Opacity and Transparency in Non-European Contexts

Abstract This chapter explores the controversial role transparency (around screening) plays in authoritarian contexts. Transparency demands are weapons that can be used and abused by those in power vis-à-vis their subjects. States and financial institutions expect transparency from aid organizations in terms of their employment affairs and financial transactions to counterterrorism or prevent money laundering. Aid organizations, however, are not only legally obliged to 'distrust' employees, partners, volunteers by means of using reasonable efforts to prevent adverse outcomes, but are also self-regulated to some extent. By screening people against various watchlists, aid organizations produce 'transparent subjects', but opacity around screening cannot but reinforce the power imbalances embedded in historical, political and legal structures. By considering the diverse power relations embedded in aid relations and the broader context of the operations of aid organizations, this chapter demonstrates that basic data protection principles—such as transparency—may simultaneously fulfil the rights of data subjects, local individuals included and endanger the security of NGO operations in conflict and authoritarian settings. However, if aid organizations cannot deliver services or function as employers because they are considered foreign agents in aid recipient countries, other human rights of local individuals may also be violated.

© The Author(s), under exclusive license to Springer Nature Switzerland AG 2024
B. Paragi, *Screening by International Aid Organizations Operating in the Global South*, https://doi.org/10.1007/978-3-031-54165-0_5

Keywords Transparency beyond data protection · Opacity · Countersurveillance · Risks of generosity

To demonstrate what totalitarianism and democracy has in common, Giorgio Agamben used the term *state of exception* introduced originally by the German philosopher, Carl Schmitt (Agamben, 2005). The concept describes a mode of government, the extensive extension of state power, which has become a deeply embedded norm worldwide since the 1920s, even in democratic contexts. Having the potential to transform democracies into totalitarian states, the 'state of exception' determines who is truly sovereign in a given realm. In the game of terrorism—counterterrorism, neither the North-South relations, nor the civil society can escape the consequences of exceptional, many times ignorant measures either. It is worthwhile to recall Chapter 2 that introduced the securitization of the aid sector briefly, and the words of the UN's Special Rapporteur on human rights and counterterrorism (UN SR HR/CT, 2023a, 12):

> when States deploy counter-terrorism or P/CVE measures they enter a realm of exceptionality where human rights deficits pervade and the normal rules of due process and procedural protections generally do not apply.

The extensive use of technology, digitalization and datafication have only complicated the matter. On the one hand, various technologies or tech-enabled mechanisms are systematically weaponized by states to enforce 'exceptionality' to counter existential threats in the civil space too (UN SR HR/CT, 2023a, 74–79, 109, 2023b). On the other hand, the use of some of these technologies (biometric technology, drones, screening/surveillance) are justified by aid organizations claiming that they provide more effective services to beneficiaries, optimize their costs or mitigate various operational, security or compliance risks. By doing so, however, they can easily contribute to generating further risks and contribute to consolidating power imbalances.

Risks and Harms Associated with Technology and Data in the Aid Sector in a Nutshell

Limiting the discussion only to the aid industry, scholars have scrutinized the beneficial and harmful impacts of technology and practices of collecting or extracting (personal, group) data for about a decade. As a result, an emerging scholarship deals with the instrumentalization of technology for both humanitarian (Sandvik et al., 2014, 2017; Slim, 2021) or development purposes (Harris, 2016; Qureshi, 2019; Walsham, 2017).

Offering a comprehensive review is beyond the scope of this section, but relevant studies deserve to be recalled. Building on insights from (critical) security studies, migration studies and counterterrorism studies, growing attention has been paid to the increased involvement of private actors in aid work through potential harms of digitalization, datafication and instrumentalization of vulnerable people (Duffield, 2016; Madianou, 2019; Sandvik et al., 2017); and the conceptualization of digital technologies as tools for biopolitics, the purpose of which is to govern or discipline populations and control their movement by providing not only incentives for voluntary participation, but also the illusion of the freedom of choice. Digital (legal) identity management systems (Martin & Taylor, 2021) and the related "financial inclusion" of the world's "unbanked populations" are not only about providing more freedom of consumer choice but also entail tighter-than-ever control over vulnerable people (Lemberg-Pedersen & Haioty, 2020, 610).

Power is an integral part of any asymmetric relation. Interactions between aid organizations and vulnerable local beneficiaries are also characterized by disparities and inequalities (Barnett, 2002, 32–46). Aid organizations' use of technology only makes otherwise asymmetric relations even more unequal by frequently turning (larger) aid organizations agents of political and business interests under the banner of humanitarian governance and in name of beneficiaries' best interests in all sorts of contexts (Barnett, 2013; Jacobsen, 2015; Madianou, 2019).

A further risk concerns the loss or disappearance of the human (being) in digitalized aid relations. While Lemberg-Pedersen and Haioty's paper (2020, 608) demonstrated how refugees' bodies are constantly "reassembled in digital terms for having a better control over the movement of digital data representing their bodies", countless studies documented the increasing vulnerability perceived by various segments of Global South populations (refugees in camps, in host communities, transit, trafficked or smuggled 'migrants'; internally displaced persons; stateless people; unaccompanied migrant children, etc.). As these people are simultaneously seen 'at risk' by aid organizations and 'as risks' mostly in migration contexts by governments and border control agencies (Huysmans & Squire, 2009), certain technologies cannot but serve both purposes by blurring the border of care and control. Humanitarian organizations' collection and sharing of biometric data not only ensures access to services, but can also be used to deny access to services or entail exclusion (Fast & Jacobsen, 2019) depending on how decisions are made and what kind of digital systems are used for identification in aid or migration contexts (Schoemaker et al., 2023).

While regulators, donors and aid organizations argue that data-enabled technologies (screening tools at least as much as biometrics-based ID management practices and platforms) help them reduce risks, others— scholars and practitioners alike—warn of the harmful consequences (Sandvik et al., 2017). Risks and uncertainties, however, are not the only factors characterizing the unintended consequences of digitalization in the aid sector. As argued by Fejerskov et al. (2023, 12) humanitarian ignorance deserves to be treated as a separate category of humanitarian non-knowledge as it equally represents intended or unintended unknowing. This observation can be illustrated by the words of an ordinary field officer[1]:

> Data protection is a huge problem within the [aid] industry for various reasons. It is common that things are not explained [to data subjects]. The industry is digitally illiterate, while we collect a lot of information, we do not understand the complexity of gathering data and the legal side of data collection.

While it is widely known that a lot is unknown regarding the use of various technologies by NGOs and related practices of data collection, processing and sharing and associated risks (Fejerskov et al., 2023; Jacobsen, 2022, 623), donors, aid organizations and their business partners seem to have a common interest in preserving certain secrets. While tech companies' legitimate interests may include confidentiality for profit-related reasons, aid organizations are in a somewhat different position

---

[1] Interview with an advisor working at a Norwegian NGO [1], Zoom, 17. December 2020.

when they confront the matter of transparency and accountability. As argued by Jordan and van Tuijl (2006) activities that are claimed to be charitable should be openly disclosed and accessible for public questioning. Citing McGee (2013, 111) on the broad consensus about the relationship between transparency and accountability:

> [the way] they relate to aid is that transparency is a necessary but insufficient condition for aid accountability. Aid transparency initiatives constitute a sub-set within the broader, longer-standing aid accountability field.

It should, however, be acknowledged that aid organizations are much better positioned to comply with transparency and accountability-related demands in democratic settings than in authoritarian or conflict-related contexts (Jordan & van Tuijl, 2006, 5). Even if control over their finances is strong due to the involvement of banks and financial services providers, civil society organizations enjoy broader autonomy in democratic countries than other sectors (finance, health care, business).

Transparency in the Aid Sector: Beyond Data Protection

Transparency, as a principle and idea, encompasses equality and balance of power both in public and private contexts serving the objectives of legitimate governance (Vrabec, 2021, 65). It has been recognized as a legal principle by nations over the past decades, the purpose of which has been to equip citizens with the right to (access to) information and right to know to strengthen democracy even beyond the border of the United States (Schudson, 2018). Due to rapid digitalization and the widespread application of technologies performing automated decision-making or using artificial intelligence, the emerging 'right to be explained' joined the right to information (Kaminski, 2019), both strongly communicating with the legal principle of transparency. Transparency, however, is also a "political and cultural ideal[that] has left secrecy to accumulate negative connotations" (Birchall, 2011, 7).

To address the politics of transparency, its contemporary conceptualizations and legal understandings are to be considered simultaneously. Transparency, as an idea or concept, is related to but not identical to transparency as a legal principle enshrined in legal instruments (Adams, 2020). The difference matters to the extent which, transparency around screening may be expected from aid organizations on ethical or moral grounds, even if transparency can be restricted legally, for example, in name of national security or international counterterrorism activities. The latter may vary from jurisdiction to jurisdiction even with the EU, notwithstanding that data protection standards are identical due to the GDPR in EU member states.

The meaning of transparency varies across disciplines entailing not only diverse interpretations, but also conflicting interests as screening illustrates. The general discourse implies that "transparency concerns the disclosure of information by a particular entity with the view to increasing visibility and accountability of this entity to a broader spectrum of persons and institutions" (Adams, 2020, 5) and denotes the conditions "in which information about the priorities, intentions, capabilities and behaviour of powerful organizations is widely available to the global public" (Lord, 2006, 5 cited by Adams, 2020, 5). Which information is disclosed depends on the state via its laws and regulations. Individuals (data subjects) are required to cooperate in producing information as any "resisting the call to be transparent to the state is automatically registered as a sign of guilt" (Birchall, 2011, 10). However, if the state—or any other actor, for example, an aid organization acting for the benefit of the public—refrains from "applying transparency to its own actions, [it] meets the charge of totalitarianism coming the other way" (Birchall, 2011, 10). This is exactly how the matter of transparency/secrecy in the context of counterterrorism determines the nature of a political regime on the democratic—totalitarian continuum. It is secrecy which ensures "a discretionary space of action exempt from the rule of law" the purpose of which is "to protect and stabilize the state" while at the same time secrecy also "opens a space of exception from the rule of law that breeds violence, corruption and oppression" (Carl Schmidt discussed by Horn, 2011, 103).

As aid projects financed by OECD DAC, especially EU donors aim to convey values, such as human rights, democracy, good governance, transparency also reflects a consensus in development and humanitarian practice—and scholarship too—that more and higher-quality information about aid disbursements (financial transactions) should have positive effects on aid effectiveness under adverse conditions, such as corruption in aid recipient countries (Christensen et al., 2011). Indeed, transparency—at least in theory—constrains the power of the remote 'agents' (state actors, policy-makers) by making more information available to the local 'principals' (the public, voters, citizens). As a result, principals—those benefiting from aid included—are better positioned to ensure that processes deliver outcomes closer to their preferences (Christensen et al., 2011). It should, however, be remembered that demanding transparency around (external, foreign) finances at least as much serves oppressive state interests as interests of local societies. If the state is authoritarian deeming a given NGOs' presence and operation a political threat or security risk, the notion of transparency may be used to undermine its presence, entire operation, or only certain projects.

Many aid organizations, indeed, operate in conflict settings and (semi-) authoritarian environments where transparency around finances (vis-à-vis the public, the beneficiaries, the employees) is demanded and used to undermine the legitimacy of organizations providing aid to poor, disadvantaged or discriminated segments of societies. The label 'foreign agent' is widely used globally to delegitimize international or foreign NGOs that justify their work, operations, presence by citing human rights. Regulating the finances of such foreign agents—demanding transparency around donations included—is one of the simplest ways to control such organizations in geopolitically diverse settings as examples from the USA, Russia, Israel equally demonstrates (Lamarche, 2019; Watson & Burles, 2018, *see* later).

Transparency as a legal principle prescribed by data protection laws (such as the GDPR) may produce equally similar unintended consequences. Taking the example of screening, if NGOs interpreted notification obligations broadly and provided information on screening to data subjects publicly, by ignoring the opportunities provided by restrictions and exemptions (in the context of laws regulating counterterrorism, national security), they may well be further targeted by governments that labelled the given NGOs as security risks or foreign agents.

No surprise that regardless of the transparency obligation of the GDPR, it was consistent across the interviews and in the workshop that aid organizations have a well-founded, seemingly 'legitimate' interest *not to disclose* the fact of screening. To illustrate the nature of the dilemma by comparison, US authorities, operating in the field of immigration control or customs, have been widely accused of and criticized for using commercial databases provided by vendors such as LexisNexis to increase their efficiency by surveilling individuals even where no crime has been committed (Biddle, 2023; Shabibi & Bryant, 2016). Applying a somewhat twisted or reversed logic, vendors such as LexisNexis can also be accused of complicity in human rights violations committed by governmental actors (DelGrande, 2022).

By engaging in surveillance-like activities for whatever legitimate purpose aid organizations, in effect, join forces with those state actors that are interested in producing 'transparent subjects' in order to govern them in name of counterterrorism and other 'gods' or 'goods'. Common is the technical capability by which powerful agents (state agencies and authorities, banks, corporations, audit and consultancy firms, NGOs) increase the transparency of individuals and the instrumentalization of ethics. Those that are not willing or not able to produce the required level of transparency—by providing information, personal data, documents or biometric data—are assumed to have something to hide in all domains, and as such "suspicious and unwanted by societal norms" (Adams, 2020, 70). It is likely simpler (quicker, cheaper) to screen individuals quietly by using the database of the screening tools to deliver the needed transparency and trust than to confront the concerned persons by raising questions on their background that reveal default distrust towards them.

Opacity around screening can also be explained by environmental complexity. Navigating across jurisdictions (prescribing 'exceptional' legal requirements for the controversial mission of AML/CFT), donors (providing funding and expecting AML/CFT compliance), authoritarian regimes (being interested in knowing their 'political opponents', that is, the local transaction partners, beneficiaries of Northern NGOs), their own mandate (implementing projects in a principled manner) and other organizational interests (preventing reputational hazards), the reasonable expectations of individuals (benefiting from jobs with aid organizations or from aid projects) and data protection laws (prescribing the transparency obligation) requires not little creativity from INGOs. Considering the power imbalances embedded in aid relations, both the acknowledgement and denial of screening might reinforce local perceptions that aid organizations are agents serving interests other than that of helping beneficiaries. The next two sections will take a closer look at it.

Navigating Among Political Regimes, Legal Jurisdictions and Financial Regulations

How do aid organizations engage with security-related regulations in various political and legal environments? Recalling Didier Fassin's words (2007, 508) "[h]umanitarian intervention has become an important mode and even a dominant frame of reference for Western political intervention in global scenes of misfortune". Hence, participation in security-related and counterterrorism activities has also been a matter of discussion within the aid industry since UN, EU and US regulations were implemented after 9/11 at large scale (Eckert, 2022; Hayes, 2012, 2017; NRC, 2018a, 2018b; VOICE, 2021). The legal and ethical dilemmas surrounding the global sanctions regime in the context of human rights (Tzanou, 2017) and humanitarian law (Eckert, 2022; O'Leary, 2021) demand NGOs to navigate among realms representing parallel and conflicting realities. Local and international NGOs as beneficiaries or coordinators of aid projects are interested in demonstrating compliance to their official donors to prevent exclusion from future tenders on the one hand, and to mitigate other risks threatening their reputation, credibility and operations, on the other hand.

However, as no Western or international intervention into another country is without its justification on humanitarian grounds (Fassin, 2007, 508), humanitarian organizations can also be easily seen as agents of Western interventionalism in many conflict situations or non-like-minded, (semi-)authoritarian settings. While aid organizations try to avoid such accusations by emphasizing their distinctiveness as humanitarian actors, their (self-)portrayal as apolitical actors make them part of the securitization game (Vaughn, 2009). After all, they can secure their 'humanitarian' profile in a securitized environment sometimes by resorting to solutions (protection, risk-mitigating measures) provided by private vendors, such as screening tools, other times working with security companies (Abrahamsen & Leander, 2016) or even military actors in conflict zones.

As a result, counterterrorism legislations—a core component of which is lists and listing—are also used against civil society actors by states having diametrically opposed opinion on terrorism and sanctions (UN SR HR/ CT, 2019, 2, 2023a, 71–72). Therefore, while screening may increase public and governmental confidence by ensuring compliance with norms and rules set by Northern donors, it also exerts coercive and normative pressures by regulating, that is, constraining NGO behaviour (Hayes, 2012, 2017). Reasonable measures, such as screening, are equally applied by larger aid organizations and used against them.

Focusing this time on the former, financial institutions (FIs), banks and service providers (FSPs) also conduct financial surveillance over clients' international transactions in line with international standards and domestic legislations (Amicelle, 2011; Rébé, 2020). Aid organizations—as bank clients—are by no means exceptions. Citing the original FATF Recommendation 8 (FATF, 2001, 4, 7), the transactions initiated by some of them are considered risky:

> Countries should review the adequacy of laws and regulations that relate to entities that can be abused for the financing of terrorism. Certain *non-profit organisations [NPOs] are particularly vulnerable*, and *countries should ensure that they cannot be misused*: (a) by terrorist organisations posing as legitimate entities; (b) to exploit legitimate entities as conduits for terrorist financing, including for the purpose of escaping asset-freezing measures; and (c) to conceal or obscure the clandestine diversion of funds intended for legitimate purposes to terrorist organisations.

The implementation of customer due diligence (CDD) and know-your-customer (KYC) procedures in the context of AML/CFT required a huge investment in resources, skills and creativity not only in the financial sector (Amicelle, 2011; Amicelle & Favarel-Garrigues, 2012), but also among larger civil society actors. Although Recommendation 8 was revised in 2016 and more recently in 2023 too by acknowledging the flaws in the original approach,[2] financial institutions keep the international transactions of non-profit organizations, aid organizations included, under tight control as documented by guidelines and reports prepared by the European Center for Not-for-Profit Law (ECNL).

As a result, non-profit and non-governmental organizations as legal entities and their high-ranking officials, board members, are subject to strict customer due diligence procedures (CDD) by banks, the purpose of which is to detect cases when actual financial transactions or patterns are not aligned to expected transactions and behaviour (També, 2021, 10). While monitoring their transactions, the banks screen NPO/NGOs' transaction partners for their adverse media appearances, sanctions lists established by UNSC resolutions and domestic sanctions lists depending on the jurisdictions the FI operates within (També, 2021). (I)NGOs as

---

[2] FATF refined its initial position ('non-profit organizations, NPOs, are particularly vulnerable to terrorist financing abuse') by acknowledging that not all NPOs are inherently high risk and some may represent little or no risk at all, yet many representatives of States, NPOs, and financial institutions continue to use it as a reference point (ICNL-FATF, 2019). On the most recent amendments see: https://www.fatf-gafi.org/en/publications/Fatfrecommendations/protecting-non-profits-abuse-implementation-R8.html.

clients are typically screened against US sanctions and terrorist lists simply because many FIs rely on US-based FIs and financial service providers in their corresponding operations (També, 2021, 14). While FIs have been increasingly rely on financial and regulatory technology to increase efficiency in tackling financial and other crimes (Arner et al., 2019), NPO/ NGOss have fallen to victim to the financial industry's tendency to de-risk in many cases. Recalling experiences from the aid industry and a recent ENCL-commissioned study by Anwar and Wesseling (2022, 10, 52–53), NPO/NGOs may equally face various difficulties opening bank accounts, delayed transactions or unexplained account closures especially if they operate internationally.

Such control over international financial transactions is not unrelated to the criminalization and securitization of local and international NGOs by governments, treating "the boundary between civil society and the state as a matter of security, particularly in relation to 'foreign influence'" (Watson & Burles, 2018, 4; see also Howell, 2014; Howell & Lind, 2009; Jackson, 2015; Lazell & Petrikova, 2020). While at least 140 governments adopted counterterrorism legislation between 2001 and 2018, such measures can also be used against civil society actors (UN SR HR/CT, 2019, 2). Indeed, INGOs are not only subject to surveillance as bank clients but may also be criminalized or securitized as foreign agents. While Muslim charities traditionally have been considered suspicious in Western countries (Malakoutikhah, 2020), certain governments—in Russia, Turkey, Israel (Lamarche, 2019) and Hungary (Nagy, 2017; Romaniuk, 2022), among others—not only rhetorically labelled but also legally designated international and local NGOs as security risks, accusing them of threatening public order or 'national values' (UN SR HR/CT, 2019, 2023a). To sum up, finances of aid organizations are equally regulated and restricted by governments (Christensen & Weinstein, 2013; Watson & Burles, 2018) and their financial institutions and other service providers (Anwar et al., 2022; També, 2021).

Aid organizations, however, may also be subject to alternative political surveillance too in highly politicised environments. Inasmuch as the international civil society has suffered the consequences of the securitization agenda since 9/11 restrictions in general (Chapter 2), aid organizations operating in Palestine are also subject to extensive monitoring and lawfare for supporting Palestinian rights (Guinane, 2021). Indeed, international and local NGOs may also be surveilled by fellow NGOs, sort of 'vigilante' organizations, such as the pro-Israeli NGO Monitor. Such organizations are not only concerned with how various foreign-funded Israeli NGOs may contribute to funding Palestinian human rights dubbed as 'terrorism' (Lamarche, 2019). As documented by Guinane (2021) legal institutions and processes are increasingly used by politically motivated civilian and governmental actors in attempts to discredit, delegitimize and eventually cut foreign funding to organizations defending the human rights of Palestinian individuals and organizations by providing aid in form of projects, CVA or other kinds of material support. And the worse the reputation or media portrayal of an aid organization or human rights NGO is, the higher the likelihood that it will appear on certain watchlists.

The screening database is not a neutral technology as illustrated by experiences because commercial screening tools, more precisely, the vendors behind and their research teams either do not necessarily assess sources for credibility in a transparent manner or it is unknown to their clients how assessment is done. Indeed, as it was introduced in Chapter 4, the definition of the 'terrorist' in the ADVERSE MEDIA category is more elusive than in the SANCTIONS category. In other words, the threshold for being listed in certain categories in the databases of screening tools is much lower than with government terrorist lists. Organizations operating and individuals living in conflict settings can do very little to get delisted (Minella, 2019) as Palestinian experiences with World-Check show (Guinane, 2021, 30–34). It applies not only to states designating certain (human rights, advocacy, aid) NGOs as terrorist organization, but also vendors (Refinitiv/LSEG, CSI, Lexis-Nexis, others) whose research teams may also create profiles of NGOs (within the ADVERSE MEDIA category) by mapping who is involved in a given NGO and in what role/position. Depending on the jurisdiction, such data about an EU/EEA registered NGOs and affiliated persons may potentially also be transferred to the US government.

Localization, Digital Illiteracy, Countersurveillance and Non-inclusion

Aid organizations operating in Global South countries or their borderlands have invested in the localization of aid work—well beyond simply offering assistance to final beneficiaries—for reasons that cannot be discussed here in detail.[3] Working with locals—as employees, volunteers, activists, vendors, suppliers or other partners (hereinafter NGO-subjects for the sake of simplicity, even if official or intergovernmental aid agencies and humanitarian organizations also extensively work with locals and even screen them)—may contribute to the local economy, even if not without side-effects. Obviously, financial transactions (salaries, rents paid, items purchased) are at least as much integral part of aid relations as non-reciprocated financial transfers ('aid', cash-voucher assistance, in-kind assistance, other forms of project aid) to final beneficiaries are.

Therefore, the question how aid organizations navigate between their mission, key elements of which are localization and participation, regulations protecting Western or international security and laws prescribing the protection of personal data raises further questions. How does screening influence solidarity between international and local organizations, actors that are being treated differently by donors? How are local individuals treated differently by aid organizations in employment context, the data protection dimension included? Can aid organizations adhere to their principles while they are securitized in various ways and for diverse purposes or are they also links in the chain of politics and security?

Localization and participation are highly relevant for the accountability of the NGO sector towards local organizations in the Global South and the individuals without whose engagement, passion or commitment aid organizations could hardly operate. As it was formulated by the UN Secretary General, António Guterres, and cited in a recent report by the UN Special Rapporteur on Counter Terrorism (cited in UN SR HR/CR, 2023a, 16):

> People wish to be heard and to participate in the decisions that affect them. Institutions could establish better ways of listening to people whom they are meant to serve and taking their views into account, especially groups that are frequently overlooked, such as women, young people, minority groups or persons with disabilities.

---

[3] Ownership, participation and localization—just as transparency—are key 'aid effectiveness' principles that mostly govern the work of development (aid) organizations (OECD, 2008). The *Participation Handbook for humanitarian field workers* is one among the guidelines containing detailed practical advice on the participation of affected people in humanitarian action (Groupe URD, 2009).

While local participation has been encouraged both in humanitarian and development contexts for almost two decades both by policies and practical guidelines (see for example, Groupe URD, 2009), increased localization and staff diversity is not without risks from organizational perspectives. Various modes of remote management may simultaneously facilitate the localization of employment and entail the risk of growing distance between various levels of staff. Although as prompted by Heathershaw (2016) the international humanitarian community should be understood more in terms of its inclusions than its exclusions due to this expansion and diversity, the unknowns of screening may complicate the picture. The conditions summarized briefly in this section carry not little relevance for studying transparency/opacity around risk-mitigating measures. Even if final beneficiaries are not screened for humanitarian reasons (Gillard, 2021a, 2021b), there are tens, if not hundreds, of thousands of NGO-subjects—the vast majority is likely a Global South citizen—that are potentially subject to screening.

Acknowledging that aid organizations suffer the consequences of the 'shrinking civil space' (UN SR HR/CT, 2019) and they frequently experience mistreatment by the governments and the financial sector during the latter's coordinated de-risking attempts (Anwar et al., 2022; També, 2021), it can also be assumed, however provocative it might sound, that local partner organizations and individuals screened by international aid organizations may equally be subject to some sort of unfair treatment, a potential result of which is exclusion, that is, de-localization, non-participation or a non-representative inclusion of local communities. This assumption can also be justified by the rich ethnographic scholarship that discusses precarious conditions for employment and the power imbalances between international donors (agencies and aid organizations) and their local partners, organizations, grassroots movements, local/national development experts (Barnett 2002: 216–219; Kamruzzaman, 2017; Mosse, 2011; Sakue-Collins, 2021; Wright, 2011).

Starting with local partner organizations, global counterterrorism measures have had an adverse impact on local civil society organizations because of political oppression, de-risking procedures implemented by local banks in charge of international transactions and their comparative disadvantage regarding compliance with conditional clauses in funding agreements. These are particularly challenging in conflict situations as illustrated by experiences of local, Palestinian NGOs. According to their experiences, OECD DAC donors, equally seem to select regions and prefer larger international aid organizations that present as little administrative burden and reputational risk as possible (El Taraboulsi-McCarthy, 2018, 6), while conditional funding is a highly political issue (BADIL, 2021).

Regarding the relationship between EU/EEA-based aid organizations and local individuals (data subjects), the impact of counterterrorism regulations and their perceived incompatibility with humanitarian principles has received far more attention (Eckert, 2022; Gillard, 2021a, 2021b; Hayes, 2012, 2017; O'Leary, 2021), than individual rights, compliance with local privacy standards or data protection laws or local privacy norms. While the GDPR can be seen as an instrument attempting to globalize privacy standards (Bennett, 2018), it should also be acknowledged that local understandings of privacy in various Global South settings remains underexplored (Arora, 2019).

According to estimations, however, national aid workers—local citizens of aid recipient countries in the Global South—are the majority of aid staff in the field upwards of 90% (Egeland et al., 2011, 40). Regardless of variations across organizations, it is worthwhile to consider that the size of the global workforce of Médecins Sans Frontières (MSF) includes about 40,000 staff employed locally (MSF, 2023). The Norwegian Research Council (NRC 2023) employs more than 15,000 humanitarians in 30 countries according to its website, while Oxfam, an international confederation of eighteen organizations networked together in 92 countries, has more than 10,000 employees and works with more than 3,000 local partner organizations.[4] Such numbers explain the 'thousands' of searches conducted by screening tools even in cases when aid organizations do not screen humanitarian beneficiaries.

Mapping the practical experiences of NGO-subjects in employment context is not easy methodologically, but the perceptions and perspectives of Northern aid professionals and volunteers have enjoyed considerable attention in academic scholarship (Fechter, 2014). The experiences of the majority of aid workers—the so-called subordinate development [and humanitarian] professionals (Heathershaw, 2016, 79)—however, has remained understudied for various reasons (Pascucci, 2019, 740).

---

[4] According to estimations, more than 630,000 humanitarian staff worked in humanitarian settings, 90% of which were nationals of the countries they were working in (ALNAP 2022, 14). This data do not include the staff of development organizations. For further data see https://www.devex.com/organizations/search.

Nevertheless, local aid workers physical presence—for their cultural and linguistic competency and differentially insured, or non-insured status—is central to the implementation of humanitarian policies (Pascucci, 2019) and development projects too (Kalfeis & Knodel, 2021). This localization, however, is rather ambiguous for it not only contributes to stronger sense of ownership and local participation, but may also imply the outsourcing of risks by aid organizations. Or, somewhat ironically, locals are provided the opportunity to take responsibility for local risks too under the banners of principles, such as participation and localization.

As a result, local aid workers—refugees working for aid organizations, iNGOs and IOs included—are increasingly in charge of implementing actual field operations and securing access to hard-to-reach areas in humanitarian contexts (Farah, 2010; Malkin, 2015 cited by Pascucci, 2019, 744). Taking the practice of 'profiling' (Duroch & Neuman, 2021) as an example, locals are exposed to greater risks than expatriate staff or white employees that are not deployed for their physical safety in certain countries in Africa.[5] The results of such measures are obviously controversial considering that 98% of the aid workers that died in 2021 were national staff (and only 2% were international), while 53% of them were employed by national NGOs (AWSD, 2022). Furthermore, most of the employment opportunities offered by humanitarian organizations are temporary and precarious as demonstrated by studies in Jordan (Fechter & Hindmann, 2011 cited by Pascucci, 2019, 750), and in Africa too, even if a lot of aid actors "were born and grew up in the target destinations of NGOs projects, sat in classrooms built with development funding" (Kalfeis & Knodel, 2021, 10). Yet, locals are usually work for lower salaries and poorer insurance conditions than internationals and they are recruited with local contracts in the countries where field missions are located (Pascucci, 2019). There is no reason to assume that their privacy-related rights, such as right to information, enjoy better protection than other dimensions of their employment.

Screening, non-notification and digital (il)literacy. Identities and identification—cornerstones of citizenship-based rights and entitlements, also duties—became increasingly securitized. While freedom, rights or

---

[5] According to the Aid Workers Security Database (AWSD, 2022) the ten most dangerous countries (in 2021): South Sudan, Afghanistan, Syria, Ethiopia, Mali, Myanmar, DR Congo, CAR, Cameron and Nigeria.

entitlements have been conditioned on legitimate identity—identification—even in democratic countries (Rose, 1999), the widespread implementation of various technologies, ICTs, biometrics, tokens enabled not only remote identification (Lyon, 2007, 124–130), but they have been increasingly used to securitize—and sometimes even criminalize—identities (people). All this is relevant from the perspective of aid organizations to as long as they also resemble 'states' [governance] in their interactions with individuals as briefly mentioned in the Introduction. Not only governments condition rights and entitlements on identification, but aid organizations too (Fast & Jacobsen, 2019). Humanitarian governance also seems to securitize identities—of NGO-subjects—by increasingly conditioning aid relations on registration, biometrics-based identification and results of screening. Aid organizations may be legally obligated to do so, but their legitimate interests cannot be ignored either. But (how) is it possible to discuss screening with screened subjects?

If screening is conceptualized as a data processing operation (*see* Chapter 3), the GDPR applies and aid organizations as data controllers are legally required to provide information to individuals—even to local staff employed with various contacts—to meet the transparency obligation enshrined in Article 5(1) and related articles, unless data controllers can document restrictions or exemptions. While the information on screening as data processing may be missing from publicly available privacy notices because the INGOs in the sample (VOICE-members) simply do not collect personal data or do not screen individuals, it is highly unlikely in the light of earlier reports (Gillard, 2021a, 46–49; 2021b; Hayes, 2017, 28; NRC, 2018a, 23–25; VOICE, 2021, 13). Responses given to the online surveys also confirmed that screening is an existing practice. Internal opacity, however, became clear only during the qualitative interviews, and aid organizations tend to explain silence over it with the low risk of exclusion. As a legal advisor at a Norwegian NGO explained[6]:

> While we do such checks continuously, by verifying the identity and background of hundreds or thousands of people annually, the likelihood of a true positive hit is very low. As the risk of exclusion [from humanitarian aid] is very low, we do not provide much information on details

---

[6] Interview with an advisor working at a Norwegian NGO [8], Zoom, 4 May and 14 June 2021.

[unless people ask about the screening clause in employment contracts, for example].

The reasons are complex, but communicating privacy and data protection matters in a GDPR-friendly manner poses a huge challenge to organizations. The matter of information provided internally to local data subjects (local employees, event participants, beneficiaries of projects) was addressed by the online survey too (Q12), which asked about the ways how aid organizations provided information about the purposes of processing and their rights when they collect or register their personal data. Like in case of other questions, the respondents could select more than one answers. The two most frequent ways of communication mentioned were oral communication ('we always provide information orally, even if people do not ask about it', $n = 17$) and the privacy notices available on NGO websites in European languages ($n = 17$). By answering this question only a few respondents reported that the privacy notices were available in local languages, for example, in Arabic ($n = 3$), whereas others acknowledged that the privacy notice posted on their websites was addressed only to a European audience ($n = 8$). While this question was considered not applicable/relevant by some respondents ($n = 7$), a few of them said that their organizations did not provide information to locals at all ($n = 3$). How information is provided, what kind of information is provided may be explained, among others, by NGO perceptions on and experiences with how locals understand the matter of data protection. To map such perceptions four questions were used (Q15m, Q15n, Q15o, Q15oo) and respondents had the opportunity to agree or disagree at a four-point scale as summarized in Table 5.1.

Acknowledging that about the third or the respondents did not consider this question relevant (perhaps because they did not collect personal data)?), an absolute majority of the remaining respondents ($n = 22$) agreed or strongly agreed the statement that local individuals do not know their digital rights (Q15m). Respondents were more divided over the question whether local individuals raise questions about the purposes of collecting their personal data (Q15n). While the majority ($n = 13$) indicated that they did not experience such inquiries, there were either respondents that agreed (or strongly agreed) that locals raise questions concerning the reasons for or purposes of data collection. With regard to obtaining an informed consent (Q15o), nine NGOs reported that they experienced that local individuals are either reluctant or scared

Table 5.1 NGO perceptions on local people's knowledge on data protection (*n* denotes the number of responses)

Statement (Q15) Our organization experienced that...	Strongly disagree (n)	Disagree (n)	Agree (n)	Strongly agree (n)	N.a. (n)
m: local individuals, in general, do not know their digital rights	1	2	14	8	10
n: local individuals raise questions about why their personal data is collected	3	13	6	2	11
o: local individuals are reluctant or scared to sign consent statement	4	9	7	2	13
oo: that local individuals cannot give a GDPR-proof consent (freely given, specific, etc.)	1	12	8	3	11

to sign written consents and 13 respondents did not face such challenges (the question was considered irrelevant by 13 organizations either not collecting personal data or using a different legal basis). Qualitative interviews also confirmed that[7]

> It is kind of "unexplainable" [using clear and plain language] to an ordinary mother in Mozambique why or how the personal data of her daughter is collected and how it is processed or protected for the imbalance in power and knowledge between the data subject and us.

In addition to the problem of digital illiteracy perceived by aid organizations, lack of human capacity may also explain why screening—one among the many other data processing operations—is under-communicated to individuals in the Global South in detail.[8] Recalling the interviews and related observations, only one or two legal advisor or compliance officer are involved in the periodic (weekly, monthly, biannual) screening of thousands of individuals, a procedure which is not necessarily well known in-house either. While larger humanitarian (aid) organizations have drafted standard internal procedures for screening criteria in line

---

[7] Interview with advisors working at the UK branch of an international NGO [9], Teams, 17 June 2021.

[8] Interview with an advisor working at a Norwegian NGO [8], Teams, 14 June 2021.

with FATF recommendations on due diligence (Muhomed et al., 2021), human capacities are limited. Such constrains, however, may also entail a limited understanding on the real-life impact of screening and related decisions on NGO-subjects.

Earlier studies, however, demonstrated that NGOs and their officials are not allowed either to understand[9] how financial surveillance is conducted by their banks—"much of what happens is not visible to [our] clients"—and opacity results "from the complex interplay of algorithms, input data and code, coupled with the diffuseness of responsibility along the compliance chain" (Anwar et al., 2022, 17 and 50). As observed by També (2021, 14) too, financial crime advisors at banks prefer not to disclose their internal thresholds and criteria to their customers (potential money launders and terrorist financers), simply "to prevent that organizations and individuals with malicious intent use such information to evade controls". It may be a legitimate explanation offered by compliance officers working at aid or humanitarian organizations too, provided that one disregards the differences between the financial and for-profit sector. Anyhow, if the NGO sector is treated as a specific—suspicious—customer segment by financial organizations (Anwar et al., 2022, 52–56), it can be reasonably assumed that advisors working with legal compliance and screening also apply a 'segmented' approach and potentially treat some of their (data) subjects as 'high-risk' individuals. More research would be needed in this regard to understand the background and consequences of such (potential) decisions.

Screening as countersurveillance? While beneficiary exclusion (as a result of screening) is a bigger concern for humanitarian organizations than for development NGOs (Gillard, 2021a, 2021b; Malakoutikhah, 2020), no aid project is implemented in an apolitical context. While fears for political repression, conflicting organizational interests and limited organizational capacities perceptions of digital illiteracy, are definitely among the explanatory factors for missing transparency around screening, the narrative of counterterrorism and legal instruments used to marginalize political opposition, journalists, civil society leaders, activists or anyone critical of state policies (Amnesty International, 2020; Hayes, 2017; UN SR HR/CT, 2019, 2023a) prompt further explanations.

---

[9] But there are guidelines available for NGOs to help them navigate access to financial services (ECNL, 2022).

Without further evidence, the question emerges if screening can perhaps be considered not only a surveillance (ensuring legal-regulatory compliance) but also a *countersurveillance* measure ensuring the autonomy of aid organizations. Following the logic of the lessons offered by the 'autonomy of migration' literature (Scheel, 2019), screening by aid organizations may also be seen as a means, the purpose of which is to appropriate tools of financial and regulatory control (lists and databases of consolidated lists, procedures and standards). Screening tools, after all, provide access to information precious to organizations under control and surveillance in various contexts.

To counterbalance attempts constraining human rights or targeting their very operational capabilities or reputation, certain NGOs engaged in countersurveillance activities even in Western contexts (Monahan, 2006).[10] Aid organizations, however, are not necessarily best placed—at least not in the case of screening tools—to disable or destroy surveillance practices for the complex set of reasons explaining their involvement in screening. Screening tools, after all, can be used for both purposes: for mitigating risks (in order to comply with laws or other purposes) and mapping the risks an aid NGO or a human rights activist may potentially mean to certain governments.

To understand interests in (counter)surveillance it is necessary to recall that "humanitarian surveillance" can be distinguished from "human rights surveillance" (Topak, 2019). While they share the ambition to "resist the spread of discriminatory and hierarchical surveillance and appropriate surveillance technologies to use them in oppositional ways" (Topak, 2019, 388), human rights surveillance aims at advancing the well-being and rights of marginalized populations in ways similar to practices of actors conducting countersurveillance. Humanitarian surveillance, however, cannot be considered countersurveillance. Rather, it is a parallel form of "surveillance that contributes to surveillance and normalizes the hierarchies between watcher and watched" (Topak, 2019, 388). While further research would be needed to explore this matter, it is highly

---

[10] Monahan (2006) originally discussed this matter in urban contexts and defined counter-surveillance as "intentional, tactical uses, or disruptions of surveillance technologies to challenge institutional power asymmetries". Organizations such as Privacy International and Access Now are at the forefront of anti-surveillance movements fighting for privacy rights.

likely that some aid organizations are simultaneously engaged in humanitarian and human rights surveillance (Topak, 2019) obtaining information on their own 'listing' from the consolidated databases. Charities and humanitarian organizations are obviously interested in obtaining information on their listings (or the listings of some of their board members, staff, advisors, partners, employees) especially considering the abundance of disinformation available on the internet, the purpose of which is to delegitimize them as illustrated by experiences of human rights and aid organizations operating in the Israeli-Palestinian space (Guinane, 2021, 31–34).

Legal compliance combined with pastoral care. Screening is usually framed as a compliance matter serving legal-regulatory, perhaps organizational, purposes. However, regardless of the purposes, thinking around and opaque communication about screening can be characterized by certain patterns typical both in domestic (welfare state) and international (humanitarian, aid) contexts. Acknowledging that depending on the context conceptual differences may apply between labels such as 'paternalistic', 'patronizing' and 'pastoral', each of these terms can be used to describe asymmetries in cases when 'care' or 'expertise' is provided to the powerless by the powerful. While historically the bishops were "the most effective protectors and pacifiers of the mob" while "at the same time they… were able to pose the question of how wealth could be best spent" (Dean, 2010, 98), their contemporary equivalent is the liberal, democratic welfare state (delivering services in exchange for taxes) and private actors offering expert assistance (care, remedies, healing, aid, advice) on for-profit or non-profit basis both inside and outside its borders. By doing so liberalism also offers opportunities "for non-liberal interventions into the lives of those who do not possess the attributes required to play the city-citizen game" (Dean, 2010, 162 and 172) or whose "backbone would otherwise 'collapse under the pressure' caused by the 'privatization of ambivalence'" (Bauman, 1991, 197).

Practices of aid organizations in general, humanitarian organizations in particular fit this logic especially when they use the 'vital interests' of people to justify organizational decisions and actions without consent (Barnett, 2002, 35). The idea and enforcement of universal human rights are usually promoted for securing international peace and stability by the UN, funded by OECD Development Assistance Committee donors, and implemented mostly by Northern aid organizations with or without local partners. While their activities are usually justified by promoting liberal values and human rights, their participation in the governance of poverty and conflict is, in effect, intervention and control wrapped as solidarity and care which serves 'empowerment', 'ownership' or 'local participation' (in case of development projects) or the purpose of mitigating suffering and saving lives (in case of humanitarian projects).

However, much of the (critical) scholarship on empathy, humanitarianism (Chatterjee, 2004; Wilson & Brown, 2009) and care ethics in general "occurred from and through unnamed locatedness in the global North" (Raghuram, 2016, 517). What local understandings of and variations within care and protection mean in the context of humanitarian ethics remain largely unexplored, if not ignored (Pallister-Wilkins, 2021). However, the lessons drawn from the tension between the broad (international, interventionalist) and narrow (local, resilience-based) conceptions of civilian protection in humanitarian contexts (Lidén, 2019) may be informative with regard to screening too, the extent to which local voices (on power, culture, complicity) cannot but remain underexplored, if the matter is not discussed with the concerned individuals.

The ethics and practices of screening would likely be different if screening was not framed simply as a security (risk-mitigation) necessity, a compliance issue (legal-regulatory compliance, after all, is not a matter of choice) or an issue challenging principled humanitarian action (a 'fig leaf' so frequently used to avoid confrontation). If screened subjects (individuals) were provided access to information on the data sources and the content of consolidated databases, they could also be potentially mobilized to resist conditional funding and (legal) demands for screening in the context of counterterrorism policies (politics)—not only in Palestine (BADIL, 2021), but elsewhere too. In other words, the real harm implied in screening perhaps is not simply exclusion from employment opportunities or aid projects (as beneficiaries), but negligence, ignorance and non-inclusion of NGO-subjects in decisions concerning their own lives, the politics of screening and the role aid organizations play in Global South settings. Recalling the mainstream 'Third World' critique of international law (Anghie, 2004; Koskenniemi, 2011; Mutua, 2000) and using Ariella A. Azoulay's provocative argument for illustration, humanitarian practice—or the aid endeavour in general—can also be read as an opportunity for "imperial powers to bestow upon themselves a general amnesty without having to pay for the crimes committed and rights violated during centuries of human trafficking, genocide, forced displacement" (Azoulay, 2017, 467).

Aid work in general, humanitarianism in particular, is part of this logic, which is further strengthened by the practice of screening. Regardless of its universally acceptable norms and principles, the agenda of localization and participation, aid work has, to a large extent, remained 'white', if power is measured by ODA (the bulk of which is provided by the five to ten largest OECD DAC donors) and decisions concerning the critical domains of aid work (evaluation of projects and programmes, deployment of various technologies, etc.). Earlier critical studies already shown how racial and other hierarchies shape everyday aspects of development work even if discussing them in everyday practice is not easy (Kothari, 2006). In similar vein humanitarian practice can also be considered an opportunity simultaneously allowing Europe to reproduce itself as 'ethical' and 'good' with the active participation of aid organization and securing control via the logics of care as argued by Pallister-Wilkins (2021). And the contemporary logic of care is unimaginable without risk-mitigation, screening and surveillance. The embodied control may benefit Global South communities too, but its prime function is to secure trust by mitigating the risks imposed by Global South conditions on white—European/Western—order and stability (Pallister-Wilkins, 2021). Screening as a risk-mitigation measure or 'reasonable effort', after all, implies that specific groups and individuals are "blamed before they have done anything, 'simply by categorizing them, [and] anticipating profiles of risk from previous trends'" (Bigo, 2002 cited by Lyon, 2007, 54), that is, they may be 'blamed' based purely on the information available in the consolidated database. Being screened only once or regularly, certain people are potentially categorized "suspicious" and "hardly innocent until proven guilty" (following Marx, 1988, 227) or as a financial-regulatory risk by default.

Such critique is relevant for screening too given the extent to which entities and individuals in the Global South are routinely—sometimes categorically—securitized in the name of (inter)national security by privileged states and aid organizations. However, while compliance is performed by law-abiding, also to some extent self-governing, aid organizations registered in the Global North, affected populations in the Global South have not been provided the opportunity to shape AML/CFT norms, rules and laws, such as IHL and IHRL, data protection regulations included, on equal terms. Following Madianou (2019), reasonable measures, such as screening, may also make aid organizations "complicit in maintaining a techno-colonial order that benefits already privileged segments" of the global population.

The politics of opacity and transparency in practice. The politics of opacity and transparency. Opacity or secrecy around screening merits at least as much attention as screening itself. While being aware of screening (as bank clients), aid organizations can somehow appropriate such practices and technologies to counterbalance democratic or authoritarian control, regulatory or financial surveillance by diverse means, such as hiring consultants and experts, reading guidelines (ECNL, 2022), sharing ideas and experiences within their network and subscribing to screening tools that provide access to precious information in the consolidated database. The database, therefore, enables the—the simultaneously screened and screening—aid organization to "see, watch and look out", but "not to be seen, watched or looked at" (Amoore, 2007, 222) by the individuals it screens.

Individuals, however, cannot appropriate 'humanitarian or development control', if they are not provided adequate information on screening—in line with, yet regardless of data protection principles. As a result, screening technologies may further alter the power relations between those subject to screening and aid organizations conducting screening by potentially reducing aid organizations' reliance on individual stories and narratives. If individuals and entities "considered violent, corrupt and criminal are neutralized or removed" by various means (Duffield, 2001, 132), among others, screening—understood as a combination of technology and expertise—can also contribute to implementing or resuming 'normal' aid-financed activities serving the interests of privileged (Northern) organizations and populations (Duffield, 2001).

Donor conditionality (mitigating risks by demanding the implementation of reasonable measures) combined with self-regulated, but undercommunicated screening by international aid organizations contributes to social and political control over Global South populations. Therefore, screening as surveillance for security purposes can also be considered a 'compliance tool' of biopolitics that—regardless of the purpose but depending on the less visible consequences—may facilitate global legibility and governability (Dean, 2010; Scott, 1998) the extent to which lists—consolidated in commercially available databases—themselves are interpreted as 'technologies of governance' (Sullivan, 2020, 56). Similarly to other contemporary digital technologies—such as various types and generations of digital ID systems (Martin & Taylor, 2021; Schoemaker et al., 2023); solutions mapping people's needs by extracting their data without their understanding (Madianou, 2019; Sandvik, 2023); various compliance tools (Kuldova, 2022)—sanctions and watchlist screening governs people by enabling aid organizations to sort and categorize them in an experimental manner which is unclear to the concerned people.

Regarding the consequences, just as identification of other states' citizens may entail their deportability in immigration contexts (Franko, 2020), screening (based on identification) may also entail 'deportation' in functional terms. Individuals whose personal data matches data in the databases can be sorted out, that is, excluded from tenders, transactions and contracts, job offers—rightly or falsely—without their awareness, understanding and participation. However, while rejected asylum-seekers and illegal(ized) migrants can somehow appropriate migration control (Scheel, 2019)—a control, which is increasingly justified by humanitarian and human rights arguments in the context of border control too (Perkowiski, 2021)—individuals enjoying the inseparable logic of 'care and control' or 'recognition and surveillance' simply do not have similar room of manoeuvring vis-à-vis aid organizations. Not just because they cannot necessarily afford quitting their jobs, not participating in aid projects or not making contracts with aid organizations, but also because their access to information on how aid organizations operate and how they make decisions is constrained as illustrated by the practice of screening too.

The hypothetical or imagined alternative—from the perspectives of NGO-subjects—is either calling for mutual and symmetric transparency (which is unrealistic considering the power imbalances embedded in the relations between aid organizations and individuals) or resistance to one-sided transparency ('being screened'), provided that they have an informed understanding of what being screened means in practice. As argued by Adams (2020, 89–93) following others, 'resistance to transparency' not only implies various individual techniques (moving away from the use of technology), but also the right to opacity, that is, "the right not to be reduced to, or rendered comprehensible/transparent by the dominant, Western filian-based order" (cited by Adams, 2020, 91). The tension between the right to opacity/secrecy vs. transparency is all the more interesting, because without the former "the subject in a democracy – a liberal democracy committed to transparency – will find herself deprived of that which confers her singularity upon her, where the singularity of the subject constitutes democracy's primary unit" (Birchall, 2011, 18).

Considering that screening is mostly justified as a legal compliance and risk-mitigating measure—making subjects visible and transparent to aid organizations, but not the way around—in order to prevent terrorism finance or other harms, the Palestinian case[11] can be further cited before the concluding remarks. Not only the six Palestinian NGOs mentioned at the beginning of Chapter 2, but also the United Nations Relief and Works Agency for Palestinian Refugees (UNRWA) has been accused of supporting terrorism by Israel, and implicitly also by donors, many of which (temporarily) suspended their funding as a consequence (as of February 2024). Considering its mandate and the number of civilians it serves not only in the Gaza Strip, but also in the West Bank and in the neighbouring countries, UNRWA's case illustrate the trap aid organizations—balancing between international laws, norms and local conditions and rights—face, especially in humanitarian settings (Blackman & Clark, 2024):

> The potential affiliations of a relatively small number of UNRWA staff with organisations like Hamas and Islamic Jihad is illustrative of a risk inherent in most international organisations and must be balanced against the vital work such organisations do providing critical services to vulnerable populations in conflict zones.... however, international organisations also fear that employees with local ties will privilege their political goals over the interests of the organisation. For these reasons, such organisations invest considerable resources in vetting staff and providing training on humanitarian neutrality, especially when they are recruited locally.

---

[11] The unprecedented massacre committed by Hamas-members and affiliated persons against Israeli civilians on October 7, 2023 (see https://www.csis.org/analysis/hamass-october-7-attack-visualizing-data), illustrates the consequences of the competition between transparency and opacity in conflict settings. Secrecy (a self-invoked 'right to opacity') was so crucial that details of the Hamas-operation was not disclosed to (would-be) perpetrators either until the last moment (Burke, 2023; Kingsley & Bergman, 2023; Rubin & Warwick, 2023). This case not only illustrates the devastating consequences of the right to opacity, but also the limited benefits of tight control, surveillance and screening. And while one may point to human errors explaining the failure of the Israeli intelligence (as opposed to technology and expertise), oversecuritization of all spheres of human experience and social relations (Zureik et al., 2011) does not help to create trust needed for (political) recognition and reconciliation, or human condition and life in general.

Although UNRWA has not been among the (mostly non-governmental) organizations interviewed for the sake of research, results of which are presented in this book, it can be reasonably assumed that it has also been screening its employees against various watchlists, precisely to demonstrate compliance and prevent the suspension of donor funding. Looking at its website it uses the heading (title) 'vetting' to communicate some, but not all, components of these processes:

- Any contribution to the Agency must comply with the UNRWA Vetting/Due Diligence Policy, as overseen by the Strategic Partnerships Division and then ultimately the Chief of Staff
- Initial checks of names of any potential suppliers and other payees against the Consolidated UN Sanctions List
- Six-monthly checks of names of all staff, personnel, donating entities, beneficiaries, vendors and suppliers against the Consolidated UN Sanctions List.[12]

Details of UNRWA screening are complex according to the cited page, but no matter how it had been arranged, it did not deliver the expected results: sorting out potential terrorists. UNRWA could have been able to identify and detect the concerned employees (participating in the October 7 attack according to Israel) by screening, *only if* the concerned staff (12 individuals of the roughly 13,000) had been previously listed on the watchlists available in consolidated databases. Obviously, if these individuals had been designated neither by Israeli agencies, perhaps under various UN sanctions regimes, nor by the researcher teams of UNRWA's service provider (the vendor likely delivering the screening tool to UNRWA) in the ADVERSE MEDIA or similar category (see Chapter 4), they could not be 'flagged' as an alert by the screening tools either. But even if they had been listed on a watchlist (mostly likely by Israel or by the vendor), considering that non-governmental organizations, their staff and activists may also be listed (if not by states opposing their work, then by service providers), aid organizations can easily find themselves in a sort of Catch-22 situation.

---

[12] https://www.unrwa.org/vetting.

The alert is alert, which makes the aid organization responsible and legally liable for distinguishing terrorists from human rights defenders—potentially also ordinary people fighting for their rights, such as self-determination—once they had been listed. However, as the quote above illustrates, many aid organizations prefer working, perhaps making transactions with and supporting 'like-minded' local people that are ready to privilege interests, norms and principles of the international aid organization over the 'political goals' prompted by their ethnic, national or religious belonging especially, if the given local community resorts to violence to achieve its goals. The case of UNRWA, which is more Palestinian than international, if measured by the demographic composition of its staff, illustrates the shrinking room of manoeuvring in the shadow of unresolved political conflicts, securitized risk-based thinking, conditional funding and digital solutionism (Berg et al., 2022; Sparks et al., 2024).

Recalling Jacques Derrida (Derrida with Ferraris, 2001, 59 cited by Birchall, 2011, 18), "[i]f a right to the secret is not maintained, we are in a totalitarian space". By maintaining the 'right to secret', Hamas-fighters and affiliated civilians not only committed heinous acts against defenceless civilians in Israel, but at the same time also resisted, apparently in a suicidal manner,[13] to a sophisticated, multilayered complex system of control and surveillance, the maintenance of which is primarily attributed to Israel by the international community and public opinion, but the consequences of which are to be borne on both sides of the conflict.

The current Israeli government may hold the UNRWA or international aid organizations responsible for providing employment opportunities to Palestinian 'terrorists', legal scholars, international courts and aid organizations may criticize and accuse Israel for mindlessly killing thousands of

---

[13] The long history of the Israeli-Palestinian hostage swaps, known not only to Hamas, but the entire Palestinian population, illustrates the «value» attributed to an Israeli citizen (live or dead) as opposed to a Palestinian by earlier Israeli governments (Ganor, 2017). For example, in May 1985 Israel released 1,155 Palestinian and Lebanese prisoners from its jails in exchange for three Israeli soldiers held by the PFLP; in October 2011 Israel freed 1,027 Palestinian prisoners in exchange for a single hostage (the release of soldier Gilad Shalit), see: https://www.aa.com.tr/en/middle-east/top-10-hostage-swap-deals-between-israel-and-palestinians/3063381#.

Palestinian children[14] and making the lives of Palestinian civilians unbearable, but the matrix of control has been maintained collectively with the support of securitized thinking and technologies that—regardless of their violent or non-violent nature—keep locals under control and divides them politically and socially for long years.[15] By doing so certain international actors not only prevented large scale, spectacular violence and revolt (with few exceptions), but have also impeded the Palestinian people's capacities to be 'experts of their own lives' and take political responsibility for the past and their future too. This politically non-harmonized 'division of labour' can be best illustrated by the observation that the Israeli security-military establishment is far more interested in maintaining the UNRWA and allowing humanitarian organizations to do their job than Israeli politicians and people on the radical right-wing end of the political spectrum (Sparks et al., 2024).

[14] According to local and UN statistics around 30,000 people, women and children included, were killed in the Gaza Strip (as of February 2024, for the most recent data see https://www.ochaopt.org/). The Israeli-Palestinian relations cannot of course be reduced to dying children, but it is beyond the scope of this book to discuss how (visible and 'permitted') violence against or the death of 'legitimate' targets (such as men/males) in the name of ideas, such as nationalism, patriotism or (national) security affects the (invisible) survivors (family members, children and women). On the long-term impact of political trauma and its (co)memoration, *see* Edkins (2013) on the instrumentalization of children for humanitarian appeals, see Suski (2009, 212) raising the question of "when we are moved by the suffering of children, we must also ask why we are not similarly moved by the suffering of adults."

[15] UNRWA is not simply and aid organization, but also the symbol of the Palestinian right to return (Berg et al., 2022). On the background, ambivalence and complexity of aid in the Palestinian(-Israeli) context *see* Tartir and Wildeman (2021) and Tartir and Seidel (2019); on donor complicity in Palestine (focusing on the Gaza Strip after the 2014 'war') *see* Murad (2014), on the limits of the applicability of international rules, standardized norms, and principles (such as territorial sovereignty and vertical partition plans) contextualizing aid work in Palestine, *see* Shenhav (2010) and for possible reconciliation *see* local initiatives such as the annual Joint Israeli-Palestinian Memorial Day ceremony organized by Combatants for Peace (https://cfpeace.org/israeli-palestinian-joint-memorial/) and the Parents Circle-Families Forum (https://www.theparentscircle.org/en/pcff-home-page-en/).

Conclusion

If a system is wrong, actors can hardly make right decisions. Screening equally serves and undermines organizational interests and the interests of innocent and/or ignorant subjects of aid organizations too. NGO-subjects—their workplace, salaries livelihood, after all—may also protected by screening the extent to which organizational interests (if not survival) depend on legal-regulatory compliance and legitimate interests to mitigate other risks emerging even in aid contexts. Yet, operations of aid organizations are dependant to a large extent on voluntarism from fundraising to implementing aid projects, no matter how professionalized their activities are. Their credibility depends on how they conform to the public image of solidarity and altruism. While screening may prevent fraud, the misuse of funds and ensure compliance with AML/CFT rules, inconsistent compliance with the transparency obligations (enshrined also in the GDPR) might also undermine trust towards those delivering aid.

If the reputation, credibility or legitimacy of aid organizations is undermined—by screening? or by screening in secret?—not only the care and protection provided to local communities and individuals may be compromised, but they may also lose their legitimacy, and as a result, donations too. Controversies around screening may entail unintended consequences on other human rights too—that may be better fulfilled by aid organizations than by neglient or (semi)authoritarian governments of aid recipient states controlling the given populations. A lot depends on the context. However, if international organizations truly promote values and norms, such as human rights (privacy rights and data protection included), they should do it in a consistent manner. After all, if resourceful aid organizations can consider withdrawal or self-exclusion from aid projects and programmes (by saying 'no' to donors demanding beneficiary screening in humanitarian contexts), should not all individuals be offered the opportunity to be 'experts' of their own lives—to make informed and autonomous decisions whether they want to be screened or not by aid organizations—even if the opportunity itself might entail non-engagement or self-exclusion?

References

Abrahamsen, R., & Leander, A. (Eds.). (2016). *Handbook of Private Military-Security Companies*. Routledge.

Adams, R. (2020). *Transparency. New Trajectories in Law*. Routledge.

Agamben, G. (2005). *State of Exception*. University of Chicago Press.

ALNAP (2022). *The State of the Humanitarian System*. ALNAP Study. London: ALNAP/ODI, https://sohs.alnap.org/2022-the-state-of-thehum anitarian-system-sohs-%E2%80%93-full-report

Amoore, L. (2007). Vigilant Visualities: The Watchful Politics of the war on Terror. *Security Dialogue, 38*(2), 215–232. https://doi.org/10.1177/096 7010607078526

Amicelle, A. (2011). Towards a 'New' Political Anatomy of Financial Surveillance. *Security Dialogue, 42*(2), 161–178. https://doi.org/10.1177/096701 0611401472

Amicelle, A., & Favarel-Garrigues, G. (2012). Financial Surveillance: Who Cares. *Journal of Cultural Economy, 5*(1), 105–124. https://doi.org/10.1080/175 30350.2012.640560

Amnesty International (2020). *AI Report 2020/2021: The State of the World's Human Rights*. Retrieved May 20, 2022, from https://reliefweb.int/sites/ reliefweb.int/files/resources/POL1032022021ENGLISH.PDF

Anghie, A. (2004). *Imperialism*. Cambridge University Press.

Anwar, T., Wesseling, M., & Soares, R. R. (2022). *New Tech, Perpetual Challenges. How Emerging Technologies for Financial Compliance Are Impacting the Nonprofit Sector*. European Center for Not-for-Profit Law. Retrieved October 15, 2023, from https://ecnl.org/sites/default/files/2022-09/ECNL%20F INTECH%20Report.pdf

Arora, P. (2019). Decolonizing Privacy Studies. *Television & New Media, 20*(4), 366–378.

Arner, D. W., Barberis, J. N., & Buckley, R. P. (Eds.) (2019). *The REGTECH Book: The Financial Technology Handbook for Investors. Entrepreneurs and Visionaries in Regulation*. (ISBN: 978-1-119-36217-3). Wiley and Sons

AWSD (Aid Workers Security Database). (2022). *Aid Worker Security Report. Figures at Glance*. Retrieved October 22, 2023, from https://www.aidworker security.org/reports

Azoulay, A. A. (2017). *Potential History: Unlearning Imperialism*. Verso Books.

BADIL. (2021). *European Union Conditional Funding: Its Illegality and Political Implications* (BADIL Position Paper). Retrieved November 18, 2022, from https://www.badil.org/cached_uploads/view/2021/04/20/eur opeanunionconditionalfunding-positionpaper-april2020-1618905422.pdf

Barnett, M. (2002). *Empire of Humanity*. Cornell University Press.

Barnett, M. N. (2013). Humanitarian Governance. *Annual Review of Political Science, 16*(1), 379–398. https://doi.org/10.1146/annurev-polisci-012512-083711

Bauman, Z. (1991). *Modernity and Ambivalence*. Polity Press.

Bennett, C. J. (2018). The European General Data Protection Regulation: An Instrument for the Globalization of Privacy Standards? *Information Polity, 23*(2), 239–246. https://doi.org/10.3233/IP-180002

Berg, K. G., Jensehaugen, J., & Tiltnes, A. A. (2022). *UNRWA, Funding Crisis and the Way Forward* (CMI Report R 2022:04). Chr. Michelsen Institute. https://www.cmi.no/publications/8574-unrwa-funding-crisis-and-the-way-forward

Biddle, S. (2023). LexisNexis Is Selling Your Personal Data to Ice So It Can Try to Predict Crimes. *The Intercept.* https://theintercept.com/2023/06/20/lexisnexis-ice-surveillance-license-plates/

Bigo, D. (2002). *Terrorisme, Guerre, Sécurité Intérieure Et Sécurité Extérieure.* Thèse d'habilitation en sciences politiques. Paris: Sciences Po.

Birchall, C. (2011). Introduction to 'Secrecy and Transparency': The Politics of Opacity and Openness. *Theory, Culture & Society, 28*(7–8), 7–25. https://doi.org/10.1177/0263276411427744

Blackman, A., & Clark, R. (2024, February 14). UNRWA Fears Are a Normal Trade-Off in International Aid. Funding Must Resume Now. Opinion. *The New Humanitarian.* https://www.thenewhumanitarian.org/opinion/2024/02/14/unrwa-fears-normal-international-aid-funding-must-resume-now

Burke, J. (2023). A Deadly Cascade: How Secret Hamas Attack Orders Were Passed Down at Last Minute. *The Guardian.* https://www.theguardian.com/world/2023/nov/07/secret-hamas-attack-orders-israel-gaza-7-october

Chatterjee, D. K. (Ed.). (2004). *The Ethics of Assistance. The Ethics of Assistance. The Ethics of Assistance. Morality and the Distant Needy.* Cambridge University Press.

Christensen, D., & Weinstein, J. (2013). Defunding Dissent: Restrictions on Aid to NGOs. *Journal of Democracy, 42*(2), 77–91. https://www.journalofdemocracy.org/articles/defunding-dissent-restrictions-on-aid-to-ngos/

Christensen, Z., Nielsen, R., Nielson, D., & Tierney, M. (2011). *Transparency Squared: The Effects of Donor Transparency on Recipient Corruption Levels.* Paper Prepared for Application to Participate in the 4th Annual Conference on the Political Economy of International Organizations for 2011. Retrieved April 15, 2022, from https://www.peio.me/wp-content/uploads/2014/04/Conf4_Christensen-Nielsen-Nielson-Tierney-01.10.2010.pdf

Dean, M. (1999/2010). *Governmentality: Power and Rule in Modern Society.* (2nd ed). SAGE.

Duffield, M. (2001). *Global governance and the new wars: the merging of development and security.* Zed Books

Duffield, M. (2016). The Resilience of the Ruins: Towards a Critique of Digital Humanitarianism. *Resilience, 4*(3), 147–165. https://doi.org/10.1080/21693293.2016.1153772

Duroch, F., & Neuman, M. (2021). *Should We Discriminate in Order to Act? Profiling: A Necessary but Debated Practice*. HPN paper. Retrieved April 8, 2022, from https://odihpn.org/publication/should-we-discriminate-in-order-to-act-profiling-a-necessary-but-debated-practice/

DelGrande, J. (2022). LexisNexis and I.C.E: An Examination of LexisNexis's Human Rights Responsibilities. *Journal of International Law and Politics*, *54*(23), 70–84, https://www.nyujilp.org/wp-content/uploads/2022/02/5-LexisNexis-and-ICE.pdf

Eckert, S. (2022). Counterterrorism, Sanctions and Financial Access Challenges: Course Corrections to Safeguard Humanitarian Action. *International Review of the Red Cross*, *103*(916–917), 415–458. https://international-review.icrc.org/articles/counterterrorism-sanctions-and-financial-access-challenges-916#footnote81_27rk033

ECNL. (2022). *Navigating Access to Financial Services for CSOs. A Practical Guidance*. ECNL. https://ecnl.org/publications/navigating-access-financial-services-csos

Edkins, J. (2003/2013). *Memory and the Politics of Trauma*. Cambridge University Press.

Egeland, J., Harmer, A., & Stoddard, A. (2011). *To Stay and Deliver: Good Practice for Humanitarians in Complex Security Environments*. UN Office for the Coordination of Humanitarian Affairs (UNOCHA), Policy Development and Studies Bureau. Retrieved October 14, 2023, from https://www.refworld.org/pdfid/4d9039e32.pdf

El Taraboulsi-McCarthy, S. (2018). *A Humanitarian Sector in Debt. Counter-Terrorism, Bank De-Risking and Financial Access for NGOs in the West Bank and Gaza*. Overseas Development Institute (ODI, UK). https://odi.org/en/publications/a-humanitarian-sector-in-debt-counter-terrorism-bank-de-risking-and-financial-access-for-ngos-in-the-west-bank-and-gaza/

Farah, R. (2010). UNRWA: Through the Eyes of Its Refugee Employees in Jordan. *Refugee Survey Quarterly*, *28*(2–3), 389–411. https://doi.org/10.1093/rsq/hdp046

Fassin, D. (2007). Humanitarianism as a Politics of Life. *Public Culture*, *19*(3), 499–520. https://doi.org/10.1215/08992363-2007-007

Fast, L., & Jacobsen, K. L. (2019). Rethinking Access: How Humanitarian Technology Blurs Control and Care. *Disasters*, *43*(S2), S151–S168. https://doi.org/10.1111/disa.12333

FATF (Financial Action Task Force). (2001). *Special Recommendation VIII (SR VIII)—Recommendation 8 (Measures to Prevent the Misuse of Non-Profit Organisations)*. For the current version see FATF (2015).

FATF (Financial Action Task Force). (2014). *Risk of Terrorist Abuse in Non-Profit Organisations*. Retrieved June 13, 2021, from https://www.fatf-gafi.org/media/fatf/documents/reports/Risk-of-terrorist-abuse-in-non-profit-organisations.pdf

FATF (Financial Action Task Force). (2015). *Best Practices Paper on Combating the Abuse of NonProfit Organisations*. FATF Recommendation 8. Retrieved April 8, 2022, from https://www.fatf-gafi.org/en/publications/Financialinc lusionandnpoissues/Bpp-combating-abuse-npo.html

FATF (Financial Action Task Force). (2016). *Guidance for a Risk-Based Approach: Money or Value Transfer Services*. Retrieved October 23, 2022, from https://www.fatf-gafi.org/publications/fatfrecommendations/docume nts/rba-money-or-value-transfer.html

Fechter, A.-M. (Ed.). (2014). *The Personal and the Professional in Aid Work*. Routledge.

Fejerskov, A. M., Clausen, M.-L., & Seddig, S. (2023). Humanitarian Ignorance: Towards a New Paradigm of Non-knowledge in Digital Humanitarianism. *Disasters*. Accepted Author Manuscript. https://doi.org/10.1111/disa.12609

Franko, K. (2020). *The Crimmigrant Other—Migration and Penal Power*. Routledge.

Ganor, B. (2017). Israel's Policy in Extortionist Terror Attacks (Abduction and Hostage Barricade Situations). *Perspectives on Terrorism, 11*(4), 2–15.

Gillard, E. (2021a). *IHL and the Humanitarian Impact of Counterterrorism Measures and Sanctions. Unintended Ill Effects of Well-Intended Measures*. Chatham House Report. Retrieved April 28, 2022, from https://www.cha thamhouse.org/2021/09/ihl-and-humanitarian-impact-counterterrorism-measures-and-sanctions/04-funding-agreements

Gillard, E. (2021b). Screening of Final Beneficiaries—A Red Line in Humanitarian Operations. An Emerging Concern in Development Work. *International Review of the Red Cross, 103*(916–917), 517–537. https://int ernational-review.icrc.org/articles/screening-of-final-beneficiaries-a-red-line-in-humanitarian-operations-916

Groupe URD. (2009). *Participation Handbook for Humanitarian Field Workers*. https://www.urd.org/en/publication/participation-handbook-for-humanitarian-field-workers/

Guinane, K. (2021). *The Alarming Rise of Lawfare to Surppress Civil Society: The Case of Palestine and Israel*. The Charity & Security Network. Retrieved September 15, 2023, from https://charityandsecurity.org/csn-reports/the-alarming-rise-of-lawfare-to-suppress-civil-society-the-case-of-palestine-and-isr ael/

Harris, R. W. (2016). How ICT4D Research Fails the Poor. *Information Technology for Development, 22*(1), 177–192. https://doi.org/10.1080/026 81102.2015.1018115

Hayes, B. (2012). Counter-Terrorism, "Policy Laundering," and the FATF: Legalizing Surveillance, Regulating Civil Society. *The International Journal*

of Not-for-Profit Law, 12(1–2), 1–40. https://www.icnl.org/resources/res
earch/ijnl/1-introduction-2

Hayes, B. (2017). *The Impact of International Counter-Terrorism on Civil Society Organisations: Understanding the Role of the Financial Action Task Force.* Bread for the World. Retrieved May 8, 2022, from http://efc.issuelab.org/resources/27481/27481.pdf

Heathershaw, J. (2016). Who Are the 'International Community'? Development Professionals and Liminal Subjectivity. *Journal of Intervention and Statebuilding, 10*(1), 77–96. https://doi.org/10.1080/17502977.2015.113 7395

Horn, E. (2011). Logics of Political Secrecy. *Theory, Culture & Society, 28*(7–8), 103–122. https://doi.org/10.1177/0263276411424583

Howell, J. (2014). The Securitisation of INGOs Post-9/11. *Conflict, Security and Development, 14*(2), 151–179. https://doi.org/10.1080/14678802.2014.903692

Howell, J., & Lind, J. (2009). *Counter-Terrorism, Aid and Civil Society: Before and After the War on Terror.* Palgrave Macmillan

Huysmans, J., & Squire, V. (2009). Migration and Security. In M. D. Cavelty & V. Mauer (Eds.), *Handbook of Security Studies* (pp. 169–179). Routledge.

ICNL-FATF (International Center for Not-for-Profit Law-Financial Action Task Force). (2019). *How to Anticipate and Respond to This and Other Unfounded Arguments About Non-Profit Organizations and FATF Standards.* ICNL. https://www.icnl.org/wp-content/uploads/Arguments-and-Counterarguments-Final-09.26.19-update.pdf

Jackson, P., ed. (2015). *Handbook of International Security and Development.* London: Routledge.

Jacobsen, K. L. (2015). *The Politics of Humanitarian Technology: Good Intentions.* Routledge.

Jacobsen, K. L. (2022). Biometric Data Flows and Unintended Consequences of Counterterrorism. *International Review of the Red Cross, 103*(916–917), 619–652. https://international-review.icrc.org/articles/biometric-data-flows-and-unintended-consequences-of-counterterrorism-916#footnoteref11_x fz9ws8

Jordan, L., & Van Tujil, P. (2006). *NGO Accountability. Politics, Principles and Innovations.* Earthscan.

Kalfeis, M., & Knodel, K. (2021). *NGOs and Lifeworlds in Africa. Transdisciplinary Perspectives.* Berghahn Books.

Kaminski, M. E. (2019). The Right to Explanation, Explained. *Berkeley Technology Law Journal, 34*(1), 189–218. https://doi.org/10.2139/ssrn.319 6985

Kamruzzaman, P. (2017). Understanding the Role of National Development Experts in Development Ethnography. *Development Policy Review, 35*(1), 39–63. https://doi.org/10.1111/dpr.12200

Kingsley, P., & Bergman, R. (2023). The Secrets Hamas Knew About Israel's Military. *The New York Times.* https://www.nytimes.com/2023/10/13/world/middleeast/hamas-israel-attack-gaza.html

Koskenniemi, M. (2011). *The Politics of International Law.* Hart Publishing.

Kothari, U. (2006). An Agenda for Thinking About 'Race' in Development. *Progress in Development Studies, 6*(1), 9–23. https://doi.org/10.1191/1464993406ps124oa

Kuldova, T. Ø. (2022). *Compliance-Industrial Complex The Operating System of a Pre-Crime Society.* Palgrave MacMillan

Lamarche, K. (2019). The Backlash Against Israeli Human Rights INGOs: Grounds, Players and Implications. *International Journal of Politics, Culture and Society, 32*(3), 301–322. https://doi.org/10.1007/s10767-018-9312-z

Lazell, M., & Petrikova. I. (2020). Is Development Aid Securitized? Evidence from a Cross-Country Examination of Aid Commitment. *Development Policy Review, 38*(3), 323–343. https://doi.org/10.1111/dpr.12426

Lemberg-Pedersen, M., & Haioty, E. (2020). Re-assembling the Surveillable Refugee Body in the Era of Data-Craving. *Citizenship Studies, 24*(5), 607–624. https://doi.org/10.1080/13621025.2020.1784641

Lidén, K. (2019). The Protection of Civilians and Ethics of Humanitarian Governance: Beyond Intervention and Resilience. *Disasters, 43*(S2), 210–229.

Lyon, D. (2007). *Surveillance Studies: An Overview.* Polity Press.

Madianou, M. (2019). Technocolonialism: Digital Innovation and Data Practices in the Humanitarian Response to Refugee Crises. *Social Media + Society, 5*(3), 1–13. https://doi.org/10.1177/2056305119863146

Malakoutikhah, Z. (2020). Financial Exclusion as a Consequence of Counter-Terrorism Financing. *Journal of Financial Crime, 27*(2), 663–682. https://doi.org/10.1108/JFC-09-2019-0121

Malkin, N. (2015). My Brother's Keeper: The Double Experience of Refugee Aid-Workers. *Journal of Peacebuilding and Development, 10*(3), 46–59.

Martin, A., & Taylor, L. (2021). Exclusion and Inclusion in Identification: Regulation, Displacement and Data Justice. *Information Technology for Development, 27*(1), 50–66. https://doi.org/10.1080/02681102.2020.1811943

Marx, G. T. (1988). *Undercover: Police Surveillance in America.* LA: University of California Press.

McGee, R. (2013). Aid Transparency and Accountability: 'Build It and They'll Come'? *Development Policy Review, 31*, s107–s124. https://doi.org/10.1111/dpr.12022

Minella, C. M. (2019). Counter-Terrorism Resolutions and Listing of Terrorists and Their Organizations by the United Nations. In E. Shor, &

S. Hoadley (Eds.), *International Human Rights and Counter-Terrorism.* Springer (pp. 31–53).

Monahan, T. (2006). *Counter-Surveillance as Political Intervention? Social Semiotics, 16*(4), 515–534. https://doi.org/10.1080/10350330601019769

Mosse, D. (2011). *Adventures in Aidland: The Anthropology of Professionals in International Development.* Berghahn.

MSF (Médecins Sans Frontières). (2023). *Who We Are.* https://www.msf.org/who-we-are

Muhomed, S., Puri, J., Stickler, H., & Sugand, D. (2021). *NGOs' Due Diligence and Risk Mitigation: A Holistic Approach.* London School of Economics and Political Science and The Charity and Security Network. Retrieved September 13, 2023, from https://charityandsecurity.org/wp-content/uploads/2021/04/NGOs-Due-Diligence-and-Risk-Mitigation.pdf

Murad, N. (2014). *Donor Complicity in Israel's Violations of Palestinian Rights* (Al-Shabaka Policy Brief). https://al-shabaka.org/wp-content/uploads/2014/10/Murad_PolicyBrief_En_Oct_2014.pdf

Mutua, M. W. (2000). What Is TWAIL? *Proceedings of the ASIL Annual Meeting, 94*(31), 31–38. https://digitalcommons.law.buffalo.edu/journal_articles/560/

Nagy, V. (2017). How to Silence the Lambs? Constructing Authoritarian Governance in Post-Transitional Hungary. *Surveillance & Society, 15*(3–4), 447–455. https://doi.org/10.24908/ss.v15i3/4.6642

NRC (Norwegian Refugee Council) (2018a). *Principles Under Pressure: the Impact of Counterterrorism Measures and Preventing/Countering Violent Extremism on Principled Humanitarian Action.* Retrieved March 13, 2021, from https://reliefweb.int/sites/reliefweb.int/files/resources/nrc-principles_under_pressure-report-screen.pdf

NRC (Norwegian Refugee Council) (2018b). *Understanding Conditional Clauses.* Retrieved March 13, 2021, from https://www.nrc.no/shorthand/stories/understanding-counterterrorism-clauses/index.html and https://www.nrc.no/globalassets/pdf/reports/toolkit/nrc_toolkit_03_reviewing-counterterrorism-clauses.pdf

NRC. (2023). *Working at NRC.* https://www.nrc.no/careers/

OECD (Organisation for Economic Co-operation and Development). (2008). *The Paris Declaration on Aid Effectiveness and the Accra Agenda for Action.* https://www.oecd.org/dac/effectiveness/34428351.pdf

O'Leary, E. (2021) Politics and principles: The impact of counterterrorism measures and sanctions on principled humanitarian action. *International Review of the Red Cross 103*(916–917), 459–477. https://doi.org/10.1017/S1816383121000357

Pallister-Wilkins, P. (2021). Saving the Souls of White Folk: Humanitarianism as White Supremacy. *Security Dialogue, 52*(1_suppl), 98–106.

Paragi, B. (2024). The Art of Screening: Reasonable Efforts and Measures at the Nexus of Aid Work and Counterterrorism. *Surveillance & Society, 22*(2), 138–159.

Pascucci, E. (2019). The Local Labour Building the International Community: Precarious Work Within Humanitarian Spaces. *Environment and Planning A: Economy and Space, 51*(3), 743–760. https://doi.org/10.1177/0308518X18803366

Perkowiski, N. (2021). *Humanitarianism, Human Rights and Security. The Case of Frontex.* Routledge.

Qureshi, S. (2019). Perspectives on development: why does studying information and communication technology for development (ICT4D) matter? *Information Technology for Development, 25*(3), 381–389. https://doi.org/10.1080/02681102.2019.1658478

Raghuram, P. (2016). Locating Care Ethics Beyond the Global North. *ACME: An International Journal for Critical Geographies, 15*(3), 511–533. https://acme-journal.org/index.php/acme/article/view/1353

Rébé, N. (2020). *Counter-Terrorism Financing: International Best Practices and the Law.* Brill

Romaniuk, S. (2022). *Under Siege. Counterterrorism and Civil Society in Hungary.* Lexington Books.

Rose, N. (1999). *Powers of Freedom.* Cambridge University Press.

Rubin, S., & Warwick, J. (2023, November 12). Hamas Envisioned Deeper Attacks, Aiming to Provoke an Israeli War. *The Washington Post.* https://www.washingtonpost.com/national-security/2023/11/12/hamas-planning-terror-gaza-israel/

Sakue-Collins, Y. (2021). (Un)doing Development: A Postcolonial Enquiry of the Agenda and Agency of NGOs in Africa. *Third World Quarterly, 42*(5), 976–995. https://doi.org/10.1080/01436597.2020.1791698

Sandvik, K. B. (2023). *Humanitarian Extractivism.* Manchester University Press.

Sandvik, K. B., Jacobsen, K. L., & McDonald, S. M. (2017). Do Not Harm: A Taxonomy of the Challenges of Humanitarian Experimentation. *International Review of the Red Cross, 99*(1), 319–344. https://doi.org/10.1017/S18163 8311700042X

Sandvik, K., Gabrielsen Jumbert, M., Karlsrud, J., & Kaufmann, M. (2014). Humanitarian Technology: A Critical Research Agenda. *International Review of the Red Cross, 96*(893), 219–242. https://doi.org/10.1017/S18163831 14000344

Scheel, S. (2019). *Autonomy of Migration? Appropriating Mobility Within Biometric Border Regimes.* Routledge.

Schoemaker, E., Martin, A., & Weitzberg, K. (2023). Digital Identity and Inclusion: Tracing Technological Transitions. *Georgetown Journal of International Affairs, 24*(1), 36–45. https://doi.org/10.1353/gia.2023.a897699

Schudson, M. (2018). *The Rise of the Right to Know. Politics and the Culture of Transparency, 1945–1975*. Harvard University Press.

Scott, J. C. (1998). *Seeing Like a State*. Yale University Press.

Shabibi, N., & Bryant, B. (2016). *VICE News Reveals the Terrorism Blacklist Secretly Wielding Power over the Lives of Millions*. VICE News. Retrieved January 20, 2022, from https://www.vice.com/en/article/pa4mgz/vice-news-reveals-the-terrorism-blacklist-secretly-wielding-power-over-the-lives-of-millions

Shenhav, Y. (2010). *Beyond the Two-State Solution*. Polity Press.

Slim, H. (2021). *Solferino 21. Warfare, Civilians and Humanitarians in the Twenty-Century*. Hurst.

Sparks, R., Harb, H., & Abdel Hamid, O. N. (2024, March 6). Gaza in-Depth: Why Israel Wants to End UNRWA and What Its Closure Would Mean. *The New Humanitarian*. https://www.thenewhumanitarian.org/analysis/2024/03/06/gaza-depth-why-israel-wants-end-unrwa-and-what-its-closure-would-mean

Sullivan, G. (2020). *The Law of the List. UN Counterterrorism Sanctions and the Politics of Global Security Law*. Cambridge University Press.

També, N. (2021). *Unintended Consequences of AML/CFT Regulation: The Challenges of Banking Non-profit Organisations*. European Center for Not-for-Profit Law. Retrieved September 1, 2023, from https://ecnl.org/publications/unintended-consequences-amlcft-regulation-challenges-banking-non-profit-organisations

Tartir, A., & Seidel, T. (Eds.). (2019). *Palestine and Rule of Power: Local Dissent vs. International Governance*. Palgrave Macmillan.

Tartir, A., & Wildeman, J. (2021). Political Economy of Foreign Aid in the Occupied Palestinian Territories: A Conceptual Framing. In A. Tartir, T. Dana, & J. Wildeman (Eds.), *Political Economy of Palestine: Critical, Inter-disciplinary and Decolonial Perspectives* (pp. 223–247). Palgrave Macmillan.

Topak, Ö. E. (2019). Humanitarian and Human Rights Surveillance: The Challenge to Border Surveillance and Invisibility? *Surveillance & Society, 17*(3–4), 382–404. https://doi.org/10.1093/ips/olz014

Tzanou, M. (2017). *The Fundamental Right to Data Protection: Normative Value in the Context of Counter-Terrorism Surveillance*. Hart Publishing.

UN SR HR/CT. (2019). *Impact of measures to address terrorism and violent extremism on civic space and the rights of civil society actors and human rights defenders*. Report of the Special Rapporteur on the Promotion and Protection of Human Rights and Fundamental Freedoms while Countering Terrorism, A/HRC/40/52. Geneva: UN Human Rights Council. Retrieved June 8, 2022, from https://documents-dds-ny.un.org/doc/UNDOC/GEN/G19/057/59/PDF/G1905759.pdf?OpenElement

UN SR HR/CT. (2023a). *Global study on the impact of counter-terrorism on civil society and civic space. Geneva: UN Human Rights Council. Retrieved August 8, 2023,* https://defendcivicspace.com/wp-content/uploads/2023/06/SRCT_GlobalStudy.pdf

UN SR HR/CT. (2023b). *Report to the Human Rights Council on the development, use, and transfer of new technologies in the counter-terrorism and P/CVE context. A/HRC/52/39.* https://www.ohchr.org/en/special-proced ures/sr-terrorism/annual-reportshuman-rights-council-and-general-assembly

Vaughn, J. (2009). The Unlikely Securitizer: Humanitarian Organizations and the Securitization of Indistinctiveness. *Security Dialogue, 40*(3), 263–285. https://doi.org/10.1177/0967010609336194

VOICE (Voluntary Organisations in Cooperation in Emergencies). (2021). *Adding to the Evidence the Impacts of Sanctions and Restrictive Measures on Humanitarian Action.* VOICE Survey Report. Retrieved January 20, 2022, from https://voiceeu.org/search?q=adding+to+the+evidence

Vrabec, H. U. (2021). The Right to Information. In *Data Subject Rights Under the GDPR* (Oxford Academic, Online ed., pp. 64–101). Oxford University Press. https://doi.org/10.1093/oso/9780198868422.003.0004

Watson, S. and Burles, R. (2018). Regulating NGO funding: securitizing the political. *International Relations, 32*(4), 430–448. https://doi.org/10.1177/0047117818782604

Walsham, G. (2017) ICT4D research: reflections on history and future agenda. *Information Technology for Development, 23*(1), 18–41. https://doi.org/10.1080/02681102.2016.1246406

Wilson, R. A., & Brown, R. D. (Eds.). (2009). *Humanitarianism and Suffering: The Mobilization of Empathy.* Cambridge University Press.

Wright, G. (2011). NGOs and Western Hegemony: Causes for Concern and Ideas for Change. *Development in Practice, 22*(1), 124–134. https://doi.org/10.1080/09614524.2012.634230

Zureik, E., Lyon, D., & Abu-Laban, Y. (Eds.). (2011). *Surveillance and Control in Israel/Palestine. Population, Territory and Power.* Routledge.

CHAPTER 6

Conclusion

Abstract The concluding chapter summarizes the main arguments of the book by reflecting on how power works regardless of political regimes. The logic implied in the chain of security explains how NGOs become links in the chain regardless of their critique concerning screening. This analysis reveals that conceptualizing screening as a data processing operation is a useful means to analyse this practice in the context of surveillance studies. The conclusion ends with a brief reflection on the limits of this research and suggestions on further research directions.

Keywords Aid organizations · Screening · Transparency/opacity · Nature of power · Chain of security

This book, hopefully, contributed to earlier research by conceptualizing screening as a data processing operation on the one hand and a surveillance tool on the other hand. The data protection dimension of screening has been combined with insights from surveillance studies to demonstrate how aid organizations—themselves potentially subject to governmental and financial surveillance—mitigate the risks of their (Northern) generosity by screening their subjects (mostly, but not exclusively in the Global South). The admitted purpose is legal compliance and legitimate interests to mitigate real or imagined risks in various contexts.

B. Paragi, *Screening by International Aid Organizations Operating in the Global South*, https://doi.org/10.1007/978-3-031-54165-0_6

The reality, however, implies balancing between the interests of larger OECD DAC donors (demanding reasonable efforts and transparency in the context of counterterrorism), organizational interests and people in the Global South that are victims of an unequal world characterized by rights and entitlements determined upon birth by chance: citizenship.

As screening is implemented by using personal data, it is a data processing operation. Aid organizations subscribing to screening technologies may use personal information to run any search in the database and the search also yields a file containing further personal data (in case of positive and false positive hits). The results may be used to identify and distinguish 'innocent' individuals from 'suspicious' ones whom the organizations do not intend to interact with. However, unlike in the case of medical screening, watchlist-screening can be used as a source of information neither for further 'diagnosing', nor 'curing' political or other 'diseases' for various reasons. Its sole purpose is risk mitigation from the perspective of the aid organizations.

Publicly available privacy notices of EU/EEA registered NGOs, usually addressed to European (Western) audiences, however, almost never contain meaningful information on screening. Acknowledging that the sample was not representative, informal discussions with aid organizations revealed that information on screening is either not provided or provided only briefly and orally to individuals. The depth of the information shared depends on the circumstances of the relationship between the organization and the person, mostly on the 'seriousness' of the position or role taken by the individuals in legal terms. In other words, decisions concerning screening—from the question of whom to screen to that of how to notify people—are made by experts, without the proper inclusion of the concerned individuals. However, 'screening in secret'—if no or very little information is shared with the data subjects—is at odds with the fairness and transparency principles guiding most data protection laws regardless of the outcome. Even if exclusion from aid projects is not of very high probability, if screening is not a common knowledge, the principle of transparency (fairness, lawfulness) and data subjects' right to information are equally affected, if not violated. Aid organizations are best placed to understand this matter as many of them suffer the consequences of bank de-risking (Anwar et al., 2022) that they themselves try to appropriate, if not resist (ECNL, 2022).

Screening as a form of surveillance is about sorting out those that might pose a risk before a contract is signed and for as long as the legal relationship lasts. Screening against sanctions, terrorist and enforcement lists is justified because of the high prevalence of financially suspicious transactions which may lead to terrorism financing or financial crimes. It may be conducted by following legal obligations prescribed by law, funding agreements, or alternative organizational interests. However, it is the lack of proper notification and discussion about this practice which facilitated the analysis of screening as surveillance. While Chapter 4 introduced the practices and the realities of screening by NGOs, the discussion in Chapter 5 focused more on the underlying effects of screening in the context of North–South relations.

Access to information by making search in screening databases may equally mean opportunities and risks as long as aid organizations are potentially required or expected to share this data (or lists) in various ways with third parties, let the latter mean commercial service providers, US governmental agencies or authoritarian governments in the Global South. As implied, screening and its communication are delicate issues not only because of the reasonable expectations and human rights of data subjects but also because data transfers further politicize (humanitarian) assistance. This likely explains why this practice is rarely discussed with or disclosed (in opaque ways) to concerned individuals.

However, by not providing (clear, specific) information on their efforts and measures to individuals that are considered risky by default, aid organizations control the discursive space. By doing so, they further consolidate images and hierarchies of generosity and gratitude between the watchers and the watched. The 'watched', playing the role of the grateful, cannot but remain ignorant, that is, not well positioned enough to raise questions and hold aid organizations accountable. The problem of course is not simply screening in terms of legal compliance or technology (Kuldova, 2022) and vague communication around it, but the content of the consolidated lists, the purposes for which they are used and the ways how screening is conducted in practice. Yet, no matter how distrustful aid organizations themselves are, as long as they sign funding agreements with conditional clauses and subscribe to controversial tools without discussing this matter with the individuals screened, they strengthen the legitimacy of the security chain that binds them and their beneficiaries too. Recalling Anwar et al. (2022, 10)

> [if] public confidence in the technology used in the financial sector [against NGOs among others] is critical to a well-functioning society, [a] lack of

confidence in these technologies could result in a loss of confidence in the financial system.

Or, inferring from the above, lack of information on and confidence in screening tools used by aid organizations may entail loss of confidence in the civil sector too. While screening makes aid organizations more accountable towards their donors—the very same actors that can be detected behind international CFT/AML instruments—it potentially undermines the trust between them and the individuals they work with. Obviously, aid organizations do not want to be accused of breaching laws or contributing to conflict by channelling money to sexual offenders or 'risky' individuals that may be associated with terrorist organizations. Therefore, people as data subjects—employees, consultants, transaction partners, potentially even beneficiaries—are usually treated with 'categorical suspicion'. It implies that the right to be recognized, supported, assisted and employed—either in a humanitarian or a development context—depends on how aid and humanitarian organizations categorize and classify individuals *before screening* and how they make decisions *after* it, based on the results of screening. Both would require further research.

As demonstrated by the findings, aid and humanitarian organization not only seem to 'overapply' legal and donor requirements in the context of AML/CFT compliance, but also under-communicate screening both internally and externally (publicly). The risk-based approach—originally characterizing financial surveillance—is problematic in the case of HOs as principled humanitarian action "contributes to organizational security by alleviating two common reasons for security incidents: mistaken identity and misperceptions regarding the roles and motivations of humanitarian organizations. However, if they cannot be distinguished from political and military [security or counterterrorism] actors, the claim that they merit special treatment disintegrates" (Vaughn, 2009, 270). This argument can be extended to other aid organizations from beneficiary perspectives, inasmuch as seeing only the 'aid' or 'charity' dimension they cannot necessarily distinguish humanitarian organizations from development organizations.

Reflecting on the limits of this research, it was neither based on proper ethnographic research conducted at headquarters of aid organizations, nor could it offer an in-depth legal analysis. Both would have required access to internal documents and procedures, policies and practices of aid organizations to explore questions, such as how aid organizations and their compliance officers make decisions, what hierarchies apply when individuals are selected for screening, what are the consequences of alerts, how the fact and results of screening are communicated with various categories of data subjects, how they document screening (as a data processing activity) in light of the rule (GDPR and related national legislation) or their own due diligence procedures, what kind of risks they see internally. As access (in the form of ethnographic research) was not an option, these questions are yet to be answered. The data gathered for the sake of this research were necessary to determine if screening is a data processing operation (it is), but data was not sufficient to analyse and conclude if EU/EEA-registered NGOs comply with the transparency obligations of GDPR. Any solid conclusion with regard to (non-)compliance with the transparency provisions of the GDPR would require the inclusion of specific laws in national jurisdictions (to see if they allow restrictions) and domestic laws in aid recipient countries in the analysis. Therefore, aid NGOs need to consider the national legislation of the countries they are registered in to see if any exemption or restriction may apply in the given jurisdiction with regard to the transparency obligation.

Transparency, however, is more than a legal principle. As EU/EEA-based NGOs and international aid organizations have the power to make both distinctions (between them to be screened and not to be screened) and decisions (based on the information they access in the database), they carry certain moral responsibly for such sorting even beyond the narrow legal domain. The potentially differential treatment of data subjects—depending primarily on organizational perceptions of individuals' digital comprehension and the nature of the legal relationship between the individuals and the organizations—raises questions to be explored in the future.

While further research would be needed to map the reasons for the lack of transparency, further limits of the methods used in this study should be acknowledged. Interviews and discussions provided valuable but limited access to information considering the fact that neither vendors within the surveillance industry (Lauterbach, 2017), nor legal advisors, DPOs, or compliance officers working at NGOs are interested in or authorized to disclose details of internal decisions for independent academic research. Confidentiality among business partners, reputational hazards and loyalty between the employer and the employee are among the factors that prevent honest discussions outside the (in)formal circles of practitioners and consultants.

Regardless of the limitations, there is a certain irony in the fact that while most civil society organizations praise the values of transparency and privacy (protection) as opposed to surveillance practices (Lyon, 2007, 169–171), considerable opacity prevails around screening. Conducting AML/CFT-related surveillance on the one hand and delivering aid to the Global South on the other hand, represent distinct domains both in practice and in theory. While surveillance implies, if not permits, certain secrecy and opacity, at least in commercial contexts or in the case of governmental agencies working for public and national security, contemporary aid work is to be guided by principles such as transparency and accountability for the sake of aid effectiveness—even regardless of the data protection dimension. Common to them, however, is the power imbalance between the watcher and the watched (in the case of surveillance) and between the care-provider (aid organization) and the cared (beneficiaries at the receiving end of aid relations). The fact that human rights and humanitarian NGOs are also watched—subject to governmental, regulatory, financial or other surveillance—explains the unescapable role they play in the securitized chain of care provision.

This book has not aspired to contribute to the scholarship on the authoritarian traits of democratic settings, institutions and arrangements, but it may have added a few ideas to the thinking on the politics of transparency/opacity in the context of aid work implemented in Global South settings by organizations simultaneously promoting democratic values and resorting to controversial technologies and databases. Obsession with risks, security and legal-regulatory compliance (Kuldova, 2022) equally explain aid organizations' decisions to screen subjects whom they voluntarily help by providing either aid or labour and other contracts. However, the distrust towards fellow human beings embodied in screening raises the question on the 'basic, pervasive evil' potentially hiding even on the generous donor side too. Recalling the poems on the opening pages of this book and as also illustrated by Kundera's *Unbearable Lightness of Being* (1984, 101; on the relationship between the literary works and their authors *see* Shields and Kabdebo, 1996; Szavai, 2011):

> A year or two after emigrating, [Sabina] happened to be in Paris on the anniversary of the Russian invasion [1968] of her country. A protest march had been scheduled, and she felt driven to take part. Fists raised high, the young Frenchmen shouted out slogans condemning Soviet imperialism.

She liked the slogans, but to her surprise she found herself unable to shout along with them. She lasted no more than a few minutes in the parade.

When she told her French friends about it, they were amazed. "You mean you don't want to fight the occupation of your country?" She would have liked to tell them that behind Communism, Fascism, behind all occupations and invasions lurks a more basic, pervasive evil and that the image of that evil was a parade of people marching by with raised fists and shouting identical syllables in unison. But she knew she would never be able to make them understand.

Non-violent forms of resistance (demonstrations, advocacy, protests, disobedience, non-cooperation, sanctions and boycotts) can be distinguished from violent forms only the extent to which the logic of separation also applies to the ways how rule and power are exercised (over the resisting or obedient subjects). Putting aside the conceptual and practical differences between democracies, authoritarian regimes, tyranny and totalitarianism, none of these are discrete (binary: either/or) options. Regarding governance and governmentality certain level of repression can be detected in democracies, and freedom is also present in authoritarian regimes (Dean, 2010, 155–204), which is further complicated by the tyranny embodied in the inescapable domination of technologies characterizing all political systems and societies. If technology-supported legibility and quantification are means of 'compliant' risk mitigation, the purpose of which is more effective governability and control over the subjects (Dean, 2010; Kuldova, 2022; Scott, 1998) only the means— the mediation of power—vary across regimes that are different in their political nature.

Civil society and aid organizations cannot but play an ambiguous role in a world where actors not only keep others under surveillance, hence control, but they themselves are kept under surveillance. Their legal status and operations are regulated by states and international norms that simultaneously also define security-related ideas and risk-based thinking as normative standards. However, considering NGOs' portrayal as advocates of values such as freedom, democracy, human rights, it is worthwhile to recall Byung-Chul Han (2018, 30 and 74)—whose work complements earlier philosophical thinking (from Nietzsche to Foucault) on power—to understand the non-violent (seemingly non-coercive, peaceful) mechanisms by which power operates:

Power as constraint and power as freedom are not fundamentally different, they only differ in the level of mediation. They are different manifestations of a single power. All forms of power are oriented towards the creation of a continuum and presuppose a self... Self-determination does not have to go hand in hand with oppression or denial of the Other. It depends on the mediating structure.

In other words, power which works *within* the other, without force and violence and power working *against* the other by means of coercion can be analysed within the same framework (Han, 2018). Depending on their self-interest democracies and authoritarian regimes on the one hand, international—global governance—structures on the other hand only use different mediating structures 'to create a continuum'. The 'chain of security' is one such mediating structure, the purpose of which is to enable security judgements in democratic settings by following "the series of translations that render financial transactions into indicators of suspicion, into evidence of wrongdoing in the chain of security" (De Goede, 2018, 35). International and non-governmental (aid) organizations and international aid projects, operating without 'oppression and denial', can also be seen as links in this security chain, which create an invisible, but inescapable 'continuum' between (Global North) donors and those individuals benefiting—or excluded—from aid projects or other forms of cooperation with international aid organizations (in the Global South) depending on the outcome of watchlist screening.

References

Anwar, T., Wesseling, M., & Soares, R. R. (2022). *New Tech, Perpetual Challenges. How Emerging Technologies for Financial Compliance are Impacting the Nonprofit Sector*. European Center for Not-for-Profit Law. Retrieved October 15, 2023, from https://ecnl.org/sites/default/files/2022-09/ECNL%20F INTECH%20Report.pdf

Dean, M. (1999/2010). Governmentality: Power and Rule in Modern Society. 2nd edition. SAGE.

De Goede, M. (2018). The Chain of Security. *Review of International Studies, 44*(1), 24–42. https://doi.org/10.1017/S0260210517000353

ECNL. (2022). *Navigating Access to Financial Services for CSOs. A Practical Guidance*. ECNL. https://ecnl.org/publications/navigating-access-financial-services-csos

Han, B.-C. (2005/2018). *What Is Power?* Polity Press.

Kuldova, T. Ø. (2022). *Compliance-Industrial Complex the Operating System of a Pre-Crime Society*. Palgrave Macmillan.

Kundera, M. (1984). *The Unbearable Lightness of Being*. Harper & Row.

Lauterbach, C. (2017). No-Go Zones: Ethical Geographies of the Surveillance Industry. *Surveillance & Society, 15*(3–4), 557–566. https://doi.org/10.24908/ss.v15i3/4.6616

Lyon, D. (2007). *Surveillance Studies: An Overview*. Polity Press.

Scott, J. C. (1998). *Seeing Like a State*. Yale University Press.

Shields, K. & Kabdebo, T. (1996). One Sentence: Illyes and Eluard. *The Hungarian Quarterly, 37*(1), 151–154. https://mural.maynoothuniversity.ie/9262/1/KS_one%20sentence1996.pdf

Szavai, J. (2011). Illyés versus Éluard. *Hungarian Review, 2*(2) https://hungarianreview.com/article/illyes_versus_eluard/

Vaughn, J. (2009). The Unlikely Securitizer: Humanitarian Organizations and the Securitization of Indistinctiveness. *Security Dialogue, 40*(3), 263–285. https://doi.org/10.1177/0967010609336194

Annexes

The Online Survey and Qualitative Interviews (2021)

To map NGOs' general experiences with data protection and GDPR an online survey and qualitative, semi-structured interviews were used. The research project was hosted by the NRCCL at the University of Oslo and funded by the Tempus Public Foundation, Hungary in Spring 2021.

The purpose of the online survey was to explore EU-based NGOs *general* experiences with GDPR in the context of aid projects implemented in the Global South. The survey was conducted from January 2021 to April 2021; 300 emails were sent out to VOICE-members which yielded 35 responses. Two questions were related to the matter of screening; the full questionnaire is available at: https://forms.office.com/r/RbA6fy5bA9.

Altogether representatives of 35 organizations filled out the survey in 2021, all of them registered in a European country and participating in aid-related activities in the Global South. Four respondents identified their organizations as purely humanitarian, nine operated in the field of development, 18 implemented projects in both fields (humanitarian, development) and four of them conducted other types of work (advocacy, for example). About one-third of the organizations ($n = 12$) were registered in a Scandinavian country, eleven NGOs were established elsewhere in Western Europe, four of them were based in the UK. Southern

Table A.1 Size of the NGOs filling out the survey

Number of employees (EU head office)	Less than 5 $n = 5$	6–20 $n = 9$	21–50 $n = 8$	More than 50 $n = 10$
Number of local employees	Less than 10 $n = 10$	11–20 $n = 3$	21–50 $n = 4$	More than 50 $n = 18$

Europe and Central Europe were represented by 3 and 5 organizations respectively in the sample.

With regard to the major funding actors, 27 respondents mentioned that their most important donors are private actors (individuals, legal entities), which was closely followed by official or governmental donors in European countries ($n = 26$) and the EU institutions ($n = 21$). Some NGOs also received funding from international organizations ($n = 14$), US governmental agencies ($n = 6$), regional actors ($n = 4$) or from other sources ($n = 6$). The geographic areas where the respondents were present concerned Sub-Saharan Africa ($n = 29$), the Middle East ($n = 21$) and Asia ($n = 21$), Latin-America and the Caribbean region ($n = 20$). North Africa ($n = 14$) and the EU's Eastern neighbourhood ($n = 14$) were mentioned much less frequently.

About a third of the respondents represented NGOs that can be considered large by the number of employees (more than 50) in the European head office, or by counting only the local employees (Table A.1).

It should also be acknowledged that not all of the respondents reported that their organizations collected personal data of *local* individuals. Question 13, concerning the use of filing systems, revealed that 25 NGOs processed personal data which was collected from or about locals. Seven respondents reported that their organizations used local subcontractors to implement projects on behalf of them (avoiding or 'outsourcing' the direct collection of personal data). Further responses varied from implementing projects in the aid recipient country in a manner (i) that did not require the collection of personal data ($n = 4$), (ii) that did not include interactions with individuals ($n = 2$), (iii) that did not include the recording any personal data on connected computers (internet, cloud, $n = 1$), (iv) other ($n = 2$).

When asked about the types of personal data (Q15b), the collection of sensitive data (revealing racial or ethnic origin, political views or religious beliefs, covered by GDPR Article 9) was mentioned by 15 organizations, while the rest either denied collecting sensitive data ($n = 16$) or considered the question irrelevant ($n = 4$). ID papers were used by 17 organizations for collecting sensitive data (Q15d), while four NGOs reported collecting and processing biometric data too (Q15e).

More about decisions concerning data collection:

Paragi, B. (2022). Challenges in Using Online Surveys for Research Involving Sensitive Topics: Data Protection Practices of European NGOs Operating in the Global South. *SAGE Research Methods: Doing Research Online.* https://methods.sagepub.com/case/online-surveys-delicate-sensitive-topics-data-protection-european-ngos.

Qualitative interviews were also used to map general NGOs experiences with data protection and GDPR. EU guidelines were followed and information was shared on the details of the project with the participants by email based on which interviewees provided their consent for participation. Names of research participants and organization have been equally anonymized, but the sample included:

[1] advisor, Norwegian aid organization; Oslo/Zoom, December 17, 2020
[2] two officials, a manager and a data protection office, European legal advocacy organization (NL); Zoom, February 12, 2021
[3] advisor and DPO, Norwegian aid organization; Oslo/Zoom, January 8, 2021
[4] manager, national branch of an international NGO, Czech Republic; Zoom, April 8, 2021
[5] director, Danish aid organization; Zoom, April 8, 2021
[6] founder and director of a human rights advocacy organization, Belgium; Zoom, March 19, 2021
[7] country director, national branch of an international NGO Austria; Zoom, April 13, 2021
[8] legal advisor, Norwegian humanitarian organization; Zoom, May 4, 2021 and June 14, 2021; and a third follow-up discussion with the participation of a regional head of risk and compliance; Zoom, November 3, 2021
[9] two officials, head of IT and a legal compliance officer, national branch of an international NGO, UK; Zoom, June 17, 2021
[10] advisor, Norwegian aid organization; Oslo, October 22, 2021

[11] project manager, humanitarian action; Swiss aid organization; Zoom, November 2, 2021;

[12] director of studies; French humanitarian organization; Zoom, November 3, 2021.

Further data was collected by means of

- a Zoom-interview with a European representative of LexisNexis Risk Solutions on 20 May 2021
- email-correspondence with an officer at CompliancePartner on 20–27 March; November 3, 20YY
- email correspondence with self-anonymized legal advisors at European Commission DG INTPA (INTPA-DATA-PROTECTION-COORDINATOR@ec.europa.eu) with whom emails were exchanged during the course of 2021 and 2022 (last email exchanged: August 17, 2022).

THE WORKSHOP: SCREENING AS A DATA PROCESSING OPERATION IN AID WORK (2022)

Closed workshop—Friday 23 September from 09:00–12:00 at the Peace Research Institute Oslo, https://www.humanitarianstudies.no/events/screening-as-a-data-processing-operation-in-aid-work/.

What does screening mean for NGOs and what may it mean from the perspective of screened individuals? How are organizational decisions made (whom to screen, when, how often)? How is screening documented as a data processing operation in the context of General Data Protection Regulation (GDPR)? How are concerned individuals notified? What are the costs and benefits of transparency? Are privacy notices (available on websites) adequate measures to communicate the act of screening from the perspective of GDPR and its transparency principle?

NGOs delivering aid are expected to screen individuals in line with conditional clauses in certain grant agreements signed with their official donors. Screening, however, is not simply a risk mitigating measure in the context of anti-money laundering (AML) and counter-terrorist financing (CFT), but it can also be considered a data processing operation as long as organizations subscribe to tech solutions providing access to consolidated databases (sanctions lists, etc.). As such, it should be clearly communicated to concerned individuals—if not to the general public— by providing enough information "in a concise, transparent, intelligible and easily accessible form, using clear and plain language" as prescribed by GDPR Article 12(1) in line with the general transparency principle Article 5(1). Publicly available privacy notices, however, rarely mention it.

The purpose of the workshop was to facilitate a discussion on relevant data protection issues focusing on the principle of transparency, right to information and data subjects' reasonable expectations. Practitioners were invited to participate in co-creating knowledge on this subject by sharing their experiences and the dilemmas they face.

The event was arranged by Beata Paragi, Associate Professor at Corvinus University of Budapest, as part of her MA-thesis project hosted by NRCCL/SERI at the University of Oslo. It is funded by the Norwegian Centre for Humanitarian Studies and hosted by two Peace Research Institute Oslo (PRIO) research groups (Humanitarianism and Security).

This was a closed, hybrid event. While a policy paper and an NCHS-podcast may follow the workshop, Chatham House rules applied during the workshop.

Privacy Notices Sampled (2022)

Organizations, the privacy notices of which contained direct or indirect reference to screening:

NGO	Country	Link to PN	Language	Contact	Screening (vetting) in PNs	Way of formulation (screening either explicitly or implicitly mentioned as a data processing operation, or as a purpose of collecting PD or as a reason for disclosing PD to third parties)
CAFOD, UK	UK	https://cafod.org.uk/Legal-information/Privacy-notice	English	General	Might be indicative of screening	"the purposes for which we will use your information includes … *fraud screening, safety, security and legal purposes*" and "*Prevention of fraud, misuse of services, or money laundering*"
CARITAS Española	Spain	https://www.caritas.es/politica-de-privacidad/	Spanish	dpo@	Might be indicative of screening	Compliance with legal obligations … *prevention of money laundering and terrorist financing*
Christian Aid, UK	English	https://www.christianaid.org.uk/legal/privacy-policy#:~:text=Christian%20Aid%20will%20not%2C%20under.giving%20your%20our%20details%20to%20us	English	dpo@	Might be indicative of screening	"We may also need to use your personal information for the *prevention of fraud* and to identify any misuse or abuse of our services"
GOAL Global	Ireland	https://www.goalglobal.org/privacy/	English	dpo@	Might be indicative of screening	Purpose: *The prevention and detection of fraud, money laundering or other crimes or for the purpose of responding to a binding request from a public authority* Or Court and the directly related legal basis: To comply with our legal and regulatory obligations

(continued)

(continued)

NGO	Country	Link to PN	Language	Contact	Screening (vetting) in PNs	Way of formulation (screening either explicitly or implicitly mentioned as a data processing operation, or as a purpose of collecting PD or as a reason for disclosing PD to third parties)
International Medical Corps Croatia	Croatia	https://internationalmedicalcorps.hr/	English	Personal	Yes	To comply with anti-money laundering, terrorism and sanctions laws and regulations, there are times when we need to confirm (or reconfirm) the name, date of birth, address and other details of our donors and business partners (including their directors, officers, board members, owners, shareholders, authorised representatives and affiliates and their circumstances). We may need to do this whether you are applying to be a new donor or business partner or have been one for some time. *This information may be shared with third-party service providers for this purpose*
International Rescue Committee, Germany	Germany	https://de.rescue.org/datenschutzerklaerung	German	general	Might be indicative of screening	To comply with statutory provisions that are mandatory for us, e.g. in relation to regulatory, governmental and law enforcement agencies with whom we work (e.g. tax payment or *anti-money laundering requirements*); to *prevent fraud and misuse of services*
Norwegian Refugee Council (NRC)	Norway	https://www.nrc.no/privacy-policy/ and https://www.nrc.no/globalassets/graphics/nrc people/privacy-notice-for-recruitment.pdf	English	dpo@	Yes (employment)	PN addressed for employees (p. 1, footnote 1): "In accordance with core humanitarian principles, NRC implements a range of safeguards to prevent or reduce the possibility of humanitarian aid falling into the wrong hands. This includes in particular those individuals and groups who are subject to sanctions imposed by the United Nations Security Council and other applicable sanctions lists. As part of this process, NRC may screen the details of the successful candidate for a position against these sanctions lists"

Organisation	Network	Country	URL	Language	Contact	Screening	Notes
Oxfam Italia	VOICE	Italy	https://www.oxf amitalia.org/pri vacy-policy/	Italian	dpo@	might be indicative of screening	Fulfil the obligations established by law, by a regulation, by Community legislation or by an order of the Authority, necessary *for the finalization of the contract* and for the *entire duration of the collaboration* (such as for example in the *matter of anti-money laundering, anti-terrorism* and other conduct contrary to current legislation)
Plan International UK	VOICE	UK	https://plan-uk. org/terms-condit ions/privacy-not ices	English	dpo@	Yes (givers, employment)	PN addressed to employees: "it is necessary to carry out *criminal records checks* to ensure that individuals are permitted to undertake the role in question"; general PN: "5. Ethical *screening* ... To do this we sometimes use profiling and *screening methods* so that we can better understand our supporters and potential supporters ... we may carry out *background checks* ... on donors and potential donors or check donations to help protect the charity from abuse, fraud and/or money laundering and/ or terrorist financing"
Save the Children Netherlands	VOICE	NL	https://www.sav ethechildren.nl/ privacy-and-coo kies	Dutch	general	Might be indicative of screening	To comply with our legal obligations (e.g. with regard to taxes, or in the event of calamities for the benefit of the police and judicial authorities)
War Child, NL	VOICE	NL	https://www.war childholland.org/ privacystatement/	English	dpo@	Might be indicative of screening	We only use your personal data for specific purposes, such as: 8. to comply with the law; 14. *to see if we can accept you as a partner or supplier;* 15. To enable the completion of an agreement with you as a company or supplier

If translated, by Google translate

The full table is available at PNs_NGOswebsites_22nov_without contacts.xlsx by 14 May 2024 (the link expires then).

The Main Provisions of GDPR Article 13 and 14

	Information to be provided where personal data...		
Art13	*Are collected from the data subject*	*Have not been obtained from the data subject*	*Art14*
1(a)	The identity and the contact details of the controller and, where applicable, of the controller's representative		1(a)
1(b)	The contact details of the data protection officer, where applicable		1(b)
1(c)	The purposes of the processing for which the personal data are intended as well as the legal basis for the processing		1(c)
1(d)	Where the processing is based on point (f) of Article 6(1), the legitimate interests pursued by the controller or by a third party;	The categories of personal data concerned	1(d)
1(e)	The recipients or categories of recipients of the personal data, if any		1(e)
1(f)	.... the fact that the controller intends to transfer personal data to a third country or international organisation...		1(f)
(2)	In addition to the information referred to in paragraph 1, the controller shall provide the data subject with the following information necessary to ensure fair and transparent processing in respect of the data subject		
2(a)	The period for which the personal data will be stored, or if that is not possible, the criteria used to determine that period		2(a)
		Where the processing is based on point (f) of Article 6(1), the legitimate interests pursued by the controller or by a third party	2(b)
2(b)	The existence of the right to request from the controller access to (...)		2(c)
2(c)	Where processing is based on point (a) of Article 6(1) or point (a) of Article 9(2), the existence of the right to withdraw consent at any time (...)		2(d)
2(d)	The right to lodge a complaint with a supervisory authority		2(e)
2(e)	Whether the provision of personal data is a statutory or contractual requirement, or a requirement necessary to enter into a contract, as well as whether the data subject is obliged to provide the personal data and of the possible consequences of failure to provide such data	From which source the personal data originate, and if applicable, whether it came from publicly accessible sources	2(f)

(continued)

(continued)

Information to be provided where personal data...

Art13	Are collected from the data subject	Have not been obtained from the data subject	Art14
2(f)	The existence of automated decision-making, including profiling, referred to in Article 22(1) and (4) and, at least in those cases, meaningful information about the logic involved, as well as the significance and the envisaged consequences of such processing for the data subject		2(g)
3	Where the controller intends to further process the personal data for a purpose other than that for which the personal data were obtained, the controller shall provide the data subject prior to that further processing with information on that other purpose and with any relevant further information as referred to in paragraph 2		4

INDEX

195

GPSR Compliance

The European Union's (EU) General Product Safety Regulation (GPSR) is a set of rules that requires consumer products to be safe and our obligations to ensure this.

If you have any concerns about our products, you can contact us on ProductSafety@springernature.com

In case Publisher is established outside the EU, the EU authorized representative is:

Springer Nature Customer Service Center GmbH
Europaplatz 3
69115 Heidelberg, Germany

The manufacturer's authorised representative in the EU is Springer
Nature Customer Service Centre GmbH, Europaplatz 3, 69115 Heidelberg,
Germany. If you have any concerns regarding our products, please
contact ProductSafety@springernature.com

Printed and bound by CPI Group (UK) Ltd, Croydon, CR0 4YY
24/04/2026
02096315-0001